MORGAN AERO 8

A BRAVE AND EXCITING NEW WORLD

MORGAN AERO 8

A BRAVE AND EXCITING NEW WORLD

Gavin Farmer

Publisher   JohnGHenry

MORGAN AERO 8 A BRAVE AND EXCITING NEW WORLD

GAVIN FARMER

First published in 2013 by JohnGHenry in association with Ilinga Books
PO Box 323
Bridgewater 5155
SOUTH AUSTRALIA
Telephone: +61 8 8339 3645   E: ilingabooks@chariot.net.au
                                          E : info@johnghenry.com
                                          www.ilingabooks.com .au
                                          www.johnghenry.com
                                          Facebook : John G Henry

©Gavin Farmer 2013

All rights reserved. No part of this publication may be reproduced or transmitted in any form or by any means, electronic or mechanical, including photocopying, recording and information storage and retrieval system without permission in writing from the publisher. The information contained in this book is true and complete to the best of our knowledge. All comments are made without any liability on the part of the author or publisher. We recognise that some words, model names and designations mentioned in the text are the property of the trademake holder. We use them only for identification purposes.

ISBN 978-0-9570223-1-7

Typeface used Minion Pro

Edited by Matthew Farmer, Wonderdog Writing Solutions, www.wonderdogwritingsolutions.com.au

Design and graphic art work by Eoin Henry

Printed and bound by Everbest Printing

This book is dedicated to the memory of Christopher James Lawrence
who was born on July 27, 1933 and passed away on August 13, 2011 aged 78 years.
Without his vision, dedication and energy the Morgan Aero 8 would never have been created

Thank you Chris

CONTENTS

Foreword		p. 11
Introduction		p. 13
Acknowledgments		p. 15
Chapter One:	A Legacy of History—Postwar Racing	p. 17
Chapter Two:	Design and Development: a Prelude to a New Beginning	p. 29
Chapter Three:	Design Aspects	p. 39
Chapter Four:	Engine and Driveline: The BMW Connection	p. 53
Chapter Five:	Getting the Aero 8 into Production	p. 73
Chapter Six:	The Release, Meeting the Public	p. 87
Chapter Seven:	The Evolution Begins	p. 95
Chapter Eight:	Aero 8 Gets a Roof—the AeroMax	p. 109
Chapter Nine:	The SuperSports	p. 119
Chapter Ten:	Racing the Aero 8	p. 127
Chapter Eleven:	The LIFECar	p. 149
Chapter Twelve:	Charles Morgan: Visionary Inheritor	p. 161
Chapter Thirteen:	Chris Lawrence: Lifetime Maverick	p. 167
Chapter Fourteen:	Where it all Began—a Brief History	p. 175
Postscript		p. 195

SPECIFICATIONS:		p. 199
APPENDIX 1:	Morgan Aero 8 Production	p. 210
APPENDIX 2:	Main Company Suppliers	p. 210
BIBLIOGRAPHY		p. 213
PHOTO CREDITS		P. 215
ALPHABETICAL INDEX		p. 219

Foreword

The Morgan Aero project has relied on so many people who have a passion. They all wanted to create a great driver's car that is also relatively practical and can be used every day. One by one these people have also become seduced by Morgan's unique position in the motor industry and by the devoted way that my co-workers at Morgan have produced each and every car for each and every customer.

One by one these supporters have pulled out all the stops to help us design and produce a great car. I am indebted to all of them, not merely for the advice and clever ideas that have been incorporated into the car, but also for their enthusiasm which has always kept me going throughout the project. All of these people are mentioned in Gavin's book but I would like to single out one special person who has given me real inspiration. This is Prince Eric Sturdza. Eric is a Morgan customer of a very special kind. Knowledgeable as a sports and GT car owner and well connected and respected in the European motor industry, Eric has made a huge contribution to the success of the Morgan Aero 8.

To name but a few of his inputs, he has inspired the Morgan AeroMax special edition, created the Morgan Aero GT3 Race team, started the Morgan Aero Owners Club and has sponsored our appearance at the Geneva Autoshow for the last 8 years. Perhaps the high point of our relationship for me was the support Eric gave to the Morgan Motor Company and the AutoGT racing team to enter all of the rounds of the European GT3 Championship in 2009. The cars put on a brilliant show during the company's Centenary Year and the engineering skill of Jean-Pierre Jabouille and the finesse and maturity of some of the best young French drivers allowed the Morgan sports car to win the first two rounds at Silverstone against stiff opposition.

This was Morgan's first full year of racing under the new rules of the FIA GT3 championship and the talented team put many podium finishes under their belt and built up massive support with everyone who loves Morgan sports cars. Now every Morgan owner knows that a Morgan is the working horse of the sports car world and the goal for Morgan has been to offer a car that can be successful in competition in the hands of the gifted amateur.

Every Morgan has a natural balance with its weight in the centre and minimal overhangs. The driver sits on the rear axle and in the old days they used to say that you drove a Morgan by "the seat of your pants." So it is very exciting to see a Morgan race in an International Championship where the competitors are driving super-cars designed and built by major manufacturers. In 2009 nobody expected a Morgan to show the way home to Ferrari, Audi, Porsche and Lamborghini but Morgans beat many sophisticated mid-engine race cars fair and square. The Morgan was also to my eyes the most beautiful and distinctive car in the Championship.

The Aero project has been a wonderful education for me, from the early days testing prototypes at Miramas or in the high Sierras above Grenada with Chris Lawrence to the collaboration with Matthew Humphries on surface design and car styling at Morgan. It has been an exciting journey and I can say that it has all been such fun. I would like to thank every single one of those enthusiasts and collaborators who have come along on that ride with me. I would also like to thank Gavin Farmer and his publishers very much for recognising the importance of the car and to congratulate him for all the hard work into pulling together all the information from so many sources to write the definitive story of the birth of the Morgan Aero 8.

Charles Morgan

Malvern Link

Introduction

For the Morgan Motor Company the arrival of the Aero 8 was something of a seachange. It created a great deal of controversy within the company's workforce during its gestation—remember, many employees at Morgan are second and third generation people who have only ever known the traditional Morgan sports cars—and continued to do so among the media, the dealers and Morgan owners.

Be that as it may, both Christopher Lawrence and Charles Morgan, heir to the top job in the company, knew deep down in their hearts that Morgan needed to embark on a road to change in whatever form it might have taken. That resulted in the definitive form known to us all as the Morgan Aero 8.

It represented not only a quantum leap forward for Morgan but for the world's automobile industry. As has become so typical of the automobile industry, creativity does not and probably cannot come from one of the big players like General Motors, Ford, Toyota or any of the rest of the major companies because of their entrenched bureaucracies and fear of over-stepping the mark in the eyes of the media and their clients. In so many ways the manufacturers, large and small, are damned if they do and damned if they don't by the hawks in the media who constantly criticise the car makers for being too conservative in their styling and/or engineering and then lampooning them when one of them dares to step outside the box! It is little wonder that such little progress has been made in so many areas of car design….

Morgan was often criticised in the media by people who did not get it where Morgan was concerned but Charles wore it with a stoic smile and kept looking forward knowing that the gamble with the Aero 8 would pay off—had to pay off! As it happened, sales of the traditional Morgan sports cars has rolled on unaffected by the Aero 8's arrival and so the sales of the Aero and its derivatives have been largely incremental to the company's business. It is in a completely different market segment from where Morgan has operated for most of their 100 years in business which was another bold step into the unknown taken by Charles Morgan.

What could so easily have backfired with the Aero 8 has been a resounding success for the company and the people who created and manufactured it. Many asked, "Will it prove to be the harbinger of further change?" We know that it has been exactly that with new versions and models evolved from it—the fabulous Aeromax and SuperSports—plus such exciting new models as the EvaGT which uses similar technology and the enchanting new Threewheeler. Times at Morgan certainly are a'changin'!

Gavin Farmer

Surrey 2013

Acknowledgements

This book would never have been published without the grateful assistance of a large number of Morgan enthusiasts including, in no particular order, Charles Morgan who is the Managing Director, the late Chris Lawrence who could best be described as a maverick engineer who did things his way, Steve Morris who is Morgan's Production Director, Mark Reeves who is the company's Development Manager, Matthew Humphries who is the resident stylist, former Sales and Marketing Director Matthew Parkin, Graham Chapman who is Morgan's senior IT man, John Burbidge who was Lawrence's assistant through much of the early work on the Aero 8; Mark Ledington Global Sales Manager, Jon Wells, Chief Designer Richard Gibson at Morgan, Richard Thorne, Managing Director of Richard Thorne Classic Cars at Grazely Green south of Reading in Berkshire; Norman Kench and Dave Houghton from Survirn Engineering at Longbridge, Birmingham; Dave Edwards, Technical Director at Superform Aluminium in Aston, Birmingham; Keith Chadwick, Managing Director at Radshape, Chris Dickinson, Radshape's Sales Engineer and John Harper who is the company's senior Production Manager; Chris van Wyk, Managing Director of Morgan Cars Australia, Richard Gilbert photographer from Malvern who shared literally hundreds of images with me, Richard Surman from London who also shared some images with me, Rob Wells, former owner of Libra Motive (Morgan dealer) for photos from his collection, and Michael Hodges from MPH Communication. Frederic O'Neill who was Team Manager and a driver for AutoGT Racing who campaigned the Aero 8 and Aero SuperSport in GT3 racing across Europe from 2007 through 2009 and was supported by Jean-Pierre Jabouille and Jacques Laffite and Prince Erich Sturdza who as CEO of Banque Baring Brothers in Geneva financed the team and who is also a good friend of Charles Morgan and an enthusiastic Morgan owner; and Hugo Spowers, a good friend of Charles and Managing Director of Riversimple.

My thanks go to all of those people for their time and patience with me. If I have omitted anyone please accept my apologies, it was unintentional and merely the result of an aging memory.

Chapter One

POST-WAR RACING

Morgan's modern racing history—in the post-World War II period at least—did not really get under way until the arrival of the Vanguard-engined Plus 4 in 1951. It had the considerable advantage of having an extremely robust 2.1-litre four-cylinder overhead valve engine in place of the comparatively small Coventry Climax 1.1-litre overhead inlet/side-exhaust engine and although not specially tuned for its life in the Morgan, the Vanguard engine endowed the Plus 4 with far more power and torque.

Managing director Peter Morgan headed a team that competed successfully in the 1951 RAC Rally, winning the team prize in that event as well as class wins in the Lisbon and Evian-Mont Blanc rallies. It was an auspicious beginning for the small company. Success in the Portuguese and British events followed in 1952 and victory was achieved in the London Rally in 1953.

In 1952 a solitary Morgan Plus 4 was entered in the 24 Hours Le Mans race but sadly the engine dropped a valve on lap three and the car was forced to retire. It was not an auspicious beginning at a venue that would later be the scene of much enjoyment.

Peter Morgan in a works Plus 4 at Silverstone, May 1954

With the availability of the higher powered, although slightly smaller in capacity, Triumph TR2 engine in 1954 the factory entered team cars in various rallies at home and abroad with privately-owned Morgans also to be found in the entry lists. Morgans participated in various rallies across England and Scotland followed throughout the Fifties with a high degree of success. A second place outright plus class wins were gained in the 1953 MCC Rally with outright victory in the 1954 Scottish Rally and another second place was achieved in the MCC Rally; a class win was gained in the '55 Scottish Rally while the following year a third placing was achieved in the RAC Rally. Peter Morgan won his class in the RAC Rally in 1957 in the new 4/4, a result that was repeated the following year.

Christopher Lawrence had a somewhat meteoric rise to prominence beginning in 1959 at the wheel of his own modified Morgan Plus 4, the redoubtable TOK 258, a car that has gone down in Morgan folklore for its racing exploits. Built in 1956, it was to have a long career in more than one guise. In an amazing run of skill, preparation and luck, Lawrence won 19 out of the 23 races he entered in the 1959 BRDC Freddie Dixon Trophy series for which he was presented with the Freddie Dixon Trophy. These performances brought Lawrence to the attention of Peter Morgan who subsequently supported him in International GT Racing.

1959 was a seminal year in Morgan's competition fortunes. Not only was Lawrence successful in winning the Freddie Dixon Trophy in TOK 258 but the factory team won the National Six Hour Relay Race and Peter Morgan took a fighting sixth place in the RAC Rally.

By comparison, the following year was somewhat barren and 1961, too, was similarly frustrating. Lawrence had a new Plus 4 Super Sport that he entered in the Nürburgring 1000 kilometre race where he did not finish although he did set a new 2-litre class lap record of 10.31, a full 7 seconds under the previous time! The highlight in 1961 was Richard Shepherd-Barron's fine second place finish in the 3 hour Grand Prix de Spa.

The low point for the year was the Le Mans' organizers refusal to accept Chris Lawrence's entry to again compete at the Sarthe circuit on the basis that the car was too old(!). Lawrence, however, suspected at the time that the Triumph works team had applied subtle political pressure to avoid any direct confrontation between their cars and the Morgan. As Lawrence commented somewhat wryly, "I am even more convinced today than I was then that that was the case." In the event the Triumph team cars took out the team prize with their prototype sports cars that were powered by a newly developed DOHC engine. Intriguingly, after the race they closed their competitions department and all that excellent design work was wasted! Undeterred Lawrence drove to Monza and entered the Coppa Inter-Europa where he finished second behind a Porsche.

1962 saw Lawrence and Shepherd-Barron again finish second at Spa and again apply for entry at Le Mans. The fiasco of 1961 was but a distant memory when Morgan entered TOK 258 for the 1962 Le Mans race. Entered as a Super Sports, it wore a Lawrence-designed fibreglass hardtop and under the bonnet was a 130bhp Weber-carburettored version of the Triumph 2.0-litre OHV engine; it competed in the GT Class. At the end of the race Lawrence and co-driver Shepherd-Barron found themselves in 13th place overall and leading the 2-litre class having driven 2,255 miles at an average of 93.96mph. After the race and post-race celebrations, Lawrence then drove TOK 258 back home to England! When one considers the meagre investment by Lawrencetune and the Morgan Motor Company when compared with the big factory efforts from Porsche and others, the results were staggering and a credit to all concerned. Not surprisingly, the factory used the results to great effect in its subsequent marketing programs.

Chris Lawrence and Richard Sheppard-Barron, winning their class at Le Mons 1962

Lawrence entered two further long distance events in 1962, the Isle of Man Tourist Trophy and Nürburgring 1000 kms but success was to elude him. He did finish both races, however, which proved the absolute reliability of the Morgan but the races showed up its deficiencies in other critical areas of design in comparison with its opposition, all of whom had vastly superior aerodynamics and more modern chassis. Lawrence finished second in the Autosport Championship however, and by the end of the season held the class lap record at every major circuit in England.

Morgan SLR racing in a club event 1964

Continuing success was experienced though 1964 when Lawrence and friend John Sprinzel collaborated to form the SLR team—Sprinzel Lawrence Racing—for which Lawrence designed and had made four Morgan SLR's featuring quite a sleek, beautiful and aerodynamically efficient body in aluminium. At the fast Spa circuit Lawrence finished third in class and lowered his lap record from 1.43 to 1.39 during the race. In the Brands Hatch Double 500 race the next year he competed in his SLR and put up a superb performance by leading for most of the first day until a front chassis tube broke and he had to pit for temporary repairs; the repair was made permanent overnight and the Morgan led all the second day of the endurance race. 1966 saw numerous successes by Lawrence in his SLR at most circuits in England; unfortunately the SLR Morgan was written off in a racing accident which sadly brought a promising chapter of Morgan's racing history to an end.

From the moment the Plus 8 was released in 1968 a revival of interest in competition from keen Morgan owners took place. It was a much faster machine than the Plus 4, having the Rover 3.5-litre aluminium alloy V8 under the bonnet, but it retained virtually all of the Plus 4's deficiencies—"It just hit the aerodynamic wall quicker!" quipped Lawrence. Nevertheless, considerable success was achieved with the Plus 8, most notably by Robin Gray who proved to be an excellent successor to Chris Lawrence. Driving a Plus 8 owned by Brian Haslam he finished second in the Modsport race at Mallory in 1972 in his first outing in the Morgan; in September he entered the same Plus 8 in the Rothmans Grand Prix at Brands Hatch and won outright. As a result of these performances Chris Lawrence bought the car for Gray to race the following year. Unfortunately it was a forgettable year for the pair although Gray did drive the legendary TOK 258 in the Charles Spreckley Thoroughbred race at Silverstone (he sat in for Lawrence who was unable to drive) and after many close dices he emerged victorious.

Chris Lawrence (Left) and Bill Wykeham discussing race strategies

For 1974, Gray set about improving the performance of his Plus 8, increasing the power through using four Weber two-barrel carburettors, higher compression, a Racer Brown camshaft and electronic ignition. He was so successful that he won the ModSports Championship that year and in TOK finished second in the Thoroughbred Championship.

With Gray's success in the Plus 8 continuing in the ModSports series, a new star, Chris Alford, emerged driving a specially prepared Morgan 4/4 in the production sports car racing series. Alford's employer, Morgan dealer John Britten, drove a Plus 8 in the BRSCC ModSports series.

Rob Wells in his Plus 8 taking the chequered flag at Snetterton

Through the race series Alford achieved seventeen out of seventeen class wins to take out the Championship! Britten, incidentally, finished second in the championship.

1976 was not a memorable year on the race tracks but in 1977 another star driver appeared, Bill Wykeham. He drove a Bruce Stapledon-prepared light weight Plus 8 in ProdSports but reliability problems with the Rover SD1 3.5-litre V8 engine dampened his enthusiasm and affected his results. Charles Morgan, the future managing director of the company, began his racing career at this time although his competing was compromised by work commitments to ITN where he was an international news cameraman. Charles competed in the Plus 8 prototype registered MMC 11 which was prepared by his close friend Rob Wells.

Rob Wells driving MMC 11 in a club event and winning

Unfortunately for Charles his 1978 season did not get off to a very good start with gearbox failure marring his Silverstone event but for the rest of the season the drivers found it most rewarding. Competing in the BRDC Production Sports Car Championship they scored six wins and a second and he was the championship winner. MMC 11 was driven in eighteen races (by Charles and Wells) for the year and won ten of them and came second in four which was quite remarkable given that the car was an eleven year old company test car!

Again for 1979 the car was shared between Charles Morgan and Rob Wells, Charles entering it in the CAV Production Sports series and Wells in ProdSports. Both experienced consistent success with Charles winning Class A for the season.

In 1980 the first 24-hour race was held in England and Morgan entered a three-car team of Plus 8s for the Willhire race held at Snetterton; the team finished third which was commendable because all three cars were stock standard and privately owned. With the assistance of the Morgan factory, Rob Wells built a rather special machine to compete in the ModSports series for 1981. A rolling chassis was provided from which Wells weaved his magic. He built a tubular steel space frame that was welded onto the original thereby dramatically improving its stiffness. He designed and made a special fully independent coil spring and wishbones rear suspension (he retained the Morgan pillars up front), wider wheels and tyres (14-ins at the rear, 10-ins at the front) and a more powerful Rover SD1 engine, the cylinder block for which was supplied by British Leyland's competition department. Gasflowed Weslake cylinder heads, a Holley four-barrel carburettor and a dry sump engine lubrication system completed the main specifications.

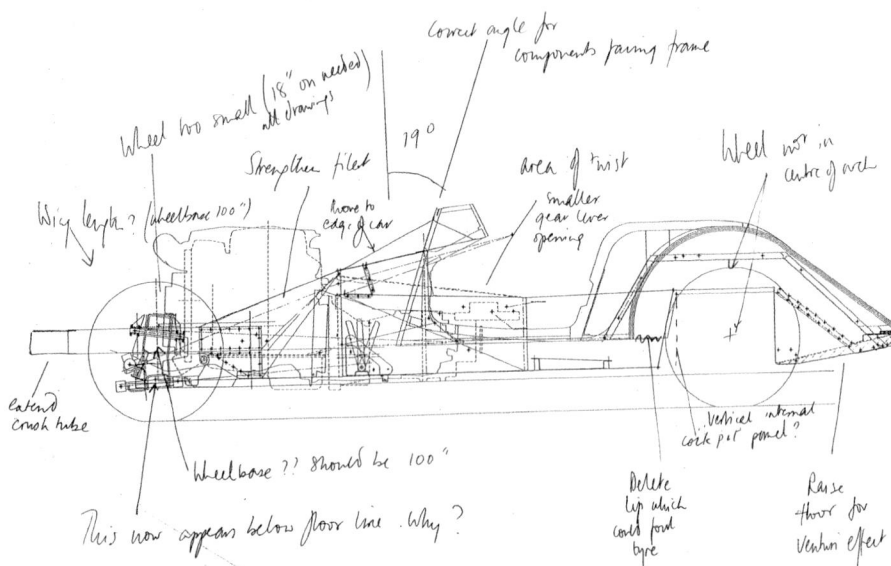

Concept sketch with various ideas on how to improve the Plus 8's track performance

Covering the mechanical components was a one-piece fibreglass body that was hinged at the rear and could be lifted up from the front to give total access for servicing. Known as MMC 3, Wells entered it in the ModSports series where he won his class no less than twelve times, was second twice and third three times, set five new class lap records and won the Championship! A new driver appeared on the scene in 1981, Steve Cole, who would prove to be a fine competitor for the marque. 1980 also saw a Plus 8 win the 24-hour race at Snetterton for the second year in a row, a result that was repeated again in 1982 with MMC 11 leading from start to finish. Cole had a successful championship winning year in 1982 in his Plus 8 and was to miss the championship in 1983 by just two points.

For the next decade Morgan sports cars would continue to be raced by private individuals and dealers looking to promote their businesses. However, apart from that exposure there were few highlights and fewer victories.

In 1995 the factory announced details of an advanced Plus 8 that was going to be the springboard for further competition participation with a car that was part-Plus 8 and part-Aero 8 although that part of the car's name had not yet been revealed. Lawrence built a race car based around the Ciebe Geigy tub but as he soon discovered, its honeycomb structure had very little integrity left in it after he had cut holes in it to accommodate doors and other access points that were vital for a working car. To anyone who has known Chris Lawrence it would have come as no surprise when he decided that he needed to completely re-engineer the tub so that it would support the structure and the mechanicals of a racing car. By mid-1996 he had designed completely new front and rear structures for the race car. Power came from a highly modified Buick V8—"I have never called it the Rover V8 engine, to me it was always a Buick," said Lawrence—that leaked oil everywhere and had a fearsome thirst for fuel. Graham Nash had prepared the engine.

Big Blue in preparation in the workshop, 1996

As part of the process Lawrence began building a race team from staff at Morgan with Mark Baldwin as crew chief, and Dave Goodwin who was a machinist there and who could make almost anything. The team later became known as the Extra Mile High Club! For much of the rest of the season the team competed on circuits all over Europe with each race being of four hour's duration. The car's Achilles heel, however, soon became obvious—the Buick alloy V8 engine which in Lawrence's opinion was "just rubbish." Three engines were blown in quick succession at £23,000 each. Despite the handicap of the engine, the car finished five out of the nine FIA GT races it had been entered in. Lawrence described the car somewhat cynically as "a mobile chicane." However, having said that he believed that the '96 season was a totally unsung part of Morgan's history.

Chapter One • Post War Racing

Big Blue in the factory workshop, ready to race, 1996

Big Blue in the pits during a race in 1996, Chris Lawrence team manager on the left with green shirt

In its first iteration, developed by Andy Rouse and Rod Harvey-Bailey, it was powered by a modified Rover 4.9-litre V8 engine that developed 385bhp at 6500rpm and 340lbs ft of torque at 4500rpm and was bolted to a Hewland six-speed gearbox driving an open propeller shaft to an Australian-made BTR Hydralock limited slip differential. Unusually for a Morgan it featured a conventional double wishbone front suspension with outboard spring damper units in place of the traditional sliding pillars; the new suspension was successfully tested at Mallory Park in February 1996. Also, the traditional ladder frame chassis had been replaced by an aluminium "honeycomb" chassis supplied by Ceiba Geigy. This rather different mechanical arrangement was hidden under a slightly modified Morgan Plus 8 body.

The Morgan GT2 was entered in a number of long distance (4 hours duration) races in 1996 BPR race series and finished five of them although the car was "well off the pace." Its first outing was in March at the Paul Ricard circuit in France where Charles Morgan achieved the amazing speed of 170mph! Morgan and co-driver Bill Wykeham completed 99 laps and were classified 28th at the finish. Two weeks later the Morgan was racing at Monza where only 48 laps were completed before a break down put them out of the race. Three weeks later at Jarama in Spain the car had to start from the pitlane and embarrassingly broke down on the first lap in front of 200 Spanish Morgan owners who had come to watch. At the Silverstone round the Morgan was punted off the circuit by a Porsche GT1 at Becketts corner at the end of the first lap and at the Nürburgring in June Morgan and Wykeham completed 120 laps to be classified at the finish while at Anderstorp in Sweden the car retired after 32 laps with Charles Morgan at the wheel. Back in England at the Brands Hatch circuit the Morgan GT2 finished 12th overall and 6th in class despite losing the engine bonnet half way through the race. Two more races were entered for the 1996 season, at the famous Spa-Francorchamps where the team added Steve Lawrence as a third driver; however, on the 87th lap the engine expired and their race was over while another DNF happened at the Italian circuit of Nogaro. Today, that car is owned by Morgan enthusiast Adrian van der Kroft.

For the 1997 season a completely new GT2 was prepared. It had a much more rigid aluminium tub-and-tube construction that was based on a bonded aluminium tub designed by Professor Jim Randle. A redesigned suspension system, wider wheels, better brakes and far superior aerodynamics to any Morgan previously raced was developed by Chris Lawrence. The power train was carried over from the previous year and the completed vehicle was ready just in time for the FIA GT meeting at Silverstone in May where the four hour race was shortened by an hour because of torrential rain. In practice Charles Morgan was a shattering 10-seconds-per-lap faster than last year but this was reduced by half in the rain, still significant. He and Wykeham were running at the finish having completed 66 laps. At the next race in Helsinki the Morgan ran out of fuel on lap 31 and therefore did not finish while at Spa in July the engine failed. At the Nürburgring in June the Morgan finished almost last and it was here that Charles Morgan and Chris Lawrence met Karl-Heinz Kalbfell and Dr Wolfgang Reitzle who were there watching their BMW-powered McLaren F1 GTR when Lawrence famously said in response to a Kalbfell joke, "We could have gone much faster if we had a BMW engine." Little did Lawrence realise the impact that innocuous comment would have!

After the race at Spa where the engine expired after only 42 laps it became obvious that the weak link in the car was the engine, not the chassis. Having had considerable experience with the small block Chevrolet V8 engine from his time at Marcos, and living in America, Lawrence dumped the Buick V8 and replaced it with an all-aluminium 6.0-litre V8 Chevy similar to the one he had used in the Marcos LM600. As he told the team, "Now you will see how good the new chassis really is!" At this point the Morgan GT2 was nick-named "Big Blue."

There were three more races for the season, one at Donnington followed by Sebring in Florida, and then Laguna Seca in California, USA. Unfortunately, because of problems with the complex dry-sump system the engine's bearings were run in warm-up so the Morgan never started the Donnington race. Sebring was a six-hour race run on an old WWII B52 bomber airfield, the track being very rough and hard on cars. For the US races Charles Morgan had been replaced by classic car journalist Tony Dron. Charles had injured the tendons of a finger and was incapacitated. The car finished the race with only minor problems which were all overcome. It DNF'd at Laguna because the driver taking the first stint—a British classic car journalist—had forgotten to lift off the throttle just before the infamous corkscrew where the car became airborne momentarily; when it landed on the third lap—it was leading the GT class after three laps—the impact caused a drive shaft to break. The team manager and crew were bitterly disappointed at this needless and avoidable disaster because they had talked about it with the drivers prior to the start of the race and all agreed to the lift off of the throttle. Not only that but the Morgan was decidedly quicker than the Porsches and most of its competitors and according to Lawrence "it made the most glorious noise I have ever heard any racing car make."

The races where the GT2 was fitted with the very powerful Chevrolet engine proved one thing—that the new aluminium tub-and-tube construction that Chris Lawrence had devised in conjunction with the completely new suspension system was well and truly capable of standing up to the rigours of racing and therefore would be more than capable of withstanding a long career as a production road car. In January 1998 the company made the decision to end the race program and concentrate on developing a production sports car, the project being given the code P8000. Today "Big Blue" is in the care of US Morgan dealer Norb de Bries of Northshore Sportscars in Chicago.

Big Blue being serviced in the pits, Chris Lawrence behind the car

Chapter Two

DESIGN AND DEVELOPMENT: A PRELUDE TO A NEW BEGINNING?

Change was something which came slowly and not very often to the Morgan Motor Company. Charles Morgan, grandson of HFS Morgan, joined the company in October 1985 following a successful and award-winning career as a television cameraman for the ITN network. However, despite this success he was always destined to become the Managing Director of the Morgan Motor Company as he was the only son of Peter Morgan who in turn was the son of HFS. Charles has two sisters who have non-executive roles in the company.

When he joined the company Charles began the slow process of learning how it was run, by whom and how he could influence it to produce cars more efficiently. According to the technical director for the P8000 project (which became the Aero 8) Chris Lawrence, "Charles always wanted to be the Morgan family member who would create a completely new Morgan sport car."

Charles Morgan managing director who was the driving force behind the Aero 8

From the early 1990s there were stirrings for change. The then model range consisted of the Ford-powered four-cylinder Plus 4 roadster and the Rover V8-engined Plus 8. Both were largely derived from the 1936 development, the Morgan 4-4, when HFS literally added a fourth wheel to his three-wheeled chassis. Very little had changed from then, or not that Morgan made mention of it.

In some ways Morgan appeared to be caught in a time warp in more ways than one. The factory was not organised along conventional (dare one say modern?) industrial lines and its product range was regarded as quaint-but-old-fashioned in a peculiarly English kind of manner. However, the catch for Morgan was that that was exactly how their clients around the world liked

CHAPTER TWO • DESIGN AND DEVELOPMENT: A PRELUDE TO A NEW BEGINNING

it. They quite clearly told Peter Morgan that modern sports cars were not what the company ought to be producing and certainly not what they would consider buying.

If there was any doubt about this attitude from their clients one only has to witness the Plus 4 Plus. This car was built under the aegis of Peter Morgan and against the wishes of the family. Although not a startlingly modern design in itself—it pales in comparison with the original Lotus Elite, for example—it was stylistically a huge step forward from the traditional Morgan Plus 4 of the time. Mechanically it was 100 per cent Plus 4 with all the compromises that brought to the model and perhaps it was that more than the coupé styling and its fibreglass body—the first and only Morgan to be so made—that made it such a dismal failure. Maybe that is why in some respects Peter Morgan took a long while to warm to the idea of the Aero 8.

During the decade which began in 1990 the Morgan Plus Eight was gradually improved with crisper steering from a Jack Knight steering rack, a new set of wheels from GKN, manufactured using their revolutionary "squeezeform" casting process and longer doors to make it easier to enter and exit. Furthermore a new 4.6-litre V8 engine gave the car more power and torque.

Morgan Plus 4 Plus the only Morgan with a fibre glass body. A very rare car

This led to a boost in sales and the potential for a number of profitable years for the company. Peter and Charles Morgan began to have the confidence to think that they might have something in the kitty to spend on developing the next generation of Morgan sports cars.

Through motor racing Charles had met Rhoddy Harvey-Bailey who specialised in improving suspension systems of other manufacturer's cars. Charles had also kept in close contact with Rob Wells, the Morgan dealer who co-drove and developed the winning Morgan +8 for the 1978 and 1979 BRDC and BRSCC Production Sports Car Championships. All three men agreed that one of the weaknesses of the +8 was the live rear axle and all had the desire to engineer a cost effective independent rear suspension system for the Morgan. Charles commissioned a prototype from Rob Wells with just such a system and ran it as a daily driver. He also took it on skiing trips to Verbier in the Swiss Alps where it was spotted by none other than the blues singer Dianna Ross. She offered to buy the car on the spot but Charles was worried that if he left the car in Switzerland he would lose the prototype independent rear suspension. This was a shame really as what she was offering to pay for the car would probably have bought a lot of prototype suspension parts.

But Charles realised that the flexibility of the traditional ladder chassis with its ash wood frame bolted to it did not offer a rigid enough platform for the pick-up points for the suspension. Charles therefore set out to find a system that would replace the steel ladder chassis

Charles's father Peter admiring Big Blue in the factory workshop

The fastest Morgan of its day, the Plus 8 had a long and successful career

complete with its tubular spring and damper bars with a much stiffer component. Because of the Morgan's mantra of light weight at all costs, this new chassis had to be lighter than the existing component—a difficult goal with so much improvement required of the specification.

The Ceibe Geigy technology that Charles was considering was used in the Ford RS200 rally car

Charles' initial research took him to Ceibe Geigy where he discovered their honeycomb material, Aeroweb 3003. This material was used for the bulkheads in the early Boeing 747 aircraft. Charles met Professor George Woodley who took him on a tour of Ceibe Geigy's aluminium prototype workshop. Professor Woodley showed Charles the tub of the Ford RS200 rally car and explained how the passenger structure was constructed from aluminium honeycomb components adhesively bonded together. Designed by Tony Southgate and developed by Ford for Group B in the World Rally Championship, this car was to become notorious for being too fast to race. The Ford RS200 was the car that crashed on the Portugal Rally in 1986 claiming the lives of three spectators.

Professor Woodley opined that the construction of the chassis was far too complex and he offered to build a much simpler monocoque that could be used as the basis of a new car. Designed to the dimensions of the exiting Morgan Plus Eight this "tub" was brought to the Morgan Motor Company repair shop where work was begun to incorporate the new suspension systems of Rob Wells and Rhoddy Harvey-Bailey.

With new larger 17-inch wheels, but otherwise completely standard Plus Eight bodywork, this car was run for a year on the road by Charles Morgan. One of its first demo runs was at Shelsley Walsh, where it climbed the hill in some style. It was painted the identical blue to the Plus Eight that won its class in production sports car racing in 1978/79. The car was extraordinarily comfortable for a Morgan and was also capable of lapping any circuit faster than the standard car with the ladder frame. However, very early on problems were identified with the honeycomb construction. It was immensely difficult to fit components on to the honeycomb tub because of the need to bond in cotton reels everywhere where two parts would be bolted together. If there was no cotton reel the aluminium honeycomb simply compressed and lost all of its strength and rigidity. Furthermore, it was noticed that as soon as any steel came into contact with the aluminium corrosion could rapidly occur.

Charles showed the car to Anthony Loades of Abbey Panels in Coventry, who at the time was building the chassis for the Jaguar XJ220. This sports car used exactly the same material, Aeroweb 3003, for the passenger cell of the Jaguar supercar. Charles was keen to understand how an economy of scale could be achieved in low volume production. Unfortunately what he saw worried him about the practicality of using honeycomb. The laboratory process of the construction of the chassis of the XJ220 meant that even at an "on the road" price of £361,000 ($580,000) the car still lost money. In addition, the car was enormous. This was in part because the honeycomb was at least an inch thick from one side to the other, so floors and bulkheads were massive components.

However, in spite of these disappointments Charles pursued his dream of an ultra-stiff Morgan, partly because the prototype was such fun to drive. He approached Andy Rouse who had a company in Coventry building successful racing cars for the British Touring Car Championship. Andy was asked if it was possible to turn the honeycomb Morgan into a race car for the new FIA GT Championships. Needless to say Rouse responded with enthusiasm and modified the prototype to accept much of the latest Touring Car technology. He fitted an AP Racing brake system and similar spring and damper units from his Nissan saloon. He delivered the car back to Morgan where it had its first shakedown run at Mallory Park.

The car lapped Mallory in 50 seconds and a decision was made to homologate it for the upcoming British GT Championship run under the FIA GT2 rules. In 1995 this Morgan Plus Eight GT2 was campaigned by the factory, driven by Charles Morgan with a team of mechanics led by Mark Baldwin.

Chris Lawrence, who had engineered the Marcos LM600 for Computacentre noticed the car on the track and inevitably he thought that he could improve it. With his long list of associations with Morgan, it seemed a natural

Big Blue in the pit garage awaiting time on the track

progression for him to join the team eventually to re-engineer the car which he did at the beginning of 1996.

Meanwhile Charles, having been shown the Jaguar XJ220, went to meet its designer, Professor Jim Randle, who had been chief engineer at Jaguar Cars. Jim had recently retired from Jaguar and was Professor of Engineering at Birmingham University where he ran the advanced castings centre. He was still keen on designing fast road cars and wanted to help Morgan. Charles showed him the aluminium honeycomb tub and Randle immediately suggested that they visit the research department of Alcan in Banbury and talk to Colin Scott. Scott introduced Peter Schiesby who explained the process of adhesively bonding aluminium. He demonstrated the design of joints that create a very rigid structure and have no danger of peel so that the two components are firmly fixed together. Alcan was keen to take this technology from the aircraft industry into automotive and had designed a complete front end of a Volvo saloon from bonded aluminium which met all the current standards of crash protection. Peter also showed Charles and Jim a film of an articulated lorry with a chassis constructed entirely from bonded aluminium. This lorry was being driven on a supply route coast-to-coast from the tip of northern Australia to the south and back again. The goal was to determine whether adhesive bonding was robust enough to withstand the most extreme temperature changes as well as the twisting and bending of the vehicle on uneven road surfaces. The rig had been in use for over ten years with no problems.

The visitors were also shown glass cases where bonded components were being continuously pulled apart by mechanical devices, these tests having been running for around 12 years. This gave Charles the confidence that bonded aluminium was not only rigid but was also durable enough for a road car. Shortly afterwards Alcan and the Morgan Motor Company signed a confidentiality agreement and it was agreed that Professor Randle, Charles Morgan and Alcan would co-design an aluminium tub made from their new material which they were also hoping to supply to the next generation of Jaguar sports cars. Unofficially Alcan were keen to try out this material on a low production run in advance of a larger project. This seemed an opportunity too good to miss and Charles reported back to his father, Peter, that Morgan could be a genuine pioneer of new technology with their next model.

Charles and Jim set to work designing the new Morgan chassis. One proviso was that the existing Morgan body should fit over the chassis virtually unchanged. Right at the start Randle suggested making the car much wider to accept standard mass production car seats, but Charles argued that this would ruin the classic lines of the sports car. Randle employed a young post-graduate student to draw the tub and together with Alcan worked out the specifications for the joints that were to be adhesively bonded. Park Sheet Metal was chosen to manufacture a prototype chassis from the new material. The monocoque had been designed on CAD so the design could be manufactured using the computer data to control the path of the laser cutter and the folds of the bending equipment. A combination of 27 individual accurate components made up the separate parts of the final chassis. Each one was drilled with a datum hole so that pegs could be used to guide assembly. Once the adhesive had been applied and the parts pegged together the chassis was baked in Alcan's own ovens according to their strict requirements for time and temperature.

The result was an extremely strong, stiff, accurate component. Park Sheet Metal delivered two chassis to Morgan, these arriving at the same time as Chris Lawrence was struggling to make a successful race car out of the aluminium honeycomb supplied by Ceibe Geigy. This was a fortuitous coincidence and Chris and Charles immediately realised that the best way to test the strength of this chassis was to run it in endurance races. It was not long before one chassis was built up for a full frontal VCA crash test and the other was being turned by Chris Lawrence into a GT2 race car.

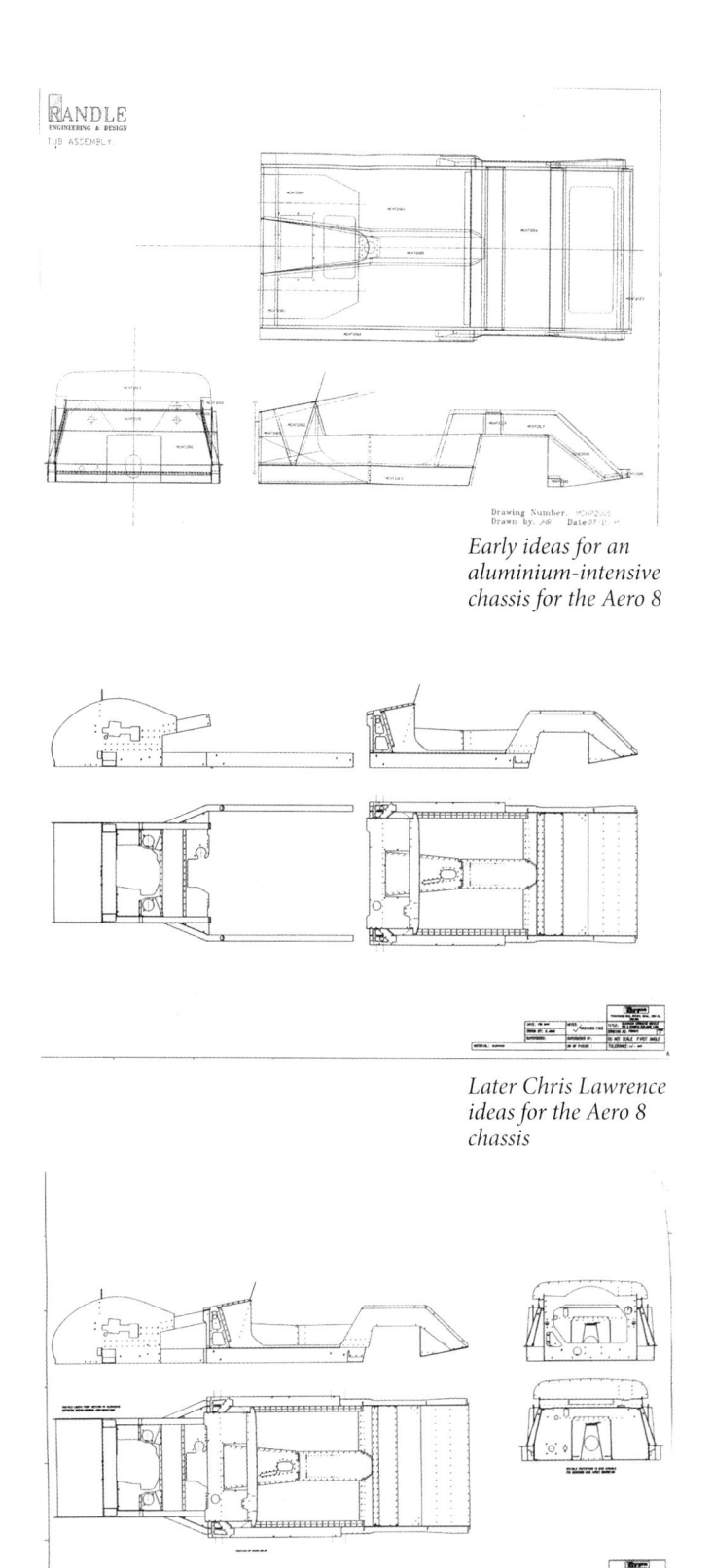

Early ideas for an aluminium-intensive chassis for the Aero 8

Later Chris Lawrence ideas for the Aero 8 chassis

Lawrence's strategy was to use the Randle tub as the basis and to add his own design frontal structure (the original tub ended at the firewall) using aluminium extrusions, carry out the necessary crash tests to satisfy the FIA rules. His cobbled up structure passed the test at MIRA (on February 11, 1997) with flying colours, there being only 4mm of rearward movement of the steering column in the mandatory 40mph frontal test.

From there Lawrence went to Park Sheet Metal in March 1997 and requested three more tubs be made to his design as quickly as possible and set a price limit—PSM responded by supplying them at £1580 each and had all three delivered by May, just two months later. Even though it was late in the season, Lawrence schemed up a completely new front frame and had British Aluminium make various extrusions to his design. Assembly took place in the workshop space allocated to Lawrence at the Morgan factory and by the beginning of June (1997) the car that can claim to be the very first Morgan Aero 8 was completed. Its purpose in life was to compete in the British GT Championship and prove Lawrence's engineering ideas for a future production Morgan.

Crash testing was successful carried out as part of the program

More "testing" of the P8000 took place when Charles Morgan and Chris Lawrence participated in the first Gumball Rally which saw them drive from London to Portsmouth and then Bilbao to the Adriatic coast in the dark blue prototype. There was an interesting overnight stop in Cannes where the annual Film Festival was being held, the two Morganistes having a hotel room next to Milla Jojovich! A year later they participated in the second Gumball Rally, again in the dark blue P8000 prototype, that took them from London-to-London via Hamburg.

CHAPTER TWO • DESIGN AND DEVELOPMENT: A PRELUDE TO A NEW BEGINNING

This is the car that Charles and Chris drove in the Gunball Rally; today it is part of the Adrian van der Kroft collection

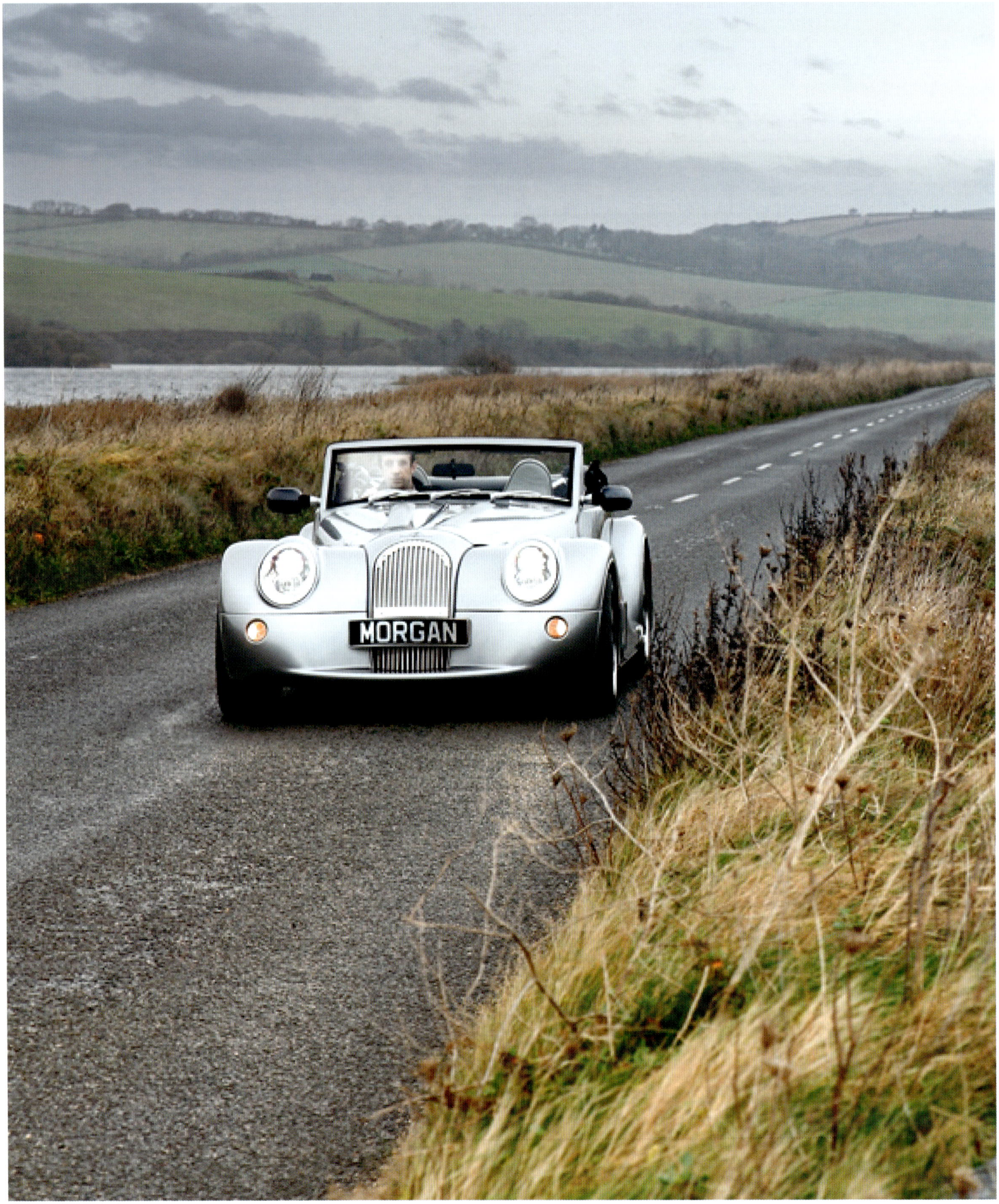
MORGAN

Chapter Three

DESIGN ASPECTS

What Lawrence had conceived was in Morgan terms more than a revolution, it was a revelation. Since the beginning of "proper" Morgan cars there had been a sliding pillar independent front suspension that had been refined only in details over the decades and the rather crude separate Z-frame steel chassis had also only been changed in minor details since the first four-wheeler in 1936. Even by the lacklustre standards of the British motor industry the Morgan was some way off the technological pace, not that Morgan enthusiasts seemed to mind or notice because they continued to buy the cars no matter what.

Change, however, had to come and it seemed appropriate that when it did it was ushered in by one of the family, Charles Morgan, and an "outsider" in the person of Christopher Lawrence, with Peter Morgan in the background quietly going along with the new direction and signing the cheques. Despite their age differences Charles and Chris found they could work well together to achieve what became a common ideal.

Following success on the race track the Chris Lawrence-conceived chassis was approved for production

There was, however, one small inconvenience. Jim Randle had ambitions to engineer and design the new Morgan sports car himself. In fact, he went as far as to bring Keith Helfet, a Jaguar stylist, to the factory with a completed scale model of what he thought the new Morgan should look like. Randle and Helfet showed it to Charles and Peter Morgan and then suggested it be called the "Randle Morgan!"

Chapter Three • Design Aspects

The problem for Morgan was that the body was not really true to Morgan's style; additionally it was wider and so could not accommodate the traditional looking cockpit and the separate wings. Lawrence and Randle had already disagreed fundamentally over the specification of the front and rear suspension. Randle wanted the car to adopt an innovative but as yet untried link between the two front wheels using a degree of mechanical anti-roll geometry while Lawrence wanted to use the upper rear suspension wishbone as the pick-up point for the rear spring and damper.

Charles was left in the middle and was told by Peter to sort the problem out otherwise the car would never be made. The resulting negotiations with Professor Randle over the design of the tub left Morgan with sole rights to the design but left Randle with the opportunity to develop a car based on the same method of construction, but using no similar parts of the Morgan prototype. Randle did subsequently engineer his own car which became the Lea Francis that was shown at the Birmingham Motor Show in 2002. He also left Morgan with a substantial Honorarium for his help in designing the monocoque of the cockpit and of what eventually was to become the Aero 8.

Charles Morgan was responsible for the styling of the Aero 8. His difficulty was in trying to modernise Morgan styling and yet retain Morgan styling cues

Lawrence had designed and proved in the intense heat and very public glare of racing a totally new aluminium-intensive frame for the new Morgan, coded internally as P8000. It consisted of the Randle tub (the passenger compartment) with massive extensions projecting forwards from the scuttle for mounting the mechanical components and for absorbing impact forces in a severe impact. Having achieved that, several steps and decisions had yet to be made, not the least of these concerned the styling of the future Morgan sports car. Charles Morgan was not the technically-minded person that his father and grandfather were; he had a more artistic leaning but nevertheless had a sufficient grasp of technical matters to know what Lawrence was talking about and would spend much of his leisure time sketching potential new cars. He had, after all, completed a pre-diploma course at the Sussex University and had a passion for the inspirational shapes made by famous carrozzeria Soutchak, Chapron and Figoni et Falaschi on Delage, Delahaye, Hotchkiss and other chassis in the 1930s. "I used to doodle all the time," he said. Three features were indelible in the designing of any future Morgan; they were, firstly, the retention of the flowing S-shaped front wing, secondly, it had to appear to be coachbuilt by ridding the body of panel joins, and thirdly it had to maintain the balance of the car with a front-mid engine, driver and passenger sitting near the rear axle and close together ("snug" was the word Charles used) so that weight was evenly divided between the wheels. By far the greatest difficulty he had was to style the car so that it looked like a Morgan and not like any other sports car. As he commented, "I was very aware of the fact that any car we might design and produce had to be instantly recognisable as a Morgan. As it was going to be a more expensive Morgan I felt it would need a leather interior with polished wood accents and I wanted to retain an arrow-shaped bonnet to connect it with Morgans of the past."

A Styling Committee was established in 1998 and comprised Peter and Charles Morgan, Mark Aston, Tim Whitworth, Matthew Parkin, Chris

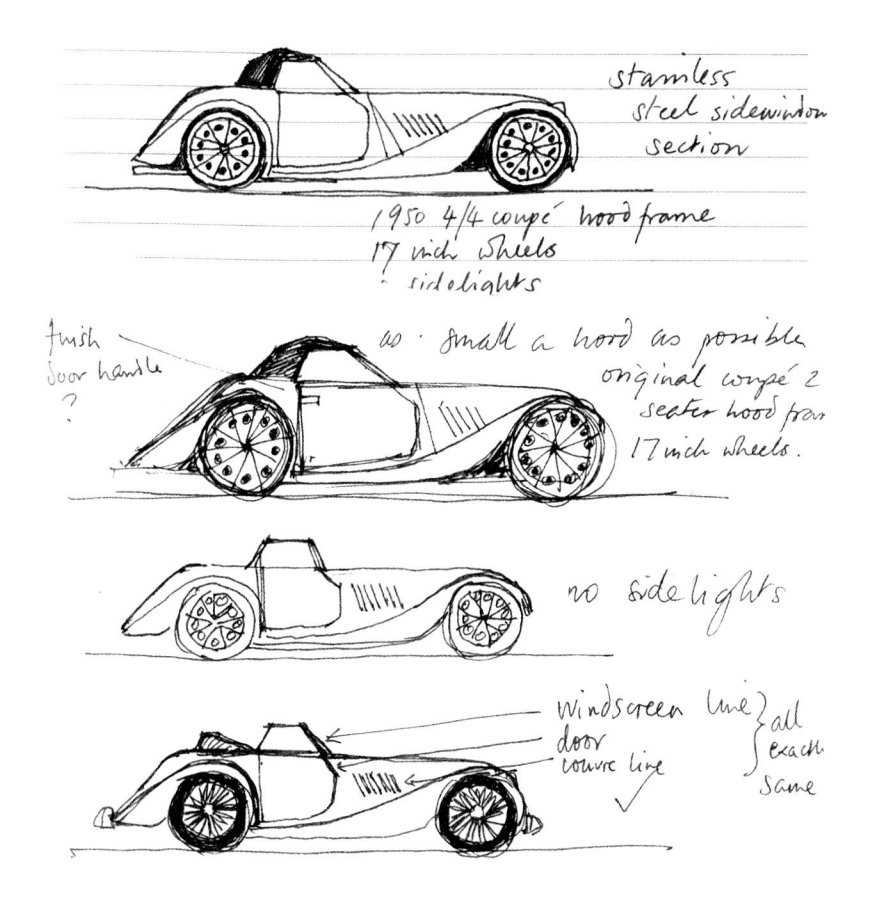

Chapter Three • Design Aspects

Lawrence, Gregor Dixon-Smith, Steve Morris and Steve Summers with Charles as the leader. All styling work was carried out in-house because the company did not have the resources to pay the fees demanded by professional styling houses or freelance consultants and besides, it felt it could not trust outside people to come up with a design that they would approve. In addition the company was always receiving sketches from art students and others but none were ever suitable. "We wanted the future Morgan sports car to possess real Morgan DNA," said Charles, "and the last thing we wanted was to have somebody else try to interpret that for us."

In communications with possible collaborators during this time the car was referred to by the company as "a new Morgan Plus Eight which features a new V8 engine, a new coachbuilt body style, a new drivetrain, new suspension and a new chassis."

Apart from making sure that the new Morgan sports car would be instantly recognisable as a Morgan there were few other hard-and-fast criteria laid down by either Peter and Charles Morgan or Chris Lawrence. More room in the cabin was, however, considered essential as was the ability for the luggage compartment to carry at least one set of golf clubs—very important for the USA and Japanese markets—and Lawrence was determined that the kerb weight of P8000 would not exceed one metric tonne or 1000kgs. During the winter of 1998 Charles Morgan in collaboration with Norman Kench and Dave Houghton, partners at Survirn Engineering, agreed upon a budget and began working on several polystyrene 1:10 foam scale models of various styling proposals until Charles was satisfied that the proportions were correct at which time a full-scale styrene foam model was made. "This process took several weeks as we—Charles and I—refined the car's shape to Charles' satisfaction and then we made a full-scale model, sprayed it with Durobild (a polyester material that can be painted) and then digitised it in preparation to making fibreglass 'splashes' of it. George Hardwick built the first car using fibreglass panels," said Houghton.

Survirn Engineering, then operating from a traditional old factory in the Birmingham suburb of Aston, was so enthusiastic about the P8000 project that it built a styling studio specifically for the Morgan in what was a scruffy old barn next to the main building. "In fact," said Kench, "we built the studio inside the barn complete with a special floor with datums." They installed the necessary equipment to digitally scan onto CAD the dimensions of the first Aero 8 prototype which were then "cleaned up" electronically. From this a full-sized styrofoam model was cut for viewing and to be critiqued by Charles and the committee. A cast iron datum floor was an integral part of the installation; a robot with a faro-arm that was manually moved around the model by one of the technicians and digitised every aspect of the P8000's shape in preparation for the manufacture of machined cast iron tooling dies.

The P8000 was not the first Morgan that Survirn had been commissioned to work on. The front and rear wings of the traditional Morgan sports cars were the first and such was the trust between the two companies that the styling studio was built "on spec."

CHAPTER THREE • DESIGN ASPECTS

During this time a range of exterior styling options were under consideration as were interiors. Charles, for example, was thinking about two interior styles that he referred to as Coupe and Sports. The Coupe was to have glass side windows that pivoted on a bolt at the front and would drop down into the door at an angle as well as the traditional use of solid polished wood and alloy much like the Figoni and Falaschi Talbots from the Classic era. He envisaged lots of hand-made details along with beautiful cream instrument faces set in turned stainless surrounds, bespoke switches, polished alloy gearbox, handbrake gate, heater controls and gear knob, Nardi steering wheel and the seats to be upholstered in light tan hand-stitched saddle leather.

The Sports would be quite different in style and feel, more in line with its intended buyer demographic by having wrap-around bucket seats in bare, polished aluminium, chassis details inside left bare, anodised brushed alloy instrument panel, and a four-spoke alloy steering wheel with leather rim. The Sports body would be slightly different insofar as its front and rear overhangs would be shorter, its wings cut away and individual aero screens would be fitted.

These ideas were all part of the path that slowly led to the definitive Aero 8 style both inside and out.

The first hand-built Morgan Aero 8 prototype

By September 1999 some Morgan dealers had seen the full-scale model of P8000 and some feedback was received that showed they were not particularly happy; they were mostly content with the rear styling with its simple round tail lights although it later became necessary to use new fog and reversing lamps. They were less than enthusiastic about the headlights that were mounted to give it a "cross-eyed" look. As far as the interior was concerned, 80 per cent of the dealers liked it.

Rob Wells, dealer principal at Libra Motive, a Morgan specialist dealer in London, was one who had seen and driven the new car (it was apparently one of the first prototypes) and wrote to Charles Morgan saying, "It was a credit to all involved. Given that the performance is achievable with anything of similar weight and power, the handling and control are exemplary. Brakes, steering and ride are all first class for what is truly a race bred car." He went on to discuss his thoughts on the car's styling saying, "I like the rear three-quarter view, the profile, all just right. I like the bootlid, rear wings, the coupé bit behind the back of the hood and the rear tunnel." Then he came to the front. "This is always going to be the most controversial part—very Cruella De-Ville. I see what you are getting at and I like the idea." He went on to say that he thought the hood and scuttle were in need of an update—"the appearance is of new wings attached to the old shape centre section."

The Morgan Aero 8 gained infamy because of its unusual head lights which gave the car a cross eyed look

Lawrence had taken two weeks off from the demands of the program to go to the American Society of Auto-Engineers exhibition in 1999 to look at the hundreds of offerings from the world's automobile industry as well as the accessory manufacturers. The aerodynamics of P8000 was concerning him, especially the problem of keeping the car's front down and in contact with terra firma at high speed. Testing at the full-sized wind tunnel at MIRA had shown the P8000 to have 80lbs of lift at the front and 180lbs of lift at the rear at 120mph which he deemed unacceptable. One of the prime causes of this was the almost total lack of frontal overhang. As

CHAPTER THREE • DESIGN ASPECTS

Morgan testing the Aero 8 in the MIRA wind tunnel to optimise its aerodynamic performance

Lawrence wrote in his autobiography *Morgan Maverick*, "Somehow I needed to get Charles to accept at least the wings being extended forward."

While wandering around in the huge hall of accessory products he happened onto the Bosch stand. Lawrence remembered, "I stood there for several minutes pondering the problem when my eyes fell upon the headlights for the new VW Beetle. In my mind I was seeking a way of bringing the leading edge of the front wings forward of the radiator and immediately I visualised these Beetle headlights mounted sideways-and-forward to give ample clearance from the front wheels and at the same time bringing the edge of the wing forward so I could put a splitter under the grille and between the two front wings and get the downforce that I needed—problem solved!"

When Lawrence returned to Malvern Link he coerced Charles into restyling the front of P8000 to accommodate the Beetle headlights. The result was certainly distinctive and unbeknown to the two men at the time would be the source of scorn and wonderment in equal measure when the sports car was publicly released. In addition to the VW headlights the team opted to use Chrysler-sourced indicator lens at the front and round lights at the rear sourced from Reed Industries because these parts had already been homologated for Europe and the USA thereby saving Morgan considerable time and expense.

At a meeting on October 31, 2000 (well after the Geneva Show) the styling of P8000, by now being referred to internally as the Aero 8 (it had previously been referred to as the "new Plus Eight"), was signed off by the Styling Committee for production following a further showing at the NEC in Birmingham. The dashboard design as conceived by Charles was unusual insofar as the six dials—two large and four small—with silver bevelled edges were grouped in a broad U-shaped nacelle that stretched from the side of the interior to about two-thirds of the way across the car. It fitted between the steering column and the underside of the polished ash wooden rail that swept across the top of the dash. Buried under the dash were the audio system and the heater/demister/air conditioning controls and vents while on the leather upholstered console was the gearshift lever, fly-off handbrake and power window switches. One of the nice touches that came with the Series 1 Aero 8 was the leather briefcase made by Mulberry, a company based in Somerset.

There were, however, a myriad of tiny details that were felt ought to be changed; for example, the gauges needed to be lowered by 6mm for better visibility through the steering wheel, the switches it was felt would look better if they were round push button types rather than rocker type—the suggestion was for the head and side lights on-off switch be a three-position turned aluminium knob with the light symbol laser etched into it, the re-positioning of the electric window switches because it was too easy to touch them with the elbow. With these changes made, the dash was signed off for production.

An early version of the Aero 8 dashboard under construction in the factory workshop

The sloping rear was nicely integrated if a little plain in comparison with the front but with its three round lights each side it was neat and inoffensive. Lawrence made an observation that would have an effect later when he said, "I noticed when we were carrying out aerodynamic tests in the wind tunnel at MIRA that we achieved better results when the wind sucked the boot lid up by about 4-inches. We spent a lot of time in the wind tunnel refining various aspects of the P8000's design to make it dynamically stable at high speed, and eventually achieved a Cd of between 0.42 and 0.45 which was probably the best for a Morgan sports car ever!"

Interestingly, after viewing the third prototype for some time its designer Charles Morgan was moved to comment, "The swoops and curves of the bodywork look like modern sculpture and I think the turned stainless steel instrument panel looks expensive particularly when contrasted with the polished ash header rail. And the vertical louvres in the wings are great while

Chapter Three • Design Aspects

the front splitter is brilliant, especially the way the radiator mesh reflects in the surface and the way the same extrusion had been used on the wings as a finisher." He continued by saying, "The front of the car looks stunning; the indicators are perfect and the headlights look truly impressive." That last comment is interesting considering the sometimes heated discussions he had with Chris Lawrence on the subject and the furore they would create in the media!

Apart from the aluminium intensive tub that Lawrence designed he incorporated several new ideas into the rolling P8000 chassis. These were "new ideas" to Morgan but they were not new to Lawrence. The front suspension was a derivation of that which he had designed for the ill-fated Monica luxury saloon car project that he had led during the early Seventies; he used a simple fabricated lower wishbone allied to a tall cast upright-cum-front hub and a long upper wishbone that pivoted on a chassis support somewhere near its mid-point. This acted upon a spring/damper unit mounted inboard; incorporated in the front suspension was centre-point steering geometry. Where the front brake discs on the Monica were also mounted inboard on stub axles for better cooling, those on the P8000 were mounted conventionally on the outside of the hub for easier servicing.

On the Monica the steering rack was positioned high, parallel to the upper wishbone so that the steering was working on the same plane as the movement of the front suspension thereby eliminating any bump steer. It was not possible to do that with the P8000 and so the rack was mounted on the lower rail of the front sub-frame. This involved some belt 'n braces engineering at first from Lawrence who recalled it with a gleam in his eye: "There was insufficient room for a conventional rack to be installed and so I thought for a moment, 'What am I going to do?' Then I conceived the idea of a tandem unit and made the first prototype one by cobbling it up from a

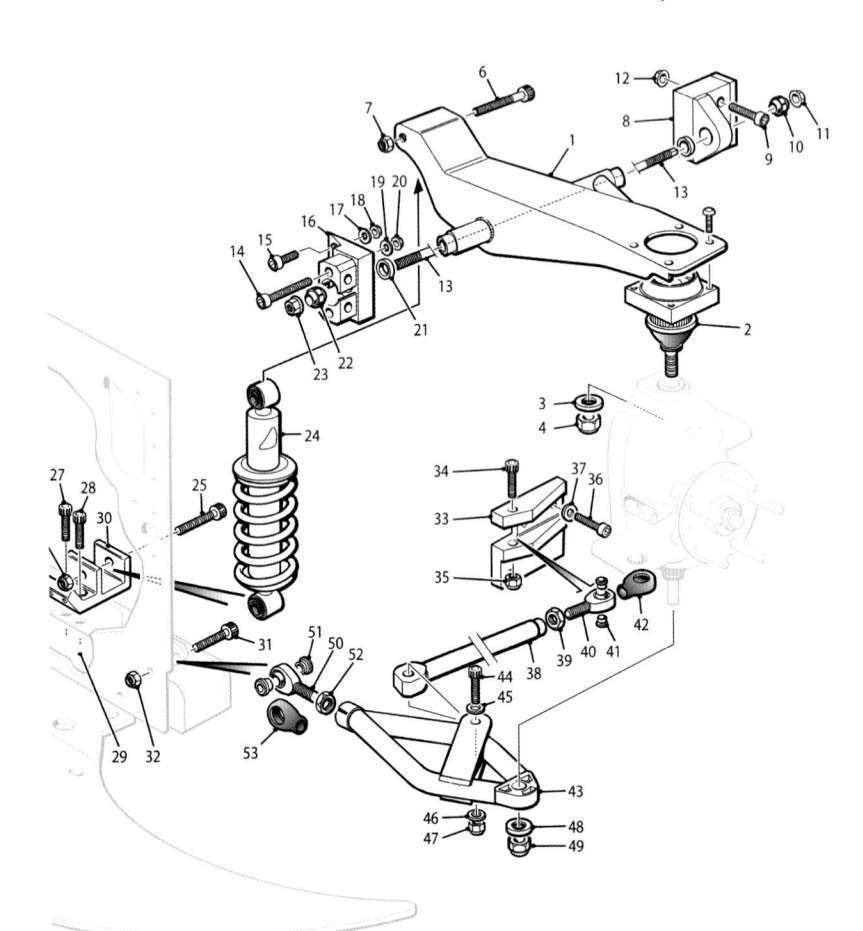

An exploded diagram of the Chris Lawrence designed independent front suspension

Ford Granada unit I'd bought from a recycling business. Jack Knight Developments in Woking ended up manufacturing it for us."

At the rear Lawrence designed a sophisticated double wishbone system that bore some resemblance to that on the Marcos LM600 racing car project that he had worked on in 1995. The most significant difference between the Lawrence system and other more conventional suspension systems lay in the way in which the spring/damper units each side operated. In a normal system the top mount would be positioned on the chassis and the lower one on one of the wishbones but in the P8000 system the top mount was on the upper wishbone and the lower one was bolted to the bottom wishbone—it worked on a ratio system. And as Lawrence commented somewhat assertively, "It works brilliantly! You can throw as much power as you like at it and it never gets fazed."

Interestingly, the Morgan Motor Company and not Christopher Lawrence patented the P8000's independent rear suspension.

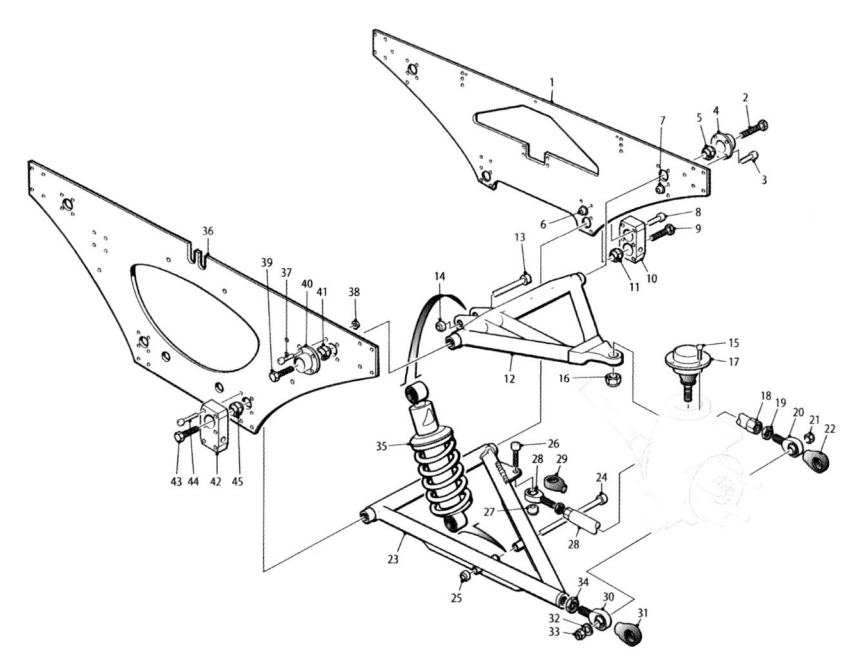

An exploded diagram of the Chris Lawrence designed independent rear suspension

With any new car development, especially one that is destined for production, there is the issue of Type Approval that must be met. At first there were two main people involved in building prototype P8000's for test and development—Chris Lawrence and John Burbidge—but as events moved forward it became necessary to add a third person who would concentrate on getting the car through the Type Approval to European Whole Car requirements. That person was Mark Reeves.

In line with Lawrence's mantra about minimising weight, he had designed a pair of lightweight bucket seats—"They were very much like racing seats," said Reeves who added, "That should surprise nobody who knows Chris Lawrence's background." However, when put to the test they failed badly. They were redesigned and we re-engineered the seat belt mounting points and these passed the test. However, for actual production bought-in seats from Restall were used—later sourced from MB Components who continue to supply them today—with a revised

Chapter Three • Design Aspects

Looks like a Plus 8 but is in fact an Aero 8 development car

seat pan to minimise the "submarining" effect in high speed impacts.

At this time, late 1999, there were three off-tools prototypes in existence and a fourth—the Geneva Show car—under construction. An interesting tale surrounds prototype number three, the first to actually look like the future Aero 8. Cars one and two were P8000 underneath but Plus 8 in external appearance.

Frontal crash tests were carried out at MIRA in November 2000 and the car passed first time. No rear impact or roll-over tests were necessary in 1999 for Euro compliance nor were airbags required and so were not fitted. Mark Reeves continued by adding, "The Vehicle Certification Agency (VCA) required that Morgan submit the car for testing to comply with European whole car type approval. A number of tests were carried out, some at MIRA and some at Milbrook, the former Vauxhall proving ground." The tests included seat belt anchorages and seat strength, tests that were carried out on a sled, occupant head impact on the dash rail, defrost and demist capabilities along with windscreen wiper coverage and front and side visibility. In addition the door hinges and locks were strength tested and the fuel tank was pressurised and the car rolled over to check for any leaks. The Aero 8 passed all tests first time which was a credit to the small team. As Reeves commented years later, "They requested that we carry out a test against the interior woodwork. This surprised us a little because the wood is on the dash, well out of range of the dummy; wood is not soft but it was attached to a hand-formed aluminium panel across the scuttle that had sufficient 'give' in it to pass anyway."

There were many other items that were scrutinised under the VCA, such as the vertical limits on forward visibility caused by the height of the cowl and bonnet in relation to the seating height, interior and exterior projections. Charles Morgan was moved to say after one of the cars had returned from VCA testing at MIRA, "Please don't let's design a car just for the VCA!"

With Bosch remapping the Digital Motor Electronics (DME) unit Morgan was able to fully comply—indeed, well exceed—the engine and evaporative emission (whole vehicle) requirements in a test carried out by the German organisation Technischer Überwachungs Verein, generally known as TÜV; it is an organisation that conducts tests on cars for roadworthiness and safety.

Problems were still being experienced with the hood, even towards the end of 1999. It was not possible, or desirable, to simply re-use the folding top from the Plus Eight because tests had shown that above 120mph it would detach itself from the car! A completely new hood was required and it took quite a deal of testing to get it near what they wanted. In the opinion of Lawrence and others who drove the prototypes there was far too much noise coming from areas like the gaps at the side, behind the windscreen, and from air forcing its way into the interior from a gap in the centre of the top of the screen.

The eventual design which was tested at high speed at Miramas had a special tensioning feature—two handles when turned raised the hood frame to tension the mohair skin. This resulted from the experience of seeing the BMW Z8 under development at the same venue. When Lawrence asked the BMW engineers how they kept the hood so tight they said, "We can't take it down!"

For production (for Series I) the hood frame was made by Radshape with all the trimming being carried out in-house.

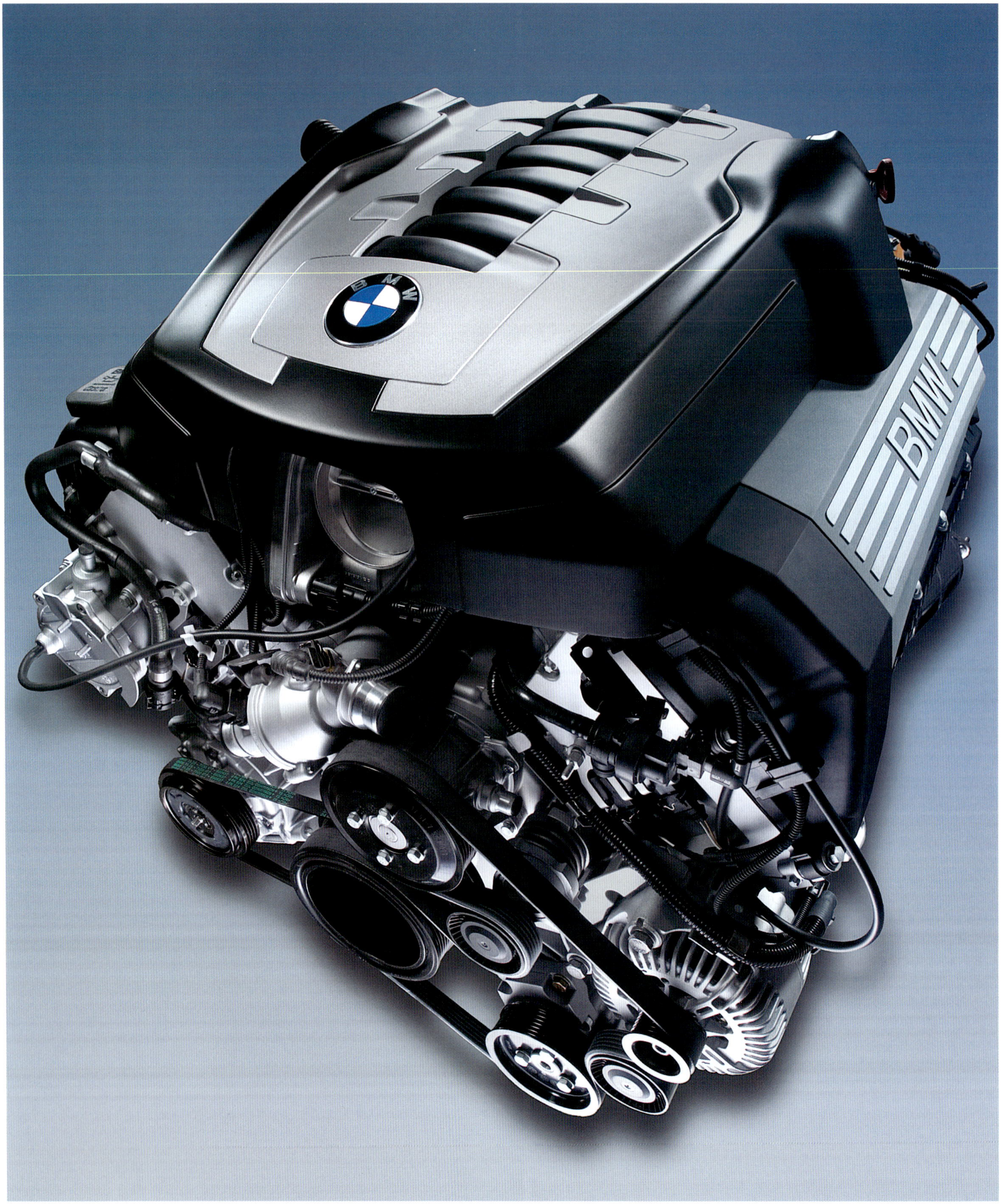
BMW

Chapter Four

ENGINE AND DRIVELINE: THE BMW CONNECTION

Both Charles Morgan and Chris Lawrence are unequivocal in their view that the Aero 8 would not be the superb sports roadster that it turned out to be without the assistance of the Bayerische Motoren Werke (BMW) AG. Having said that, it must be acknowledged that the Morgan Motor Company had many unique attributes that endeared it to clients and industry personnel alike. One of the most significant aspects if its history is that it has never built its own engines, it has always relied on the broader automotive community to be generous enough to build engines in the tiny numbers the company has needed them. Early suppliers included motorcycle manufacturer AJS and proprietary engine makers JAP and Coventry Victor as well as the Ford Motor Company in both the pre- and post-war years.

After the cessation of hostilities in 1945 Morgan began a long association with the Standard Triumph Motor Company in Coventry who supplied the company with the Standard Vanguard 2-litre OHV in-line four-cylinder engine for the Plus 4 before switching to the more powerful Triumph TR3 version of the same engine in 1953. This engine was a completely new design from Standard that powered cars beginning with the "humpy-backed" Vanguard saloon first shown at the 1948 Earls Court show. Sir John Black discontinued all other Standard and Triumph models in line with the Attlee Labour Government's policy and concentrated all export efforts on the Vanguard. His engineering team began development of the engine in late 1943; it was based around a cast iron cylinder block

This is a cut away illustration of the Standard Vanguard four-cylinder OHV engine as used by Morgan

and an 8-port cylinder head (also in cast iron) with a forged steel three-bearing crankshaft. Of particular note, for an English engine from that era, was the use of pushrod operated overhead valves and "wet" cylinder liners. It powered Vanguard saloons, estate cars, wagons and utilities until 1961 when it was phased out in favour of a completely new 2-litre OHV six-cylinder engine that was far more refined. Along the way it also powered other low volume production cars, Morgan being one of them, as well as hundreds of thousands of Ferguson tractors.

In 1968 Morgan announced the Plus 8 powered by the ubiquitous Rover (nee Buick) light weight aluminium alloy V8 engine of 3.5-litres capacity. This sports car was extremely quick, particularly in acceleration where the comparatively light weight of the whole car contributed to a marvellously tactile experience for the driver. Top speed was limited by the engine's ability to pull the high top gear ratio, and the car's poor aerodynamics. It was at the time the fastest Morgan ever and one of the fastest English sports cars made.

Since then the company has had various agreements in place whereby engines have been supplied by Rover's Powertrain Division (the K Series four-cylinder engines in M16 and T16

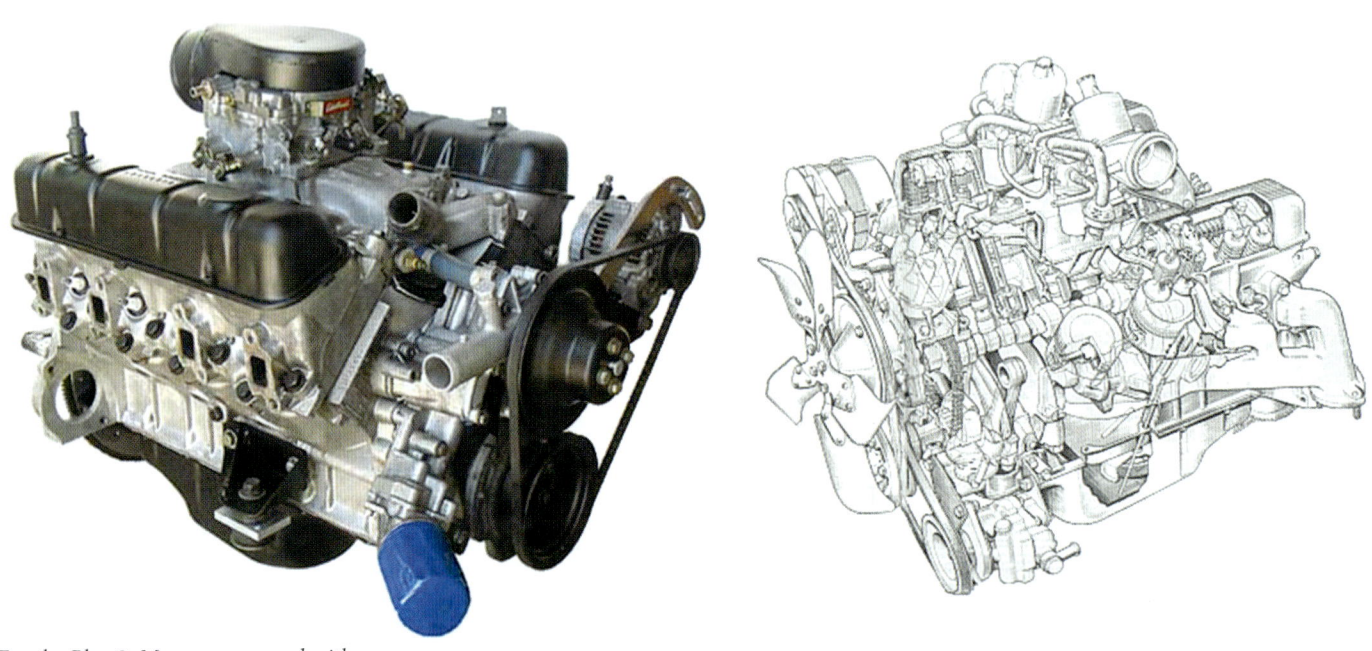

For the Plus 8 Morgan arranged with Rover to buy their aluminium alloy V8 engine--a master stroke

guise) as well as with Fiat in Italy who supplied both its 1.6- and 2-litre Aurelio Lampredi-designed DOHC in-line four-cylinder engines for the 4/4 between 1981-85 and the Plus 4 from 1985-87.

During the early 1990s Charles Morgan, with the knowledge and support of his father, began casting around the world's automobile industry for a new engine to power a sports car that existed only as an idea in his mind at that time. Several manufacturers were approached—BMW, Audi, Mercedes-Benz, Jaguar, Lexus—with varying degrees of success. His main criteria were for a combination of weight, physical size as in its height-width-length, power and torque characteristics, cost and what gearbox was available. Rover had notified Morgan in 1996 that their alloy V8 would not pass the known emission requirements for 2000 and beyond setting in (slow) motion the search for a replacement engine for the Plus 8 and Charles' future sports car.

Audi was keen but their engine, the 4.2-litre DOHC unit as used in the A8, was down on power and was physically much bigger and heavier than Charles believed desirable for his as yet unrealised new car. Having said that Audi later came out with a more powerful and lighter version but by then it was too late; the other mitigating factor against the Audi engine was that it was designed for either front-wheel drive or all-wheel drive in conjunction with an automatic gearbox. The Jaguar V8 was discounted on the grounds that it was unavailable with a manual gearbox of any description at that time. Having said that, it was not the package that the BMW was and the people at Jaguar were less than enthusiastic about supplying Morgan. Much the same attitude was experienced with the people at Mercedes-Benz although their engine was much heavier and vastly more expensive than the others. Lexus was keen but they had no experience in dealing with outside companies like Morgan even though from Morgan's point of view their engine, a 4-litre DOHC alloy V8, was very suitable; however, as with Audi and Jaguar, there was no manual transmission available to go with it. The other problem for Morgan if they had gone with Lexus was one of geography—the supply line would be more than 8,000 miles long!

For the Aero 8 Morgan considered the Mercedes-Benz V8 (above), the Lexus V8 (below) and the Audi V8 (bottom).

Eventually after much discussion the company settled on BMW because as Charles put it, "It was by far the best engine given its size and power versus its relatively light weight, but the clincher for me was the availability of it with the Getrag six-speed manual gearbox." A single example of the BMW M60 4.0-litre quad-cam V8 engine was purchased in March 1994 together with a Getrag six-speed manual gearbox and installed in a Plus 8 chassis "for purely speculative test purposes," as Charles put it. The transaction cost Morgan a considerable sum of money (rumoured to have been something like DM12,000) for the package that also included two lambda sensors, two additional catalysts, a Motronic unit, ECU, air mass meters, power steering pump, fan and fan clutch and an intake muffler. Engineers Rudolf Handlgruber and Manfred Magliotti from BMW Steyr in Austria were responsible from the BMW end.

After due consideration a contract was signed for the 4.4 litre BMW V8 engine

It was this Plus 8 that Lawrence saw when he visited the factory late in 1996 and about which he was so scathing in his opinion.

How Morgan and BMW came to be linked is one of those fascinating tales of the car industry. Before BMW bought an interest in the Rover Group early in 1994, Morgan had approached Dipl.Ing Rudolf Handlgruber of BMW Motoren in Steyr at the Geneva Motor Show to ascertain whether BMW would be interested in supplying V8 engines to Morgan. A visit was arranged between the two companies whereby members of the Vorstand at BMW came to Malvern Link to view the premises and after further discussions an agreement in principle was reached.

Four years later and journalist Mike Rutherford, writing for *Auto Express* magazine, raised the question as to whether BMW's Bernd Pichetsrieder might be looking to add another British car company to its corporate portfolio. Both TVR and Morgan were mentioned. However, Pichetsrieder assured Rutherford, "TVR, no. Morgan? It's a family-run business and the chairman, Peter Morgan, is a friend of mine. Whenever he wants help from BMW he'll get it." At a meeting in Kitzbuhl, Austria in 2000 he told Charles Morgan, "You are the only people outside the BMW Group that we would allow to have the V8 engine."

The next contact with BMW was incredibly informal given the German's sense of occasion but unbelievably it set the tone for what has blossomed into a firm and friendly, and yet at all times highly professional, relationship between the two companies and their representatives. By a coincidence of fate, at the 1997 Nürburgring round of the European GT Championship BMW Motorsport was there supporting private teams that were running the McLaren F1 GTR. The head of BMW Motorsport at the time was Karl-Heinz Kalbfell who was accompanied at the event by Dr Wolfgang Reitzle. Kalbfell remembered, "There was this unusual car in the race, the Morgan and I was impressed upon hearing that one of the heroic drivers was none other than Charles himself." As it happened, the pit garages for the Team Schnitzer cars and Morgan were adjacent to each other. Naturally in moments of comparative calm the teams chatted and chided each other, all good naturedly of course. At the end of the race in which the BMW team finished well in front of the Morgan Plus 8 driven by Charles Morgan and Bill Wykeham, Charles and Chris Lawrence happened to bump into Kalbfell and Reitzle. The Germans said, "It is good that we won, but even better that you finished!" to which Charles Morgan and Chris Lawrence responded, "If we'd had a BMW engine we would have won the bloody race!" All four men laughed at the riposte but the incident remained in their minds for some time afterwards.

A month later Kalbfell visited Morgan in Malvern Link and assured Charles Morgan and Lawrence that he would personally work on their behalf to gain permission for Morgan to have use of the BMW V8 engine.

A key man in the negotiations was Karl-Heinz Kalbfell, a Morgan enthusiast

But as Kalbfell remembered more than a decade later, "Charles asked me if he could buy a BMW race engine. I discussed this with my chief engineer Paul Rosche but he was not too convinced about the opportunity mainly because of the cost and support from BMW M GmbH. But I stayed in contact with Charles and the relationship became closer when our involvement with Rover became deeper."

Kalbfell, as is known in motoring circles, is an English car enthusiast and a Morgan owner—he and his wife Marianne love to go driving in the countryside in their black Morgan Plus 8. As he said, "I thoroughly enjoy my Morgan; it is an exhilarating car to drive fast in the country!" He also appreciated the way in which Morgan sports cars were made, the craftsmanship and olde worlde atmosphere that was alive and well in Malvern Link but which had been expunged from the automobile business virtually everywhere else in the world and most certainly from BMW.

Kalbfell was approached again in late 1997 and by this time he had been re-assigned from BMW M GmbH to BMW AG as the head of marketing and product strategy where he led the BMW Product Circle that included responsibility for customer projects such as engine sales to external clients. "It was a lucky coincidence that I could support Charles' requests to get the BMW V8 as a successor to the Rover V8," said Kalbfell in correspondence with the author. By May 1998 arrangements had been made for Charles and Chris to meet in Munich with Dipl. Ing Manfred Christian who was in charge of BMW's engines sales and based at the company's huge plant in Steyr, Austria, together with Dr Schmidt who was head of engine development at the FIZ, Dip-Ing Wolfgang Hall who was a gearbox specialist and Gunther Ranzinger who was an electronics engineer. Another senior BMW engineer, Dipl. Ing. Chris Schausberger, was not at that original meeting but he was to remain close to the project and together with a small team within BMW was to be the "realisation partner for Charles" as the Germans put it.

A Confidentiality Agreement was signed between the two companies on January 20, 1998 and between then and the year 2000 the two companies held many discussions and a contract for the long term supply of engines to the Morgan Motor Company was eventually agreed on about a year later. A most interesting aspect of these negotiations was the fact that until then BMW

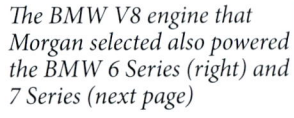

The BMW V8 engine that Morgan selected also powered the BMW 6 Series (right) and 7 Series (next page)

had not supplied any other company with its V8 engines; they had been for the exclusive use of BMW's automobile range.

Charles Morgan was involved in all the discussions and negotiations with BMW from the beginning and on several occasions Chris Lawrence attended as his Technical Director.

Released in 1992 to power various 5, 7 and 8 Series' BMWs, the M60 engine family was upgraded to M62 status in 1996 which saw the V8 engines increased in capacity to 3.5- and 4.4-litres and for them both to adopt the company's VANOS system of variable valve timing on the intake side. Mated to the M62B44 engine was to be the Getrag S6 D420G six-speed manual gearbox, something that was absolutely critical to Charles Morgan's decision to go with BMW. It had gear ratios of 4.227 for 1st gear, 2.506 in 2nd, 1.669 in 3rd, 1.226 in 4th, 1.00 in 5th and 0.828 for 6th with a tiny 6-inch tall gearshift lever on the centre console, each shift being little more than a flick of the wrist to accomplish. Drive went via a one-piece propeller shaft to the rear-mounted differential that ran a 3.08:1 axle ratio that gave 28.44mph per 1000 rpm in sixth gear.

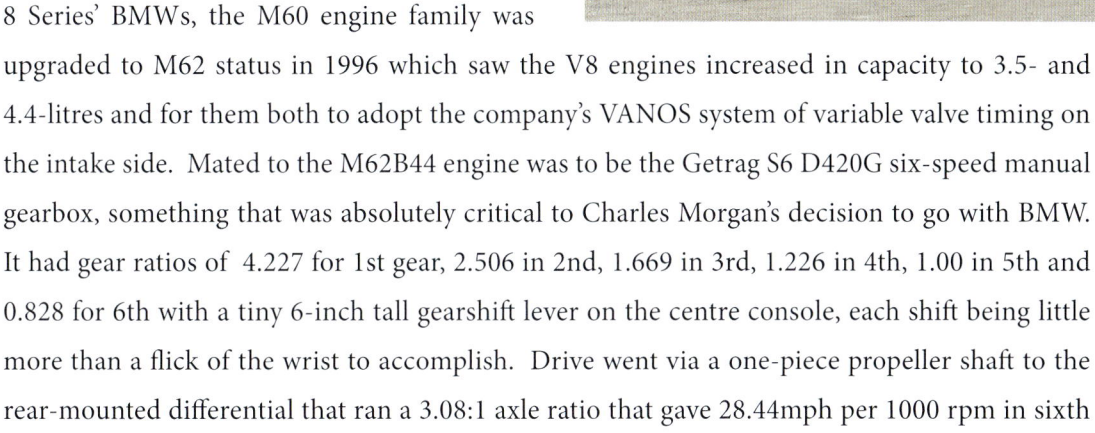

While Lawrence was building prototype #1—actually the second prototype as "Big Blue" was technically the first—news filtered through that BMW wanted to send a team of engineers to Malvern Link to supervise the engine installation. "We proffered a polite-but-firm 'No' to that one!" commented Lawrence who added, "It died a natural death after that but it did bring a great guy into our orbit—Gunther Ranzinger. He and I quickly became friends and had a great respect for one another. We're still friends to this day."

As Lawrence soon found out, the fitting of a physically large V8 engine into a classic long and comparatively narrow chassis was no walk in the park. Car #2, like Car #1, consisted of Lawrence's innovative aluminium chassis under a modified Plus

A superb technical illustration of the N62 V8 engine as used in the Aero 8

8 body—it was wider and the wings and bonnet were a one-piece fibreglass moulding. The biggest problem was the BMW cooling system which was bulky. BMW were insistent that Lawrence use the engine-driven fan from the 540i but as he somewhat wryly commented, "It was a huge piece of windmill!" It simply would not fit so a uniquely Morgan solution was devised in which the actual 540i radiator—"Aluminium, plastic end covers, beautifully made, very light in weight, delightful"—was squeezed in with dual thermo-electric fans to dissipate excess heat when required. In a quiet and private moment the Germans acknowledged that the Lawrence solution was superior to theirs!

The next challenge for Lawrence was the exhaust system which on the 540i was bulky and had four catalytic converters to meet the emission requirements. Working alone he hand fabricated a triple-skinned system that would bolt up to the V8 engine and clear—just—the chassis; it replicated the BMW system but went in a different direction. Lawrence made three of these systems by hand.

Boysen was the company in Germany that manufactured exhaust systems for BMW and a visit was arranged for Lawrence and Ranzinger to meet with their manufacturing engineer. Lawrence took one of his systems with him and when it was shown to the Boysen representative he inquired as to who made it. "I did with these hands, a mallet and a welding kit!" said Lawrence with all due modesty. Apparently this admission deeply impressed the Boysen man and helped in them giving Morgan a good deal for the exhaust system. Initial discussions with the company had indications of a multi-million Pound contract that was way beyond Morgan's ability to afford but as Lawrence commented some years later, "I am sure BMW 'leaned on' Boysen which resulted in the cost being most reasonable from Morgan's point of view," and as he added, "The exhaust systems were beautifully made." Boysen's contract with Morgan was for them to supply a complete exhaust system for the first 300 Aero 8s. However, the contract for supply has been extended to cover all production of the BMW-engined Morgans.

Having sorted the exhaust system, the next hurdle to be overcome centred on the electronic engine management system. Robert Bosch AG was the manufacturer and supplier to BMW. However, the problem for Morgan was that the Digital Motor Electronic (DME) system needed to be completely recalibrated for the Aero 8 as the car was considerably lighter and had different performance criteria to any BMW. Bosch requested a car as soon as possible and they wanted it for at least a year to develop a Morgan-specific system.

Charles Morgan had agreed to Bosch's request without really knowing where Lawrence was in his prototype build program. Suddenly a sense of urgency crept over the program because Lawrence had taken nearly 7 months building Car #2 on his own. Clearly he needed assistance if Bosch was to get its car within a reasonable time. John Burbidge was seconded from the workshops to work with Lawrence and between the two of them Car #3 was built in 16 weeks—it was left-hand drive, did not have power steering and was painted dark green, a very British colour!

That Morgan became the "toy" of a man Lawrence described as "an absolute boffin," a young man by the name of Thomas Mössner who developed a completely new electronic system that apparently included cruise control—"In a manual sports car, idiotic!" stated Lawrence.

At this time another new "recruit" joined Lawrence's team in the person of Dave Goodwin who was charged with the responsibility of entering all the engineering data onto Morgan's new computer that included CATIA software to enable direct downloading of data between Munich and Malvern Link.

Not long after Car #3 had been completed and despatched to Bosch in Stuttgart, Charles Morgan and Chris Lawrence received a call from Gunther Ranzinger who informed them that BMW management had decided that they could not supply Morgan with engines after all. At that point three engines had been received and a further five were in transit.

Upon inquiring about this change of heart the issue turned out to one of security. The department within BMW that was responsible for developing and protecting the electronic security system that is imbedded in each BMW system had not been informed that the tiny sports car manufacturer, Morgan, was being sold engines with no clearance from the department head to have access to BMW's security codes. As Lawrence commented years later, "Since BMW had implemented the system across their wide range of vehicles no car had been stolen and they were reluctant to let this tiny British company in the Malvern hills have it because they were sure that the unthinkable would happen."

Charles Morgan personally dealt with the situation that took several weeks to resolve.

An integral part of the agreement with BMW allowed Morgan test and development time at the company's huge proving grounds at Miramas in the Camargue area in the south of France between Arles and Marseilles in what is often referred to as lavender country; it was a 40-minute drive from Marseilles. L'Autodrome de Miramas had been built in the 1920s (at around the same time as the more famous Montlhery circuit on the outskirts of Paris) and inaugurated in 1923 with a motorcycle Grand Prix and in 1926 hosted the French Grand Prix but few other significant events were held at the circuit and the original owners walked away in 1941, its remoteness meant that it seldom held a major event and fell into disrepair.

In 1970 the French tyre manufacturer Kléber Colombes took over the idle facilities and invested heavily in upgrading the circuit and other track surfaces in line with their need to prove their tyres. BMW purchased it from Kléber in 1986 and proceeded to further improve and expand the facilities by considerable investment in new roads, uprated high speed oval, handling circuit and buildings. Interestingly, initially the company had planned to excavate the old (original) circuit surface until some of the engineers involved realised that it was perfect for testing BMW prototype's suspension and roadholding on the undulating and rough surface and so it was left as it was.

The most challenging road at Miramas is what is called the "ring motorway" or the "Anneau d'Istre," a 3.9 mile (6.3kms) circular track with banked curves that allows very high speeds to be maintained for extended periods of time

Over the winter of 1998/99 Lawrence set out for Miramas with two prototypes—Plus 8 Aeros, cars number 1 and 2—with not a little trepidation wondering what kind of a reception they might receive from the German engineers who worked there. The group from Morgan comprised Lawrence, Mark Baldwin, John Burbidge and Dave Goodwin while Gunther Ranzinger joined them from Munich and Thomas Mössner came down from Stuttgart in "his" Plus 8 Aero. Charles Morgan flew over to join them three days later.

Chris Lawrence's fears were completely unfounded as they were greeted extremely cordially, checked through security and escorted to a garage that was spotless and allowed them to get on with their tasks. "That facility at Miramas was astonishing; I had never seen anything like it and felt very humble," said Lawrence of the experience.

Much of the first day was spent establishing accurate data and calibrations for the ECU on car #2. Car #1 was taken out onto the outer circuit where Lawrence, accompanied by Ranzinger, went through a number of performance checks including a number of laps of the banked high speed circuit at 260 km/h (160 mph). The afternoon was spent on the three ride and handling tracks which Lawrence described as "enormous fun."

"When we got back there was a bunch of BMW guys standing nearby having watched these two old fashioned British sports cars roaring around their track. I offered the French Director of Miramas, a Mr Froment, and the German Director of engineering a drive of the cars which naturally they accepted. They went out onto the handling circuit and were gone for ages, eventually coming back with huge grins on their faces," remembered Lawrence of that first day.

The week at Miramas also indirectly helped Lawrence to solve another ticklish problem that concerned the car's steering column. Lawrence related, "We had two keys—one for the BMW system and one for the Rover steering column that we were using up until then—and it was an awkward lashup to say the least. BMW had refused to allow us their steering column-and-ignition assembly (that security thing again) for fear of litigation as it was a safety item. Anyway, when we arrived back at Morgan there were three BMW columns on my desk—obviously one of the Miramas people saw the stupidity of the situation and strings were pulled to get around the rigid internal system at BMW. I said a quiet thank you in the direction of Munich!"

Since then, BMW has supplied Morgan with its steering column along with the M62 V8 engine and Getrag S6 D420G six-speed manual gearbox.

One of the issues that arose during high speed testing of the Plus 8 Aero concerned the temperature of the gearbox oil; it was a problem BMW was also experiencing with their Z8 prototypes. They had solved it by the simple addition of two air scoops under the car that directed air flow over the gearbox and kept it much cooler; it was suggested Morgan do the same which they did and the problem was solved, too. At the same time the gearbox casing was modified to provide a small front "chamber" to stop oil surge during acceleration. This was important because on the skid pad the Morgans were generating 1.05-to-1.10g compared with the best BMW at between 0.95 and 0.98 and under full acceleration in first gear the first motion shaft was starved of oil and liable to break.

Chapter Four • Engine And Driveline : The BMW Connection

Morgan choose the Sierra Nevada mountains in Spain for much of their hot weather testing

Where BMW carried out its hot weather testing at a facility of its own in Death Valley, USA, Morgan used the Sierra Nevada mountains near Granada in Spain. Interestingly, at the same time Mercedes-Benz engineers were there testing their forthcoming smart cars. Lawrence and his crew went there in July 1999, mid-summer, where the daytime temperatures reached 42° Celsius. The test consisted of flat out drives up and down the mountains and then rush into the main square of the town and park the car with the engine still running for half an hour. This was done several times with little ill-effect on the car but the same could not be said for the crew!

Back at Miramas several weeks later Lawrence had hooked up sensors on the gearbox and wired them into a laptop computer. Out he went onto the banking with Ranzinger holding the laptop and taking readings as Lawrence reeled off lap after lap starting with five at 100mph followed by five at 120mph, then five at 140mph and fifteen at wide open throttle which meant a speed in the vicinity of 165mph. With three laps to go the windscreen began to collapse in on the two occupants! Lawrence kept his foot flat on the accelerator and shouted to Ranzinger to use his free hand to hold the windscreen up…. At the end of the fifteen laps the car was parked in a shed where it was left to idle for 20 minutes.

Ranzinger climbed out of the prototype as white as a ghost! He has never forgotten the incident nor forgiven Lawrence!

Interior noise levels had to be lowered; the target set was to achieve 85db but as Lawrence somewhat wryly observed at that stage, "At current levels, buyers should be supplied with ear defenders to comply with legislative requirements!" Noise was apparently being generated from the driveline and differential as well as the exhaust system.

Chapter Four • Engine And Driveline : The BMW Connection

Consideration was given to modifications that were necessary to the soft top to ensure acceptable noise levels at 120mph. Lawrence had sourced hood catches from America—they were off the Chevrolet Corvette—that were strong enough to withstand the enormous forces generated at high speeds and yet were affordable for production. The new hood, designed by Chris Lawrence and made for Morgan by Radshape (the actual frame) and the inner hood was mohair-lined which included a waterproof membrane. A properly designed quality hardtop was also designed and featured a glass rear window with a heating element for demisting purposes.

Testing continued at Miramas and highlighted many areas for further development, development that Chris Lawrence knew had to be carried out as the P8000 was to be unlike any previous Morgan in every way. The power steering was found to be too direct at 2.4 turns lock-to-lock and so it was altered to give 2.8 turns; at first a Ford power steering pump was used but this proved to be unsatisfactory and so a ZF unit as used by BMW was specified that gave better "feel" and as a bonus the car seemed to possess superior directional stability.

Heat, noise and water leaks persisted despite several attempts to overcome them. "What surprised me," said Lawrence, "was the enormous amount of heat that the BMW V8 engine generated. We found we had to sheath the wiring loom, heater pipes and other components to protect them and not jeopardise their function." Even the air conditioning unit suffered in hot weather tests by shutting down when under-bonnet temperatures reached a certain (very high) level.

Lawrence and his team returned to Granada in July 2000 with cars #1, 2 and 3. Car three was a P8000 in most respects but the body exterior panels were made from fibreglass and was taken to Granada in Spain for hot weather testing in a covered trailer so that press photographers in England would not see it. It was also fitted with an integrated air conditioning system—a Morgan first. After a lengthy session of photographs Lawrence set off early the next morning and did several runs up the mountains but was unable to get the temperatures of the coolant and oils hot enough; it was suggested by Ranzinger that he (Lawrence) drive the whole way up the mountain in second gear. After lunch to honour Lawrence for his 67th birthday, he took the car to the top of the mountainous road by himself but still the car was not behaving itself and doing what was required; half way up the mountain he stopped, turned around to drive back down to the town and completely forgot he was in a left-hand drive country and came down on the left (wrong) side of the road. On a blind bend he crashed head-on into a milk lorry that was coming up the other way! In a very real world test of the P8000's structure it passed with flying colours, Lawrence suffering only a broken nose and some associated blood loss.

Noise from the wide tyres was prominent, there was still the issue of transmission shunt and on the left-hand drive prototype (Car #6?) the pedals were too far offset, the spring/damper settings were felt to be too hard and there appeared to be certain inconsistencies in the conversion from right- to left-hand drive where interior fittings were concerned as there was insufficient room under the steering wheel for the thighs and the foot well was very tight as well as the pedals being offset to the left causing the driver to sit out of alignment with respect to the seat and steering wheel.

As mentioned earlier, the Camargue was a vast area in the south of France that was totally flat, there were few geographic features to be seen which meant that any breeze was felt on the test tracks at Miramas. The Plus 8-bodied cars were particularly susceptible to wind gusts blowing between the trees and buildings but once they began testing proper off-tools P8000s the problem disappeared as those cars were supremely stable no matter what the conditions.

In all Lawrence took prototype Aeros to Miramas on six occasions where they were thrashed mercilessly and came up trumps despite the abuse heaped upon them. Car #2 racked up 140,000 miles of testing and Car #6—the second with actual Aero 8 bodywork—totalled 160,000 miles of testing.

One thing was absolutely undeniable—the Aero 8 was the most tested sports car ever to proudly carry the Morgan winged badge. As far as Chris Lawrence was concerned the Aero 8 was now ready for production.

THE BMW V8 ENGINE FAMILY

BMW were aware of the need to fill the yawning gap that existed in their engine range between the aging 3.5-litre six-cylinder engine that had been in production in various capacities since 1968 and the relatively new 5.0-litre V12. In 1984 a series of studies commenced that led to the M60 family of V8 engines that became available in the 5 and 7 Series sedans at first in 1992 followed a short time later by its availability in the 8 Series coupe. Dr-Ing Karlheinz Lange was in charge of the program and Dipl-Ing Reinhard Hoffmann was responsible for the engine's design and development that had a number of targets that were deemed desirable; for example, a reduction in fuel consumption and thereby in CO_2 emissions and the complying with the strictest international emissions legislation, reduced weight, modular design to permit vehicle-specific derivatives, to improve its functionality and reduce customer-relevant costs, to strengthen the dynamic driving experience no matter in which BMW model it was installed and to have a high potential for further development.

Two M60 engines were available at the release—a 3.0-litre unit (84 x 67.6mm, 2997cc, 218bhp at 5800rpm) and a 4.0-litre (89 x 80mm, 3982cc, 286bhp at 5800rpm) option. The smaller V8 was available in the 530i and 730i sedans and a small number of 830i coupes were built as test vehicles (believed to have been around 30 units) but never sold as the performance was well below what an 8 Series buyer would have expected. Sales volumes of the 3.0-litre cars were small by comparison with the 4.0-litre version that went under the bonnets of the 540i, 740i, 740iL and the 840i.

The new M60 V8 engines were very much state-of-the-art from an engineering and manufacturing point of view. The cylinder block used the traditional 90° V angle and was a one-piece deep skirt design featuring a closed top deck, the casting being made from an aluminium alloy with no liners at all. The cylinder bore surfaces were created by breaking open the hard silicone crystals using special soft honing tools while the pistons were cast using a temperature sensitive aluminium alloy with valve pockets included in the head and a microscopically thin iron coating that allowed them to run in direct contact with the honed bore surface.

The cylinder heads were made from low pressure cast aluminium with four-valves per cylinder inclined to each other at 30.5° with cross-flow porting; the combustion chambers were fully machined and the valve covers were made from aluminium alloy as was the complex intake manifold. Individual pencil ignition coils provide the spark.

The fully counter-weighted and balanced five-bearing crankshaft was manufactured from spherical graphite cast iron for the 3.0-litre engine and was forged for the 4.0-litre unit with induction hardened main bearings. Connecting rods were sintered forgings made to strict tolerances to minimise weight variations and were "cracked" during the manufacturing process (a world first by BMW), machined and then bolted over the big end to form a perfect joint.

Mounted at the front of the engine were the various ancillaries driven by a maintenance-free twin-belt arrangement; the main 6-groove belt drove from the nose of the crankshaft the water pump, alternator and power steering pump while a secondary 4-groove belt drove the air conditioning compressor; both belts had a linear tensioner with hydraulic damping in their path.

As was the case with all BMW engines, engine management that encompassed all facets of the operation from monitoring the fuel-air mixture through to the ignition process and emissions was controlled by a Bosch-supplied computerised system, labelled Digital Motor Electronics (DME) and in the M60 it was version ME3.3.

In 1996 the company uprated the engines to 3.5-litres (84 x 78.9mm, 3498cc, 235bhp at 5700rpm) and 4.4-litres (92 x 82.7mm, 4398cc, 286bhp at 5700rpm) and given the new designation of M62. Included in the upgrade was the use of a Bosch DME 5.2 electronic management system.

And in 1998 the M62 engines were the recipient of a VANOS variable valve timing unit on the front of the intake camshafts which boosted power slightly to 245bhp at 5800rpm for the 3.5-litre engine and remained the same 286bhp at a lower 5400rpm for the 4.4-litre unit. The Bosch DME unit was now up to version 7.2.

Development and evolution continued with the engine designation changing to N62 in 2001. At this time the V8 and the new V12 (introduced in 2002) was part of a new V-engine family that had a commonality of around 75 per cent. Capacity remained at 4398cc but two new developments appeared: bi-VANOS and VALVETRONIC, the N62 being the second engine to utilise this technology. BMW made much of these new technologies. Where previously the VANOS system had operated only on the inlet camshaft, bi-VANOS operated on both camshafts in conjunction with the revolutionary VALVETRONIC system.

This was a system that replaced the conventional butterfly valve that had been used in the intake systems of engines since the beginning of the modern era. VALVETRONIC altered the amount of lift for the inlet valve and could vary the opening of the valve from 0.4mm to 9.0mm depending on the driver's demands as registered by the electronic module attached to the accelerator. The dual benefit of this new system was that it reduced fuel consumption and engine emissions at the same time without compromising the engine's performance. Accompanying this new technology came uprated Bosch DME units—ME9.2 in 2001 followed by ME9.2.1 in 2002.

The final evolution of the BMW V8 engine, as it applies to Morgan, is the N62B48 which appeared in 2005. For this version the cylinder bores were widened slightly to 93mm and the crank stroke lengthened to 88.3mm for a capacity of 4,799cc. On a 10.0:1 compression the engine now developed 367bhp (270kW) at 6300rpm and 370 lbs-ft (490Nm) of torque at 3600rpm with the ECU now uprated yet again to ME9.2.2 and in 2007 to ME 9.2.3.

Although BMW itself has gone down the turbocharging route with its use of the V8 engine, a special arrangement has been accommodated between the two companies whereby BMW manufactures the non-turbo N62B48 V8 engine specifically for Morgan which reflects the respect each has for the other.

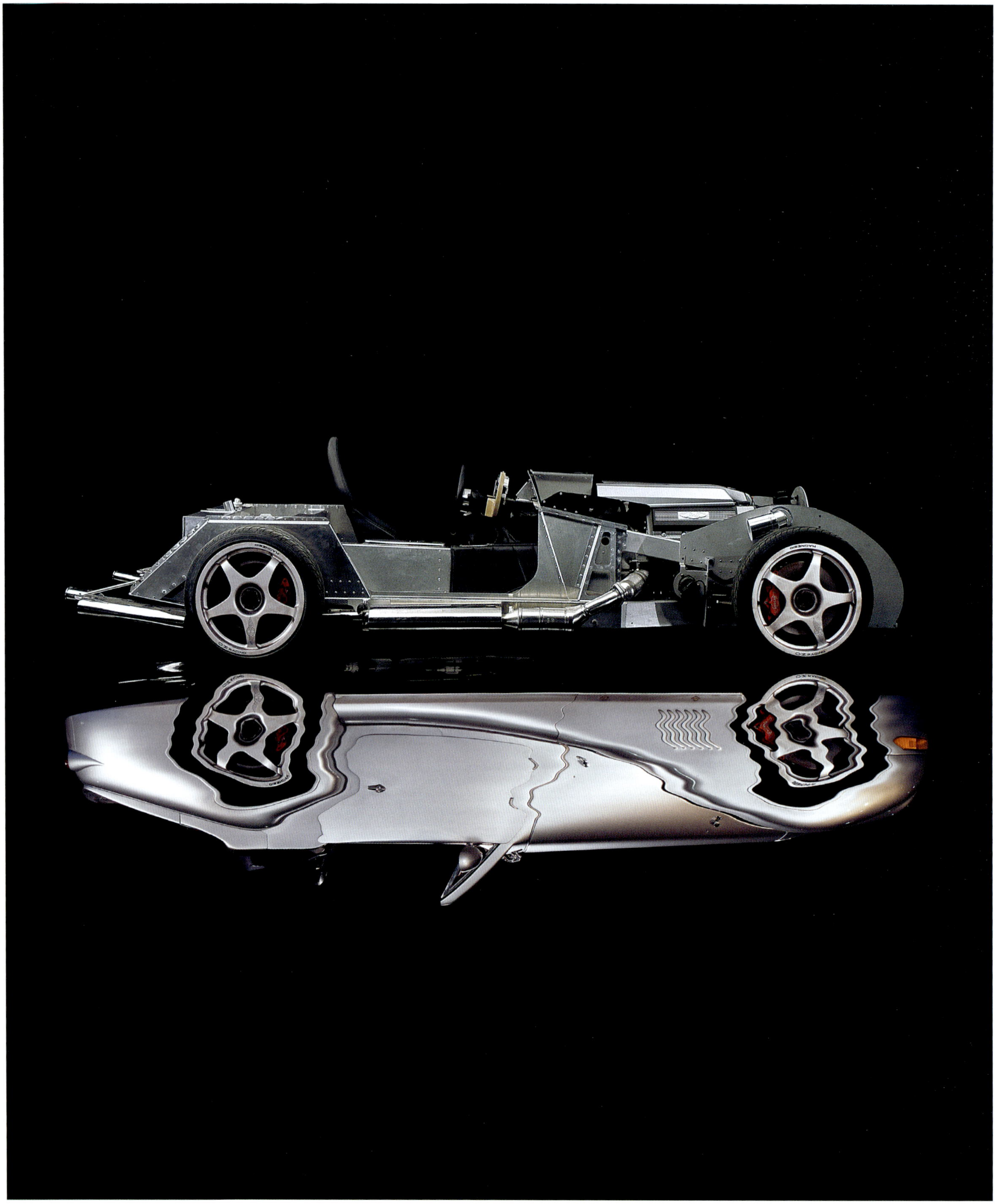

Chapter Five

GETTING THE AERO 8 INTO PRODUCTION

Industry analyst Sir John Harvey-Jones visited Morgan at their Malvern Link factory in the early 1990s and took the traditional walk around the factory with Peter Morgan to observe how a Morgan automobile was made. Harvey-Jones was apparently appalled at what he saw and said so on his television show *Troubleshooter* at the time. "Morgan must modernise or die," he proudly prophesised. Morgan, to its credit, did not take the bait and stoically went about its business as it had for the previous 85 years.

Morgan's production facilities have changed little over the past half century, they are simply a series of low, pitched roof red brick buildings with painted wooden doors in which leather, wood and metal artisans go about their daily tasks as they have happily done for decades.

Since assuming the role as Managing Director, Charles Morgan has instituted a range of changes that have significantly increased the efficiency of production. That has been achieved without the installation of any mechanical robots or the installation of any "modern" assembly lines or anything like that, but simply looking at various processes with the operators and working out new and better ways of carrying out a particular task or set of tasks. Charles had sought advice from an outside company, Strategem, to assist in implementing change in the company's work practices that would ultimately lead to a more efficient production process. As he commented some years later, "We had a young workforce who

Mass production was never what Morgan was about, each car being constructed with care by craftsmen

73

Chapter Five • Getting The Aero 8 Into Production

was not only trained in the art of coachbuilding but who also understood the need for modern efficiency measures to support their craft." A further growth of the company could be seen in its adoption of new computer technologies under the broad umbrella of AUTODESK. Design and development of new ideas and new models are schemed in 3D on a computer screen and "proved" before any time and labour is invested. According to Jon Wells, Morgan's Senior Designer, "This new technology which we have embraced at Morgan reduces new model development time significantly and enables us to plan the best way in which to manufacture any new part or model."

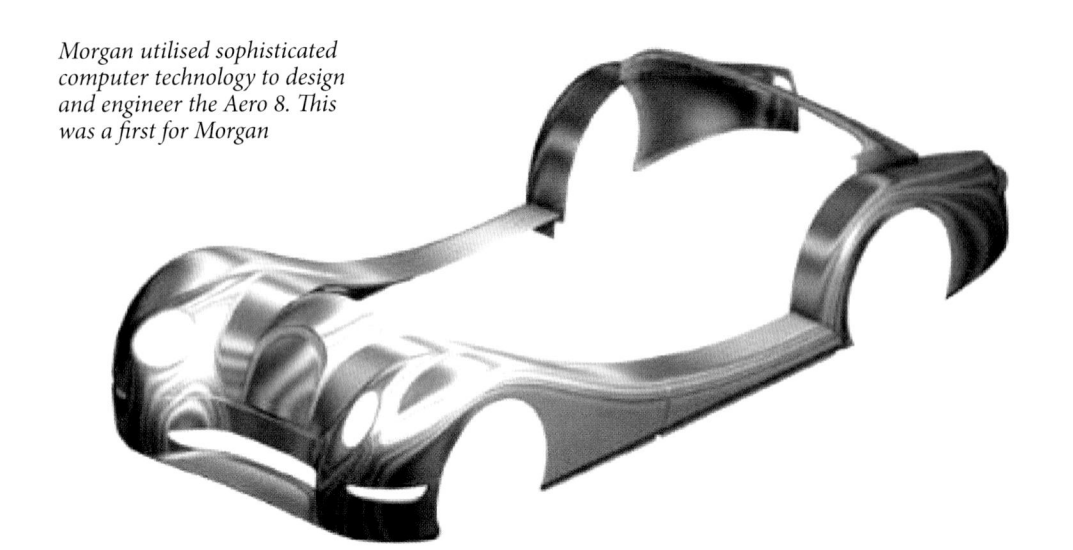

Morgan utilised sophisticated computer technology to design and engineer the Aero 8. This was a first for Morgan

Production at Morgan per day can still be counted on both hands and that will never change; and neither will the largely cottage craft methods that are now assisted by modern tools and the out-sourcing of some major components. Waiting lists are down from around four years to about six months, although this varies depending on the model and specifications ordered. No matter how Morgan goes about manufacturing its sports cars and no matter how much supposed "experts" might criticise the company the fact is the system Morgan uses works for Morgan.

Having proven beyond a shadow of doubt that the P8000 prototypes could take anything handed out to it through the most gruelling test and development program the company had ever conducted, by far the most challenging step was to take the hand-made prototypes from the Experimental Department to Production and build the new sports car in series.

As history has shown us, it is this critical step that often brings promising designs to grief. Motoring history is littered with excellent concept and prototype cars that never saw the inside of a showroom because the people involved either under-estimated the amount of capital required to take the next step or were unable to raise the necessary capital.

Chapter Five • Getting The Aero 8 Into Production

Strategem, in collaboration with Morgan's management team, identified the fact that although the company wanted to build more cars and make greater profits it did not want to lose the unique position that it was in; it definitely did not want to adopt the mass production and out-sourcing that Sir John Harvey-Jones was advocating because that would contradict the core values of the company. A key to the change was the adoption of a form of the Japanese Kanban system that accurately matched production of cars to the needs for the different components and their usage on a daily basis together with a new layout of the production processes through the factory. Effectively this meant a reduction in the batch sizes which in turn significantly reduced the amount of capital tied up in inventory.

Production of the Aero 8 took place in a new building at Malvern Link; Steve Morris (below) supervised the process

Notwithstanding that, the new P8000—now known as the Morgan Aero 8 evoking a name from the company's glorious past—had to be integrated into the company's system. This meant that Steve Morris, Production Director, had to synchronise the purchase and delivery of the myriad items, large and small, that would go to make up the new sports car. It also meant that the company would have to invest in a completely new final assembly area that would incorporate a state-of-the-art paint shop. Supplied by Junair Limited from Manchester, its construction began in late 2001 and was completed in mid-2002. This was just in time for the production of the first customer cars which became available in July 2002. The investment by Morgan in the facility was reportedly in the vicinity of £660,000—a sizeable amount in addition to that also invested in the new sports car itself.

75

Chapter Five • Getting The Aero 8 Into Production

The decision to construct a new assembly area specifically dedicated to the Aero 8 was taken by Charles Morgan and Steve Morris who both felt that such a facility was necessary for the new car in view of the elevated expectations of the buyer in the market segment they were now targeting. The paint shop was state-of-the-art at the time with touch screen controls and a sophisticated air extraction system for cleanliness, worker-friendly environment and for recycling of the water and paint. New hydraulic hoists, ramps and a sophisticated laser wheel aligner together with dedicated work benches for specific assemblies—dashboard and doors, for example—were part of the fitting-out of the area.

Supplies of the BMW engine were under way following the signing of the Agreement between BMW AG and Morgan Motor Company by Charles Morgan on behalf of the company and Dr Reuil and Dr Goschel on behalf of BMW AG. Engines would arrive from BMW's Munich plant (where all the V8s were made) in stillages containing four engines each all carefully packed and protected to prevent any movement and damage in transit. The schedule agreed between the two companies was for the engine deliveries to be monthly. Despatched separately from Getrag GmbH in Untergruppenbach near Heilbronn in Baden-Württemberg, BMW's supplier of manual transmissions, would be an equivalent number of gearboxes that would be bolted-up to the engine at Morgan.

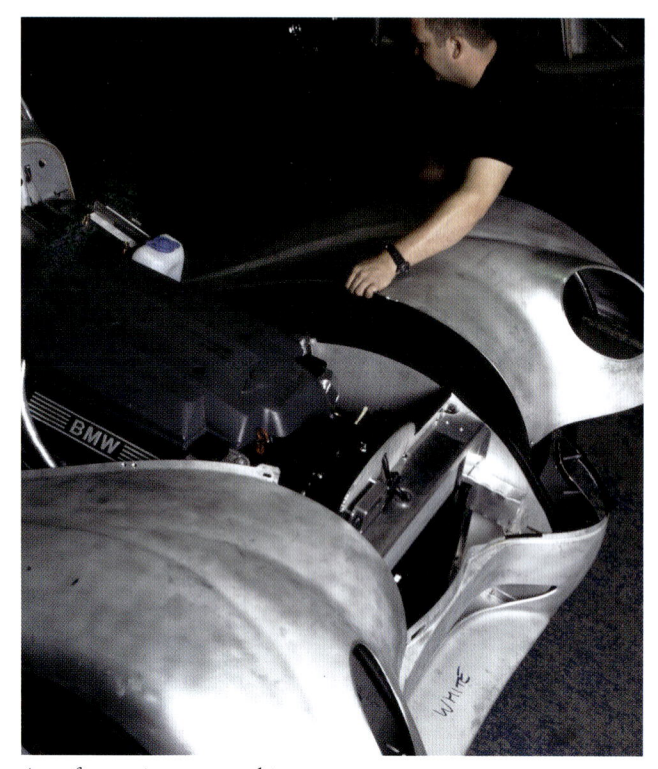

A craftsmen is seen attaching a guard above and below are BMW V8 engines awaiting installation in a chassis

In addition to engines and gearboxes BMW agreed to supply Morgan with its own steering column complete with steering lock and electronic security system that "reads" the key.

Also coming in to the Malvern Link workshops were more major items from Germany—Boysen in Altensteig just north of the Black Forest supplied the custom-made exhaust system and Kromberg & Schubert who have several plants all over Germany and in Austria (Oberpullendorf is the component source for the Aero 8) supplied the complete wiring loom, again a loom developed

76

and manufactured specifically for Morgan and the Aero 8. Again the numbers required were tiny—around 15-20 per month—but the companies all collaborated willingly on the Aero 8 project because the engineers involved loved the car!

As previously mentioned, the power assisted rack and pinion steering was sourced from Jack Knight Developments in Woking while the front and rear suspension systems were sourced from Droitwich Aluminium.

Back in England, other suppliers geared up to manufacture their contribution to the Aero 8. Radshape, situated in an industrial estate in Aston, Birmingham, agreed to invest in the necessary machinery and tooling to build the aluminium intensive chassis for the car and to deliver them in batches of five to Malvern Link.

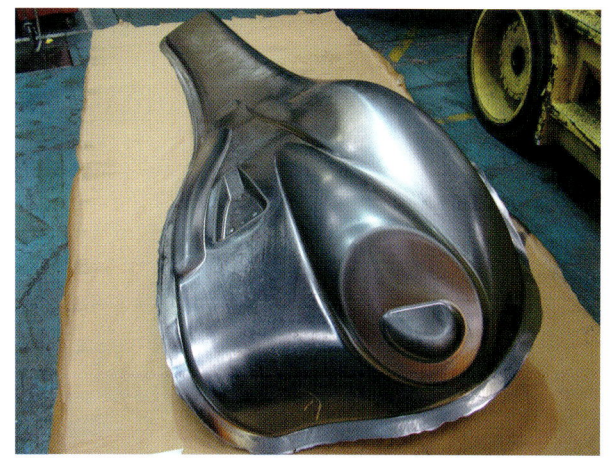

Superform Aluminium manufactured many panels to extremely tight tolerances

The link to Radshape was interesting as was its history. Established in 1967 it was a fabrication company operating within a wide range of market sectors including aerospace, automotive, rail, electrical and general engineering offering solutions from prototypes through to complete project management and small scale production runs. It had also been a contractor to the Ministry of Defence (MOD). The company originally specialised in the manufacture of radiators, hence the name, but today it has broadened its scope and is a fully ISO certified supplier to a number of industries. It has capabilities in aluminium bonding using Alcan's AVT technology, CAD using CATIA V4 and V5, CNC folding, CNC machining, CNC punching, coded welding, laser cutting and other operations that make the company ideal for short or medium production runs, prototyping and engineering for production.

Radshape had been a Tier 1 supplier to Rolls-Royce and Bentley since 1967 and in recognition of this now supplies all brightware and spares for the current Bentley range and was a key supplier of components for the Queen's Bentley State Limousine presented to her in 2002. The company was also involved in designing and manufacturing the aluminium space frame for the radical Gibbs Aquada.

Production Director at Morgan, Steve Morris, was well aware of the company and its capabilities as he was good friends with their sales engineer Graham Chapman; he was also aware of Chris Lawrence's dissatisfaction with the quality of work from Park Sheet Metal. As the P8000 project gathered momentum within the company Morris made the connection to

This is the Morgan Aero 8 rolling chassis as displayed at several motor shows

Radshape through Chapman. Soon, Chapman and another sales engineer from Radshape, Chris Dickinson, were frequent visitors to Morgan and took a keen interest in P8000 and the work of Lawrence, Baldwin, Reeves and Burbidge. In fabricating components for the future Aero 8 Lawrence found that he needed a laser cutter and it was this need that brought Radshape and the Morgan Motor Company together.

A sample chassis to Lawrence's drawings was made and it was said to have been a vast improvement over those previously supplied. As Lawrence said, "The standard of work from Radshape was one hundred times superior, they did a really good job and I was very pleased with their efforts. The people there were straight-forward and honest which I liked."

Morgan bought a license from Alcan Aluminium, the giant Canadian manufacturer of aluminium products, to buy sheets of their 5083 aluminium which was 2mm thick with a special surface coating (referred to as PT2) sourced from the company's new (in 1998) factory located outside the village of Nachterstedt, a little way east of the Harz Mountains near the ancient UNESCO-listed town of Quedlinburg in central Germany. Prior to the fall of Communism in 1989 it was in the former East Germany. As part of the rebuilding of the economy of the region Alcan invested more than DM 250 million in the aluminium rolling plant, with the Morgan Aero 8 being the world's first coachbuilt car produced using the material.

Discussions progressed during 1999 with Charles Morgan and Simon Marland, then managing director of Radshape, agreeing the two companies collaborate on the manufacture of the future Aero 8. Marland was hesitant—"I could see that Morgan was heading into unknown territory with their P8000 car and Charles was asking me to carry most of the investment for the manufacture of the chassis. I was very nervous but was eventually convinced by Charles that it would all be worthwhile." Keith Chadwick, who replaced Marland as MD at Radshape, later described the relationship between the two companies as a "voyage of discovery."

A unit price for each chassis was agreed and Radshape began investing in the necessary machinery and tooling to manufacture it in small volume. "There was another company in England with the technology to do what we wanted based in Worcester but they were only interested in high volume production, not the tiny numbers we were talking about," commented Lawrence who was perfectly happy with the arrangements made with Radshape.

The company invested considerably in new equipment, from an oven manufactured by Cooper Heaters and capable of holding two chassis tubs, a Bollhof riveter, Zwick pull tester, two TRUMPF TruBend 5130 press brake machines, a TRUMPF TruPunch 5000 punching machine that was accurate to ±0.01mm. In all the investment was rumoured to have been around £300,000. This commitment meant that some 20 per cent of the company's floor space was dedicated to just one client—Morgan. Intriguingly, at the time of making this investment Radshape did not have a firm order from Morgan! That is the ultimate trust, trust that saw up to 30 per cent of Radshape's turnover at one point coming from Morgan.

As part of the refit of their factory, the section dedicated to Morgan was partitioned off from the rest because of the need for absolute cleanliness; large plastic drop sheet "doors" were used to keep the air separated and other operations were in enclosed areas. This was necessary because any impurities on a surface could ruin the bonding.

The many aluminium pieces that go to make up the chassis of the Aero 8 were cut, punched and then formed on the press brakes before being transferred to the bonding cell for what is described as

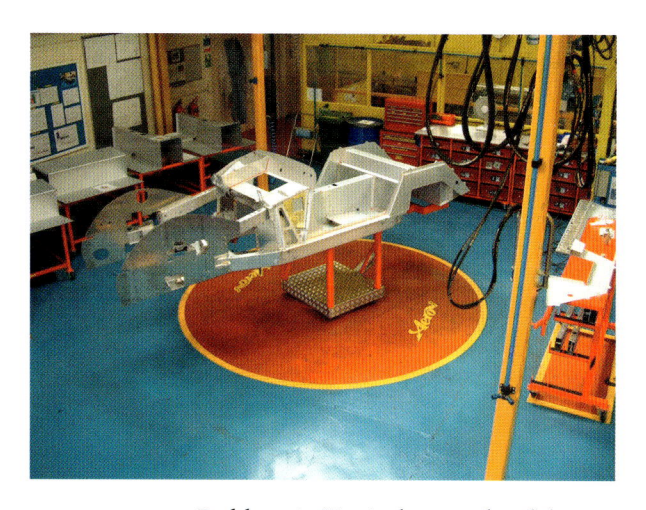

Radshape in Birmingham produced the aluminium chassis using advanced technical solutions

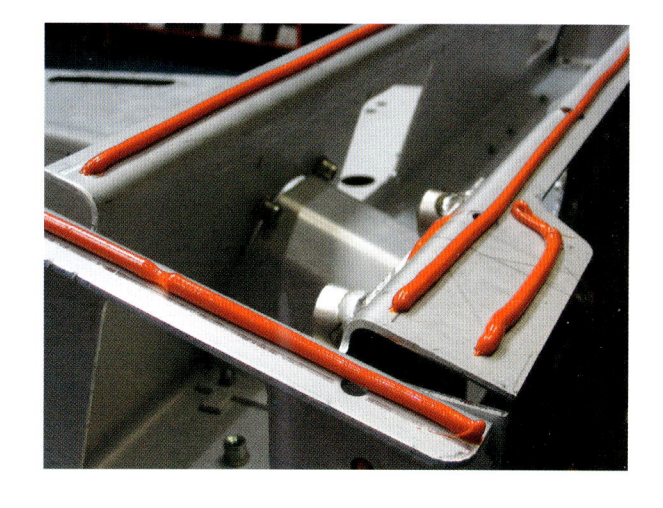

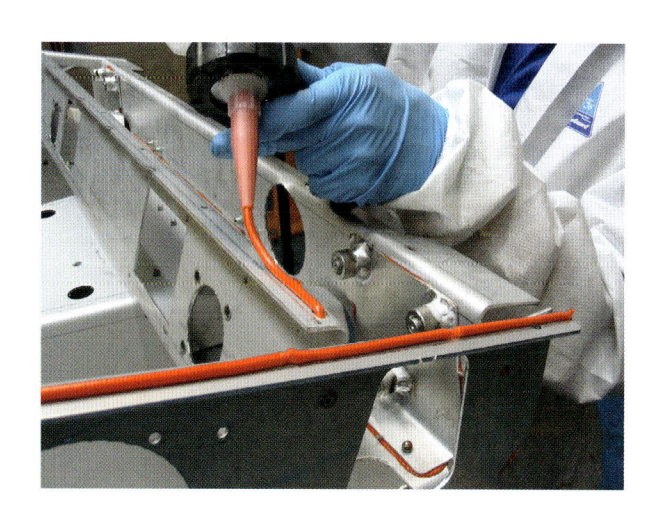

CHAPTER FIVE • GETTING THE AERO 8 INTO PRODUCTION

a "wet build" and once this process had been complete the chassis was placed in the curing oven for 20 minutes at 180ºC. John Harper, Radshape's resident expert in this new technology, said, "The temperature is critical as is the amount of time in the oven. We take sample pieces from off-cuts from the same chassis material and subject it to stress tests when it has cooled down and we have never had a failure. Interestingly, with the software we're using now we can work out the profiles of the materials to cut in an hour where previously it took days." He continued by adding, "We build the chassis tub to an accuracy of ±0.25mm, well within the design tolerances specified by Morgan."

The various panels that require gluing had applied to their mating surfaces an application of a Dow Automotive adhesive known as XD4600. In addition the panels were riveted using the Bollhoff gun that punches in the rivets noiselessly with minimal damage or stressing of the surface. Once in place the rivets (there were over 700 in the early series Aero chassis) were impossible to drill out such was their strength and hardness. Morgan insisted that this bonding technology, which was originally developed for the aircraft and aerospace industries, be supplemented by the rivets even though they were possibly unnecessary. Harper commented, "It might have something to do with the tradition at Morgan but Aston Martin, for example, have no qualms about relying entirely on the adhesive in their aluminium chassis."

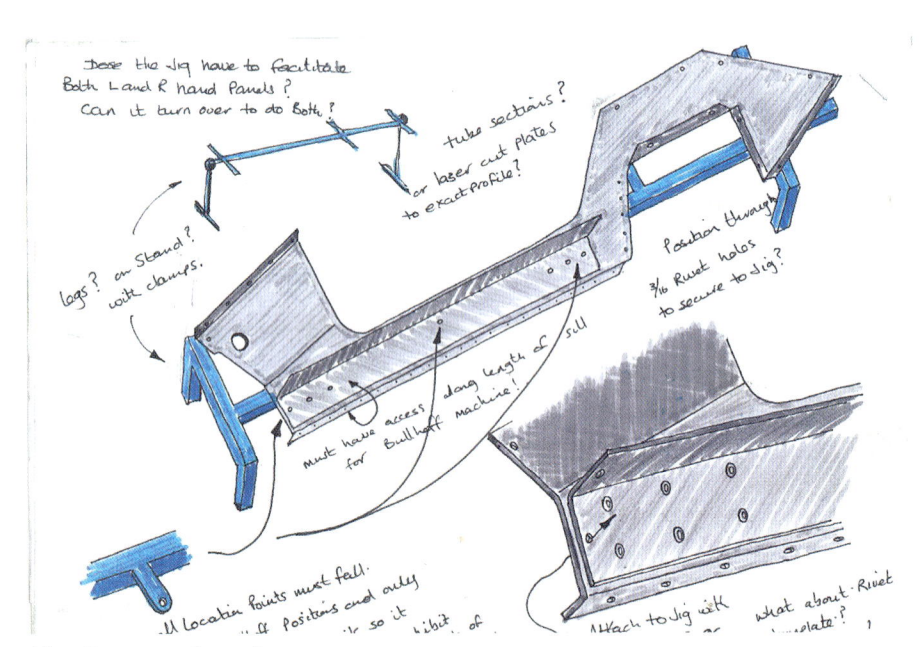

This illustration shows the thinking proccess behind the tooling required to manufacture the chassis at Radshape

Two key employees at Morgan during this period were Graham Chapman and Derek Jones. Chapman was a former long-time Radshape employee having worked for the company for 11 years but was so impressed with what he could see Morgan was going to build (and was intimately involved at Radshape) that he asked to become a Morgan employee. To better understand the man, you should know he used to own a Morgan Plus 4 until family pressures forced its sale. His background was in manufacturing, not design. Until Chapman's arrival at Malvern Link the company had never employed anybody with these skills.

Chapter Five • Getting The Aero 8 Into Production

Jones had worked at Morgan for six and a half years and joined the P8000 project in July 1999 to take Lawrence's drawings of the aluminium tub from AutoCAD 2D onto CATIA 3D, a sophisticated CAD software program used by most of the world's automobile manufacturers. Charles Morgan and Lawrence soon found that they had to upgrade the company's computer system to run CATIA so that they could quickly link to BMW's system in Munich, Miramas or Steyr, wherever they had to communicate with engineers to do with any aspect of the performance of the P8000 prototypes. Radshape also had to join the party.

Initially Chapman and Jones fed as much information as they could into the CAD database and, critically, began looking at ways and means of producing the many components less expensively and soon had a portfolio of changes that needed to be made.

The next process which had to be addressed was the forming of the various aluminium panels that made up the P8000's shape. If tradition was to be followed the long and delicately curved front and rear wings plus the doors, louvred engine bonnet, nose cowl, top rear panel and front splitter panel for the car would have been hand-formed over leather clad dollies in-house by one or two of the company's long-serving craftsmen. However, where the P8000 was concerned Steve Morris said, "We really wanted this Morgan to be different, not only in its style and specification and performance, but also in the way in which it would be made. We were going seriously up-market with P8000 and knew that buyers would expect a very high standard of build quality. That meant that it had to be made on quality tooling that would give a consistently high standard of finish. Having said that, we had been working with a company called Superform Aluminium since 1998 manufacturing the front fenders for the traditional Morgans."

Superform Aluminium located in Worcester—8 miles from Malvern Link—was approached to work with Morgan on the manufacture of the many panels needed to "clothe" the aluminium intensive chassis. Driven by technological innovation, the company was exploring the use of a property of a material known as super plasticity. This is the ability of a material to exhibit very high elongation at a controlled strain rate. Technical director Dave Edwards said, "Cold aluminium might exhibit 25 per cent elongation at maximum whereas

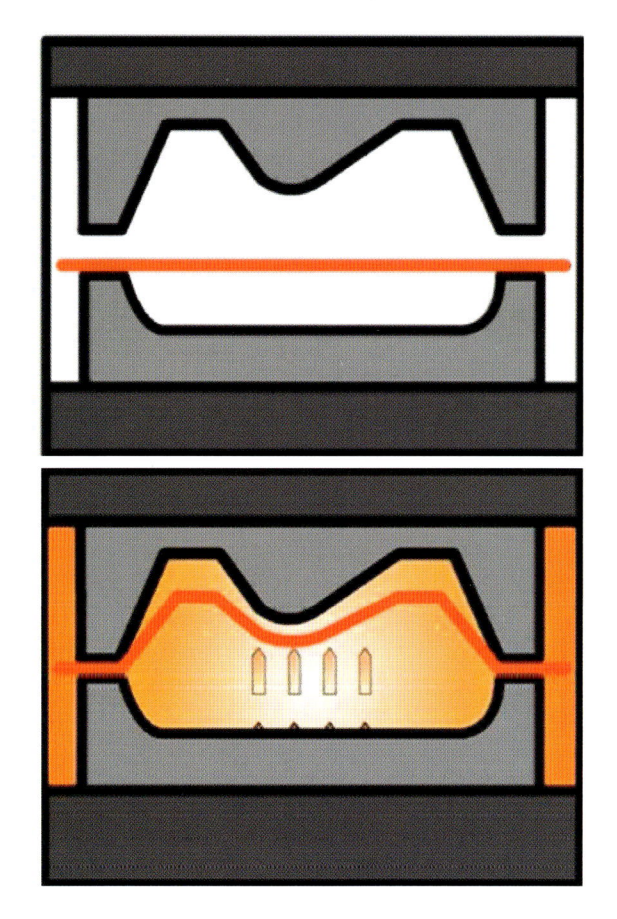

Chapter Five • Getting The Aero 8 Into Production

super plastic aluminium can exhibit an elongation of up to 1000 per cent. However, 200 per cent is most practical for manufacturing purposes." The aim of these studies was to investigate a process of vacuum-forming aluminium panels into quite complex shapes, initially for the aerospace industry, that evolved out of studies carried out by metallurgists in Academia. Initially it was almost exclusively utilised by the aerospace industry because of the enormous costs involved but gradually further research uncovered new and slightly different ways of using the technology so that it was affordable by more companies over a wider spectrum of commercial activities.

The attraction of 5083 aluminium from Alcan—5083 is a generic name for the material, not an Alcan name—was that it was highly resistant to corrosion, a property that appealed to the marine industry and to Superform for application to the automobile world.

Superform was keen to join with Morgan in the manufacture of panels for the Aero 8. As Edwards said, "Morgan's volumes were small enough for us to work together harmoniously without the budget getting out of reach for either of us. Besides, we'd grown used to each other having been a supplier to them for some years with the traditional models."

The key to the Aero 8 was the curves and shapes of the outer skin which required tools with a long draw. Edwards, described by Charles Morgan as "a genius," created tools that would remove the distortion out of the sheet aluminium as it was being formed.

Using their patented Super Plastic Forming process the very fine-grained aluminium sheets were heated to 470°C (as Edwards commented somewhat wryly, "Another 50°C and they'd melt!") by hot air blowing over them. This makes them soft and pliable and then air pressure at around 150psi pushes the panel onto a steel die to the exact shape required. This process will produce a front wing, rear wing, bonnet or roof with unerring and repeatable accuracy, something not attainable using hand methods. Using this patented process the sheet aluminium will stretch and bend without deforming which is quite remarkable.

82

Chapter Five • Getting The Aero 8 Into Production

Besides the Morgan Aero 8, Superform Aluminium manufactures components for Aston Martin's V8 and DB9 ranges using the same technology as well as Bombardier and other companies in the aerospace world.

On the mechanical chassis side of P8000 there were many bridges to cross. The Chris Lawrence-conceived rack and pinion steering system had to be manufactured as no such compact system was available off-the-shelf. Jack Knight Developments based then in Woking, was a long established company well-known among the race and rally fraternity for its five- and six-speed manual gearboxes to suit a wide range of makes and models, plus its ability to design, engineer and produce low volume components as required. It had achieved legendary status in its field.

Lawrence liaised with the two key people at JKD—Kevin Dempsey, Managing Director, and John Emptage, Engineering Director—who both rose to the challenge. They took Lawrence's rather crude (but workable) cobbled parallel-rack steering idea and over a period of four months sourced a contractor to cast the complex housing and set up their own machines to carry out the various machining, drilling, tapping and honing operations required to produce the finished article. As Emptage said, "This was no ordinary assignment. Chris, whom we both knew, had devised a really neat solution to his steering problem and we were keen to run with it. After a couple of minor issues we made a beautifully finished rack that we were proud of. Unfortunately for us when Chris left Morgan they began to gradually phase-in readily available components and our steering rack was one of the early casualties of that program. Kevin and I were both extremely disappointed as I believe was Chris."

Arrangements were made with a company for the manufacture of the fabricated tubular steel lower front wishbone and the upper rocker arm as well as the arms for the rear suspension. The rear axle assembly was a unit that bolted up to the chassis and included a sheet aluminium frame to which was bolted directly the BTR limited slip differential unit (sourced from Australia), the upper and lower wishbones together with the drive shafts from GKN and the

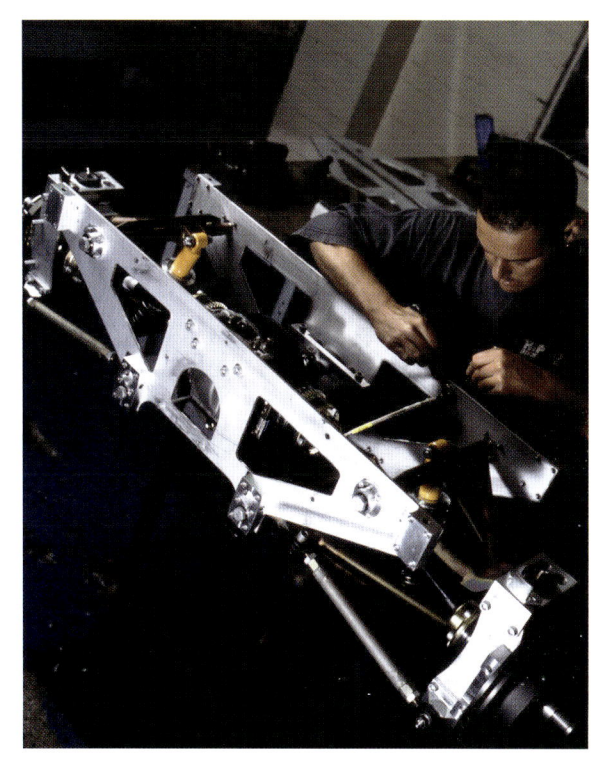

The Series I Aero 8 had the unique Jack Knight rack and pinion steering system

83

Eibach springs that enclosed the Koni dampers. The whole assembly of components was hand assembled into a unit for bolting to the chassis at Morgan.

As for the front suspension, the upper wishbone that functioned as a rocker arm acting on the inboard-positioned spring/damper unit (Eibach and Koni respectively, as at the rear) was a large tubular steel fabrication that was connected to the front hubs via a ball joint, and the lower wishbone, also a tubular steel fabricated part. These were all made by a company in Droitwich. The front hubs were interesting insofar as they were made up from one large aluminium casting that had to be carefully machined and drilled before a number of other parts were bolted to it, the centre of the main component being machined to accept the inner-and-outer wheel bearings. The rear wheel hubs were a similar modular construction. The OZ alloy wheels were held on by a large single central hub bolt, much like on a competition car.

Below is an exploded diagram of the many components that go to make-up the Aero 8 chassis. This is Series II

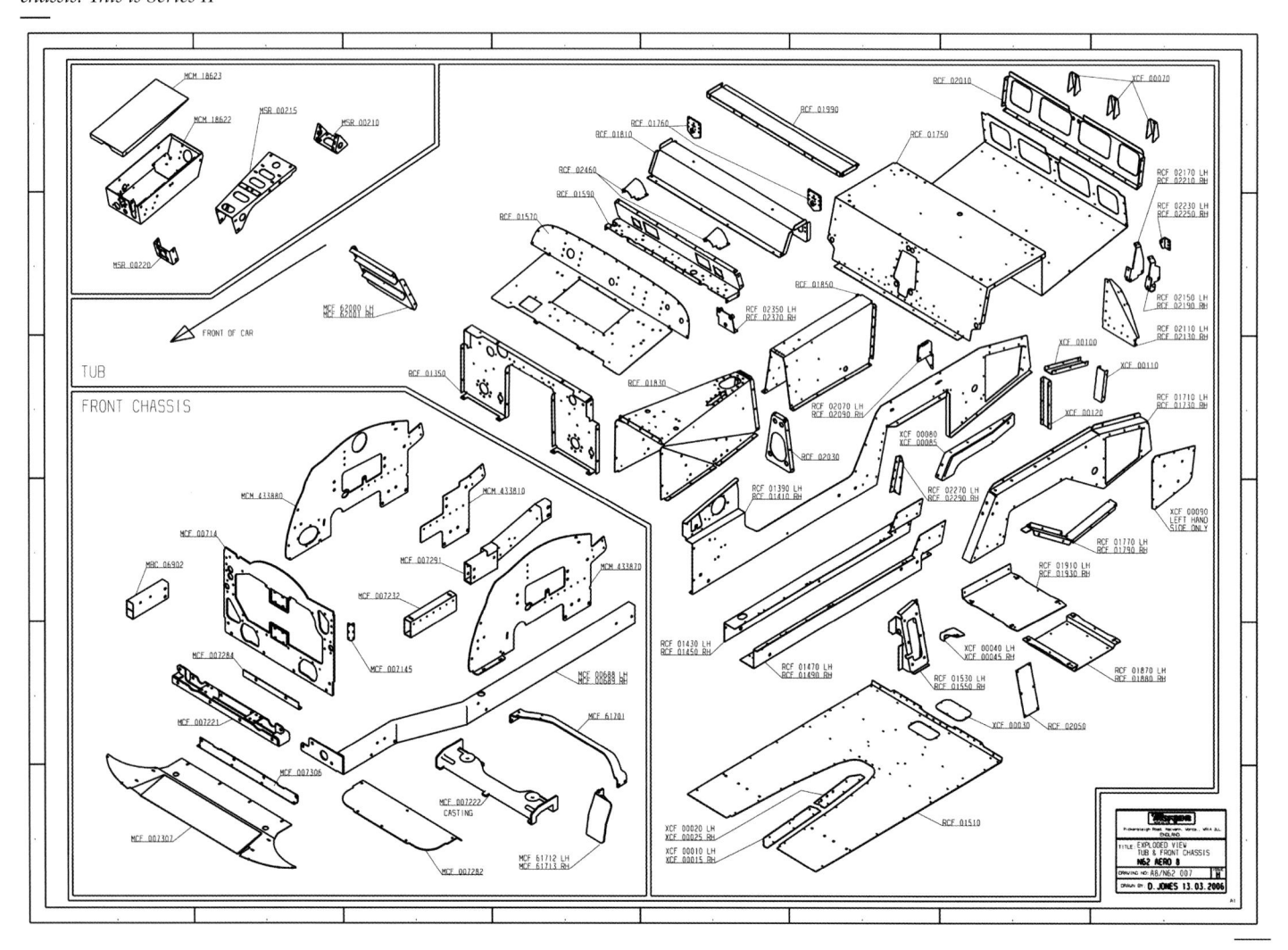

The braking system was bought-in from AP Racing in Coventry, a division of Brembo, the famous Italian company, and consisted of huge 330mm ventilated rotors at the front, 306mm ventilated rotors at the rear clamped by four-pot aluminium calipers at the front, two-pot calipers at the rear. Morgan and AP Racing, represented by engineer Richard Joyce, had been collaborating on the braking system since early 1999.

The interior of the Aero 8 comprised two comfortable leather upholstered bucket seats, carpets on the floor made by Marstons and a new style dashboard made by a company by the name of Frazero. It comprised a set of VDO instruments in a small binnacle under the polished walnut ledge at the base of the windscreen. Instruments included large diameter matching speedometer and tachometer plus minor gauges for fuel contents, engine coolant temperature, engine oil pressure and temperature as well as various warning lights and switches. In a slightly difficult-to-reach position on the transmission tunnel were the controls for the heater/demister—air conditioning from KL Automotive to Morgan's specifications was optional—and the audio system. This was based initially on an Alpine system but modified for Morgan, it consisted of the main unit plus six speakers sited around the cabin area for best effect, top down or up.

Morgan sports cars have always had a folding top that may or may not have kept all the elements at bay and often was a trial to erect. For the Aero 8 that was going to be capable of 160+mph the folding hood was going to have to be something special to cope with the forces generated at speeds above 80mph. The top on the Plus 8 was only good for 120-125mph before it broke clear of its fasteners and destroyed itself so clearly a far stronger top was going to be required.

In keeping with its position in the market, and Morgan's intent to market the Aero 8 as a luxury high performance sports car, it meant liaising with a far wider range of suppliers than at any time in the company's history. Not only was a premium audio part of the car's specification along with air conditioning but electric windows, exterior mirrors and remote central locking. Robert Bosch supplied the electric window mechanisms and the remote "blippers" were a part of the BMW security package. Pilkington Glass supplied the electrically heated front windscreen and side windows.

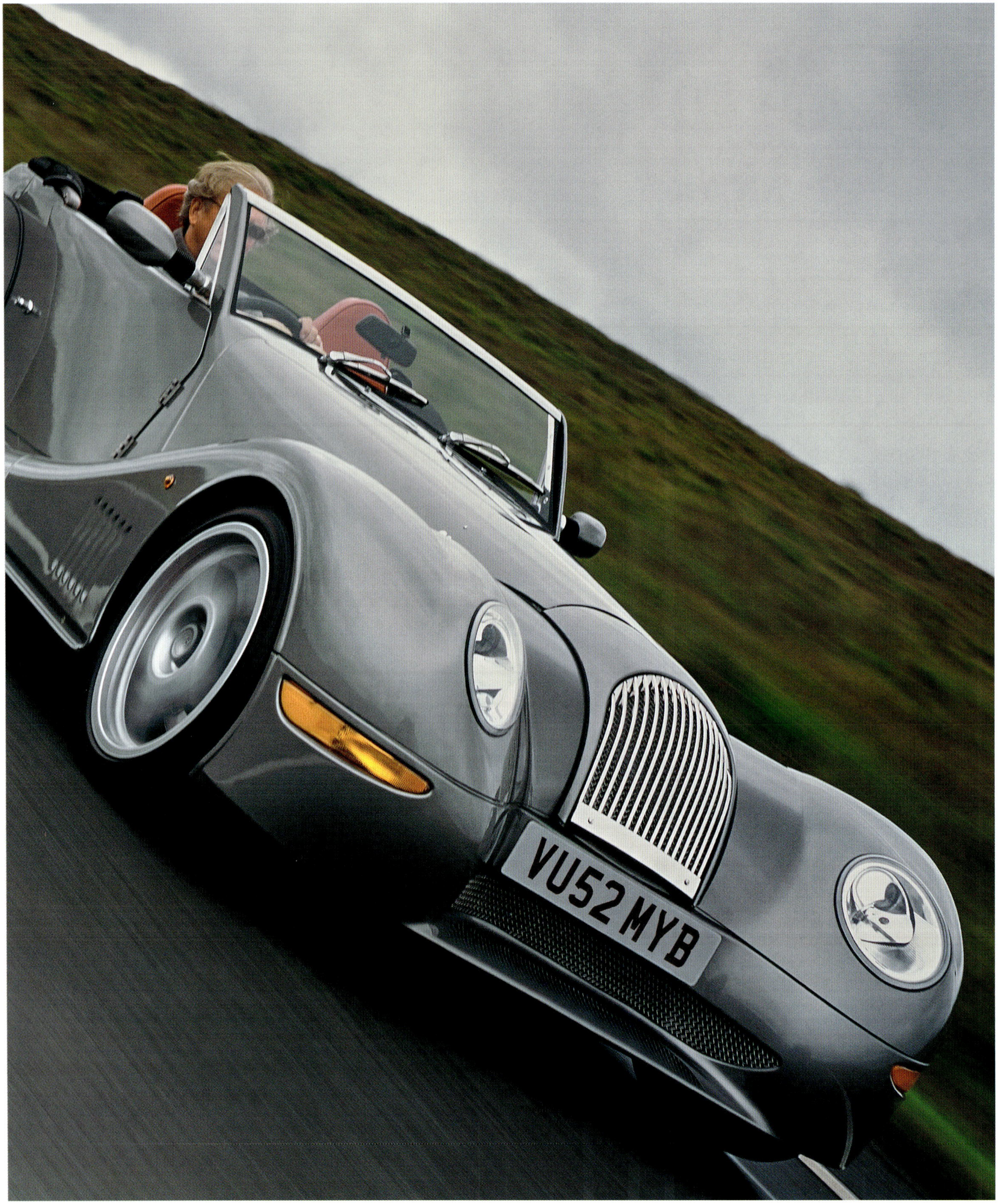
VU52 MYB

Chapter Six

THE RELEASE AND MEETING THE PUBLIC

Charles Morgan had decided that he wanted the Aero 8 to be released at the Geneva Motor Show to be held in March 2000. In the months leading up to the event a degree of panic was going on behind the scenes as there had been a hold up with the supply of front fender panels from Superform Aluminium. At the last moment the decision was made to make them from fibreglass (done by Survirn Engineering and George Hardwick) in order that the car could meet its public; after all, the stand space had been booked and paid for.

As well as the show preparations, Charles Morgan had contacted the managing director of Saab AB in Trollhätten, Sweden, seeking permission to use the name Aero for his new sports car. The name had been applied to a sporting Morgan three-wheeler in the 1920s and then usurped by Saab in the 1990s to be used on a sporting variant of the Saab 900 that was later rebadged as the 9-3. Despite this Charles took the time and courtesy to contact Saab who willingly gave Morgan permission to use the name on their new sports car.

Morgan's turn to present to the assembled international media at Geneva was scheduled for three o'clock in the afternoon, traditionally a potentially dangerous time for a manufacturer because the journalists would have been on the go and listening to a dozen or more such presentations since eight o'clock in the morning. Tiredness from all the walking, jadedness from hearing the same old clichés trotted out to the sound of ever louder music and gorgeous, leggy young

Morgan released the Aero 8 at Geneva with high acclaim from the world's media

Chapter Six • The Release And Meeting The Public

Mervyn Carter (Sales Engineer), Graham Chapman (Product Director), John Harper (Innovation Engineer), Bill Howarth (Innovation Engineer), Charles Morgan (MD of the Morgan Motor Co), Simon Marland (Managing Director), Peter Grant (Sales Director), Robert Nash (Innovation Engineer) from Radshape standing with their creation.

The rolling chassis on display at Geneva

attendants often led to them giving the afternoon shift less than their full and undivided attention.

The size of the Morgan stand at Geneva was minuscule when compared with the acres of space accorded—indeed, afforded by—the major manufacturers and even some of the lesser lights bought more space than their products perhaps deserved. Matthew Parkin, former Sales and Marketing Director, was responsible for the stand and the layout of exhibits with advice from Chris Lawrence who had insisted that a bare rolling chassis be part of the display. As he said in *Morgan Maverick*, "I pushed and pushed for the chassis to be on display as I feared that too many people would take one look at the car and wander off thinking that the Aero 8 was merely a slightly upgraded body on the old-fashioned Morgan steel chassis."

The stand comprised an Aero 8 under a white satin cover on a turntable with the Morgan wings proudly facing where the crowd would be and on the other side was the rolling chassis there for the world to see.

At the appointed time on the schedule the media assembled near Morgan's stand. Charles Morgan was standing proudly by his lectern accompanied by Chris Lawrence as his Engineering Director, Gunther Ranzinger from BMW who was the Project Manager Electronics within the BMW Group, Michael Urbschat, Vice President Powertrain Engineering with responsibility for the V engines in the BMW Group, Matthew Parkin who was then Director Sales and Marketing at the Morgan Motor Company, and David Goodwin who was the Project Manager Electronics at Morgan.

Following his speech to the media, who were apparently standing 10-deep, in which Charles described the new sports car—it had yet to be revealed—as "the result of the biggest development project ever undertaken by the Morgan Motor Company, that it was

CHAPTER SIX • THE RELEASE AND MEETING THE PUBLIC

"a major financial and emotional investment for Morgan" and that it was a "collaboration between Morgan and BMW that represented the best of British and German skills in engineering, invention and craftsmanship." He also stressed three key innovations embodied in the car: firstly, that it was one of Europe's first AIV's—aluminium intensive vehicles; secondly, that it was powered by the best V8 engine in the world—the BMW 4.4 litre M62 B44 and its associated Powertrain that had been developed specifically for Morgan; and thirdly, it was the most aerodynamic car the company had ever built with a Cd of 0.39 as measured in MIRA's wind tunnel. Charles expanded on each of these points and after 7 or 8 minutes of speaking gave the signal for his two daughters—Harriet and Kate—to whip the covers off the new car.

For a moment there was stunned silence and then one by one the media began applauding the new Morgan Aero 8. For many of them this was the highlight of their time in Geneva. Here at last was a real sports car from Morgan of all companies!

As Charles agreed and most of the journalists knew, this new sports car was the first major new development from the company in sixty years, since the arrival of the first four-wheeled Morgan in 1936 in fact. Until the Aero 8, all production Morgans—Plus 4, Plus 8, 4/4 et al—were simply derivatives of that 1936 design.

This is the Series I interior

A press release and some photographs were handed out to all the media present while the small Morgan team was inundated with questions from the by now frantic media who could no longer contain their enthusiasm. Intriguingly, in the printed release material the car was referred to as the Morgan Plus 8 Aero. The opening paragraph of the release read, "The Morgan Motor Company has unveiled a stunning all-new 150-mph supercar,

89

the Plus Eight Aero, which will be the new flagship of its distinctive range of sports cars when production begins in July (2000). The new car's world launch at the Geneva Motor Show marks the culmination of a three-year development program to create a high performance contemporary sports car to complement Morgan's existing range of traditionally styled cars." The release went on to discuss the Plus Eight Aero's all-aluminium chassis design, its exhilarating performance and innovative features. For patient Morgan clients that July 2000 production start-up date would prove to be elusive—the company missed by a year!

Autocar carried an article in its March 8, 2000 issue filed by Chris Rosamond and titled "So how about this, Sir John?" a clear reference to the infamous television show in which Morgan featured, and subtitled "Modernise or die, the hard-hitting industrialist told Morgan. Here's its response: an advanced supercar in retro roadster drag." The article, not surprisingly, described the car in some detail and was generally positive in its opinion of the new Aero 8.

Crowds thronged around the Aero 8 at Geneva

A staff journalist from *CAR* wrote an introductory piece in the May 2000 issue headed "New Morgan: the eyes have it." The sub-heading read "Controversially styled British newcomer with high-tech chassis and BMW engine leaves opinion divided." The writer was one of the first to publish an opinion—usually negative—about the Aero 8 when he wrote, "A curious amalgam of wind tunnel honing and house-style retro, the Aero 8 is marked by a bizarre shovel nose and modern (from the VW Beetle) ellipsoid headlights. Angled aggressively inwards, the result is cross-eyed and, according to one journalist at the unveiling, it 'looks as if the car has hit a telegraph pole head-on'. " He continued by adding, "The Aero 8's sills and extended running boards also looked clumsy compared with current cars (he never mentioned which, *author*), being entirely flat." He went on to describe the aluminium chassis and a connection to Jim Randle which was rather curious; he ended his pieced by saying "The Aero 8 goes on sale in July and there's currently a 36-month waiting list."

The American magazine *Road & Track* published a piece written by Ian Norris complete with two photos of the blue show car, an interior shot and the bare rolling chassis in its May 2000 issue. His comments were interesting, saying "The reaction was mixed. The first thing you noticed was the car's odd cross-eyed stare, the result of headlamps faired-in for aerodynamic cleanliness. People were so struck by the headlamps that they failed to appreciate just how far Morgan had jumped from the Thirties of last century to the Zeroes of this one." He continued, "The shape is an almost-successful marriage of traditional style and modern technology, with front and rear ends obviously shaped in a wind tunnel, linked by a center section that's totally Morgan. The result is disquieting to the traditionalist, but will likely bring the Morgan brand to a new, younger customer." Norris ended his introductory piece saying "The good news: it's US-legal. The bad news: it won't arrive here for another two years."

Ray Hutton writing in *The Sunday Times* in November 2000 opened with the statement "The Morgan Aero 8 doesn't look much, but on the road it's a swan." As he wrote in his appraisal of

Chapter Six • The Release And Meeting The Public

the car, Morgan enthusiasts had certain expectations insofar as their cars must look like something from the 1930s, provide wind-in-the-hair experience, and be individually handcrafted. He added, "Creating a high-tech 21st-century Morgan is therefore a very tricky business. For years, the company in Malvern Link, Worcestershire, rejected the idea of a completely new car as too difficult; besides, it had orders for its traditional models extending five years ahead."

After a description of the features of the Aero 8 Hutton headed unerringly back to the issue of its styling and wrote, "Even the most committed fan of the old models will appreciate the leap forward that the Aero 8 represents in performance and road behaviour. Whether they will like its shape is another matter—and a sensitive one, because the new-old style was created by Morgan himself.

"His inspiration was the classic French and Italian roadsters but, sadly, Morgan has not achieved their elegance of line. The demands of aerodynamics for a 160mph car may be partly to blame, but the inset headlamps make it look cross-eyed, there is an awkward 'shelf' between the wings, and the drooping, squared-off tail is at odds with the generous curves of the front."

Similar themes were to be read in practically every newspaper and magazine around the country, indeed, around the world as the so-called experts—the journalists—zeroed in on the Aero 8's distinctive styling.

American styling commentator, Robert Cumberford, writing in *Automobile* magazine said of the new Morgan's styling, "The problem with the new car lies in its styling, a ham-handed amateur attempt to combine Thirties shapes with contemporary racing aerodynamics. I presume that the new shape works very well for penetration and downforce and that it has been seriously developed, but its look, not to put too fine a point on it, is absolutely disgusting." He continued by comparing Morgan with Porsche as two family-owned companies that have each pursued a particular shape for decades, met every legal requirement and participated in racing programs without destroying their ambience. Until now. He added, "Morgan is now trying to peddle a racer with a blobby, cross-eyed nose that ensures aerodynamic downforce for a clientele that may enjoy a burst of speed from time to time but appreciates more a gentle top-down trundle through the countryside in a pretty car."

While he might have some knowledge of car styling Cumberford exhibited a typically American misunderstanding of who or what a Morgan enthusiast or client really was.

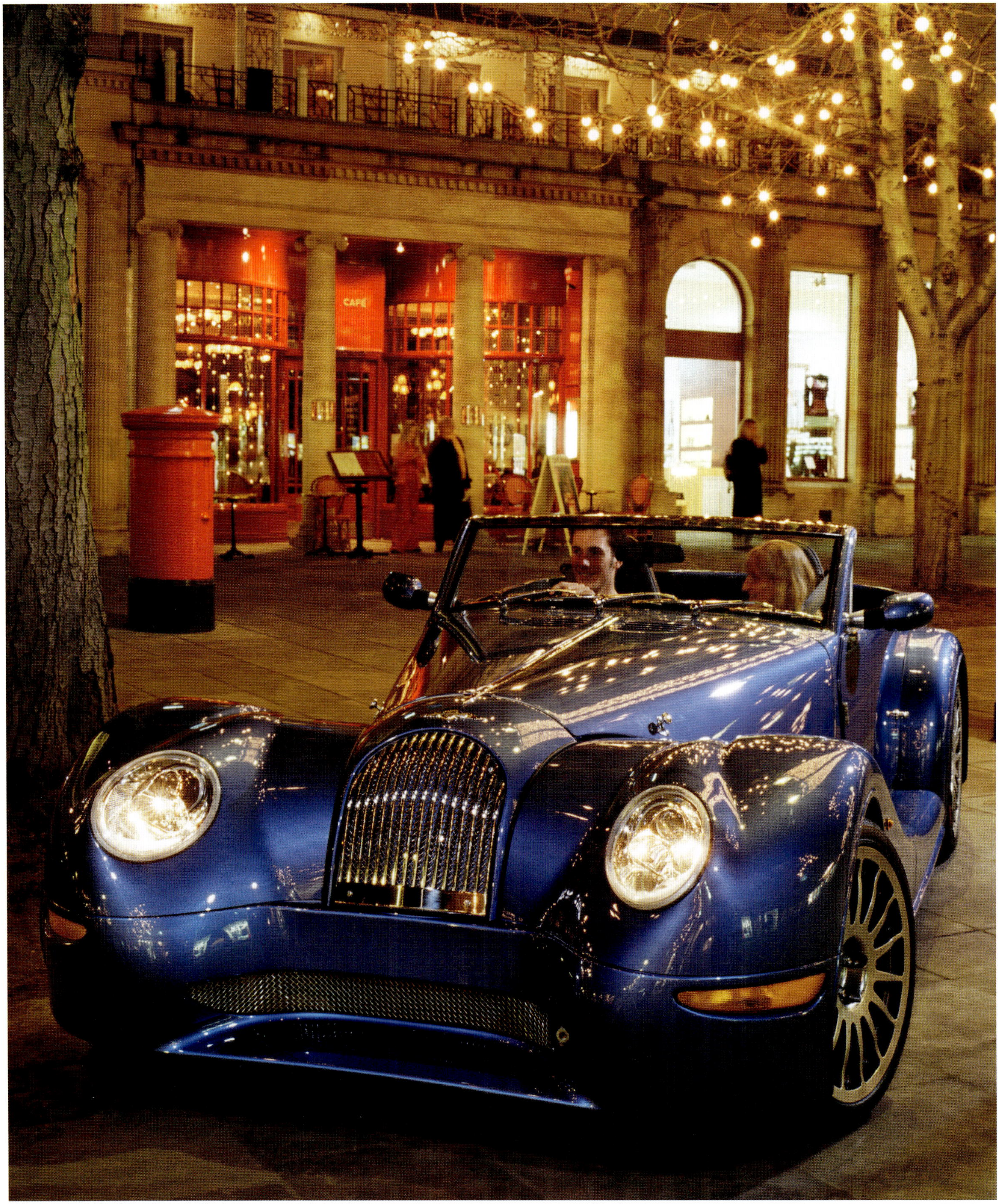
CAFE

Chapter Seven

THE EVOLUTION BEGINS

As originally conceived by Chris Lawrence and Charles Morgan the Aero 8 was both a revolution and a revelation. Not only was it expensive to manufacture it was also complicated. Although to some degree Lawrence cannot be blamed for that as the need to meet ever-more stringent legal requirements inevitably meant complication one way or another. Lawrence had a very clear vision of what he wanted the Aero 8 to be and, importantly, how it would be. To say that he was not concerned about production costs would be unkind to him but there was very little compromise in what Lawrence conceived and had manufactured by the Morgan Motor Company. As a result the Morgan Aero 8 Series I was a very "pure" high performance sports car.

Having achieved the revolution it became time for the evolution. Almost every automobile that has ever entered production has undergone a constant process of evolution, or maturation. It is inevitable with any company and product that has, or will have, a long production life. The Morgan Aero 8 would be no exception; like its siblings it would undoubtedly have a very long life (although as it happened nowhere near as long as the Plus 8, for example) and undergo a myriad of changes, some of which would be part of the normal evolutionary process while others would be forced onto the company and the car by external factors, mostly in the form of legislative requirements dictated by various Governments.

With the Series III Morgan introduced head lights from the MINI which required re-profiled front guards

In late 2003, barely eighteen months after production had begun, the Board made the decision that the company would re-enter the American market. This set in motion a series of events at Morgan that were unprecedented in the company's long history.

The decision to market the Aero 8 into the vast American market meant that the homologation process would have to be carried out from the beginning. Initially the Aero 8 had been designed around the requirements of the European Union (EU) legal requirements but for America the bar would be raised considerably.

That most European of US magazines, *Road & Track*, published an impression drive in 2003 of what was probably the only Aero 8 in the country, it having been imported by Bill Fink of Isis Imports in San Francisco. Morganiste Dennis Simanaitis (he owned a 1965 Plus 4 four-seater at the time) wrote the article and after the usual rant about the headlights—"It's only from front three-quarters that those oddly contoured headlights look goofy to me"—he went on to praise the car for its 21st century specifications and wonderful road dynamics.

East Coast-based *Car and Driver* magazine carried out a full road test of an Aero 8 in its November 2003 issue under the by-line "The Old British groaner gets a stunning makeover."

The car had been loaned to the magazine by Morgan's East Coast agent, Cantab Motors, who indicated their expectation of receiving stock to sell by the spring of 2004 at a retail price of around USD$95,000. The writer was rapt about the Aero's low weight and continually compared it to the Chev Corvette Z06 as well as mentioning the Dodge Viper, Mercedes-Benz SL500 and the Porsche 911. Much of the testing was carried out at the Summit Point Raceway in West Virginia and it was here that the car showed its true mettle. Not only did they find the chassis extremely strong and up to modern stiffness standards but that there was a precision to the car's handing they had not expected. Not only that, but they found that they did not need to down-change to keep the Aero 8 on the boil around the track—the V8 engine's power and torque combined with the car's light weight saw some rapid acceleration and lap times.

In preparation for entry into the American market Morgan had to pass stringent Federal requirements including crash testing

Against the clock *Car and Driver* recorded 3.1 seconds for the 0-50mph run, 4.2 seconds to 60mph, 5.3 seconds to 70mph, 6.6 seconds to 80mph and nearly broke the 10-second barrier for the 0-100mph run which took 10.4 seconds; the standing ¼-mile was run in 12.7 seconds at 110mph while braking from 70-0mph was accomplished in 178 feet which was far longer than the Z06 Corvette, for example, that used only 162 feet from the same speed. Fuel economy was a thirsty 15mpg for city driving, 31mpg for highway driving while on the skidpan the Aero 8 achieved 0.96g. When the magazine hit the newsstands and subscriber's mailboxes it created quite a storm of interest despite some gripes which included the front styling (surprise!), the awkward manual soft top operations, the fit and finish of some interior items and the heat generated by the exhaust catalytic converters that was transferred to the sills and made getting in and out a hot operation!

Chapter Seven • The Evolution Begins

Despite the accolades from the enthusiast motoring press Morgan was faced with the most difficult process in meeting and passing the many US impact tests if it was ever to be serious about sales in North America. This meant that SRS airbags would have to become part of the Aero 8's specifications, one for the driver and another for the passenger. To pass this test the structure behind the dashboard had to be altered to spread the load when the airbags exploded on impact. As Mark Reeves, Production and Development Manager said, "We found that we had to make only minor modifications to the structure and it passed without difficulty. What we did have to do was add an ECU to control the airbags and at the same time we redesigned the fascia to go with the wider body and added knee bolsters on the lower part of the dash."

By far the most effort in terms of time and resources—man-hours and money—was devoted to "tuning" the aluminium structure to meet the various requirements that involved frontal, rear and side impact, 40 per cent frontal offset, and moveable offset. In all Morgan had to crash test some 21 or 22 cars to satisfy the US Federal requirements making it the second major investment by the company in the Aero 8.

"In all of these tests the cars were painted a blue and yellow colour and there were two anthropomorphic dummies seated inside. We'd passed the front and rear impact tests but in the side impact the passenger dummy was grazed by the tiniest amount by the door which meant that we failed and had to come back later and re-try which was a real disappointment," commented Reeves. And as his colleague Jon Burbidge added, "The other problem we had was with the seat runners that failed the frontal impact test because of the tremendous deceleration over such a short time and distance. The g-forces were so high that they were pulling the seats runners and belt mounts out of the floor! By reinforcing the mounting points and using load limiting seat belts we were able to pass the test."

An outcome of the side impact test was the widening of the body by around six inches and modifying the way in which the doors were mounted. Reeves and Burbidge both commented, "We had to reinforce the side of the tub and add a cast aluminium member to which the doors would lock and bolt, plus we added a beam in the door. We needed the extra space to pass the test but also to widen the interior to better suit the needs of the US buyers who tend to be physically bigger than the Europeans." By widening the body it was necessary to fit three windscreen wipers to sweep a sufficient area of the screen to pass the visibility and wipe/wash tests. As a result of the tests the seats were no longer sourced from Restall but from MB Components whose seat incorporated a D-loop in its structure that prevented an occupant's body from "submarining" under the seat belt.

To pass the rear impact requirements the rear of the tub had to be extended by approximately four inches which meant that they could leave the fuel tank in its original position under the luggage boot floor.

Included in the homologation program were a number of mechanical changes that Reeves and Burbidge felt were required as part of the Series II upgrade. For the American market the Aero 8 was upgraded to the second generation of the BMW V8 engine, from the M62 to the N62, that was still of 4.4-litres capacity but had the added refinement of BMW's wonderful VALVETRONIC system that had the combined benefit of improving engine efficiency—better fuel economy with lower emissions—and engine response to accelerator input. Even though the N62 engine had been homologated by BMW it did not carry over to Morgan and so the Bosch DME unit had to be re-mapped to meet the US requirements. Part of the emission requirement was that of evaporative emissions from the fuel system itself that were limited to 0.5 grams of hydrocarbons over three days—"It was whole new ball game for us," added Reeves, "because you have to look at every pipe and every join in the whole system; you have to go through it with a fine tooth comb and examine every part in detail. We could not afford to fail as it is such an expensive process." These tests were carried out at a facility in Wallace, Houston, Texas.

Similarly there were requirements regarding On Board Diagnostics (OBD III) that were obligatory by the Californian Air Resources Board (CARB) and this had to be proven by Morgan because CARB would not allow Morgan to carry over the results from the BMW program. "That meant we had to undergo the same multi-million dollar test program as a major manufacturer who can amortise the cost over hundreds of thousands of units. We did not have that luxury," said Burbidge who added, "We had to conduct the tests in the heat and humidity of Houston, Texas, using contract people under my supervision. We began the program in mid-2003 and had to run it for 100,000 miles and simulate aging of the components to check for leakage and so forth. It was a long (18 months), laborious task that was hugely expensive for us."

Considerable re-specifying of the running gear took place concurrently. "Chris Lawrence's ideas resulted in the original (Series I) Aero 8 being a very pure sports car," said both Reeves and Burbidge, "but it was very expensive to produce because many components were unique to it and complex in their design. Feedback from our dealers told us that while this was good and made for a very individualistic car, it also made for one that was more expensive to service and maintain for the owner."

Despite protestations from Lawrence, changes were made to the technical design and specifications of the Aero 8. The greatest saving (for Morgan) came from the substitution of the expensive (and bespoke) Jack Knight Development's rack and pinion steering system with one that was sourced off-the-shelf from ZF. The new rack and pinion was a "conventional" unit similar to the one used by Ford on their Scorpio sedans in Europe and included in this change was the use of a MINI electric pump (also from ZF) to energise the hydraulics within the rack replacing the engine-driven pump on the Series I that had proven to be unreliable.

The decision had been taken to fit the Aero 8 with ABS brakes as a standard fitting. Bosch was involved and in consultation with Morgan suggested that the complex four-piece hubs be replaced by a one-piece aluminium casting that would incorporate new wheel bearings and the sensor for the ABS. The result was a much cleaner looking part that was lighter and considerably less expensive to produce. Together with this change was the replacing of the centre-lock wheel fixing with a five-bolt conventional hub, a change which necessitated modified OZ alloy wheels. In a similar vein, the rear hub uprights were also made as single-piece units from cast aluminium.

Where the front suspension was concerned, the positioning of the lower ball joint and the angle at which it was working was changed and the lower mounting point for the coil-over-damper was repositioned inboard slightly which changed the operating ratio, these relatively minor alterations having to be made to accommodate the new steering rack. Burbidge was quick to point out, "We have remained faithful to Lawrence's original centre-point geometry so the driving characteristics remain the same."

At the rear, more detailed changes had to be made to improve the refinement of the driving experience. The major change was to bolt the BTR-sourced Hydratrak differential's nose to an additional piece of laser-cut structural aluminium that was rubber-mounted to the original sub-frame thereby filtering out a considerable amount (but not all) of the noise that this unit was generating and feeding into the tub structure. The added benefit of this change was to virtually eliminate driveline shunting that was always present in the Series I.

The other major change from Series I to Series II had to do with the accessibility to the engine for servicing purposes. In the Series I the floor of the engine compartment was fully enclosed and was structural which in itself was fine but it meant that if any parts needed replacing—a power steering pump, for example—the engine had to be supported while the underside of the car was removed. Reeves and Burbidge redesigned the structure so that on the Series II the engine was mounted on a substantial new cast aluminium cross

Chapter Seven • The Evolution Begins

member (complete with Morgan wings logo!) and then the underside of the car closed off for aerodynamic purposes by bolt-on panels. As was pointed out by Reeves, what was a 2-to-3 hour job at the dealer was reduced to 40-45 minutes. Included in the Series II upgrade was a raised bootlid that improved the appearance of the Aero 8's rear and added several inches to the depth of the boot itself thereby increasing luggage carrying possibilities.

The Series II, which retained the controversial VW headlights, replaced the original on dealer showroom floors in May 2003. The Series III came along in September 2004 and incorporated the first exterior styling change to the Aero 8. During the design process for the AeroMax, resident stylist Matthew Humphries had decided to alter the frontal aspects of the car but without sacrificing any of the individuality for which the Aero 8 had become infamous. He decided, in consultation with Charles Morgan, to replace the VW headlights with those from the MINI and to mount them ever-so-slightly higher and further apart on the front fender. This required manufacturing new front fenders, and a new splitter was required because the parking/indicator lens were now round. The rest of the Aero was unchanged. Other running changes at the time included a new hood mechanism and a larger rear window for improved rearwards visibility and there was more sound deadening material applied during construction.

Many Morgan enthusiasts added the Aero 8 to their Morgan fleet, as shown below

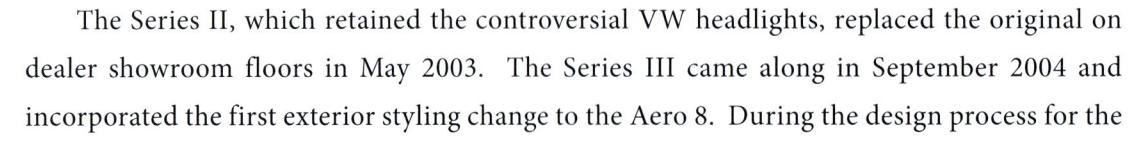

In talking with Keith Chadwick, Chris Dickinson and John Harper at Radshape, their enthusiasm for the Aero project was infectious, still after more than eight years of involvement. As Chadwick said, "Initially we were simply responsible for the chassis up to the bulkhead, but now we build up the front end too and install sound deadening material." He continued by saying, "Over the years we have suggested around 600 ideas for improvement, more than 60 per cent of which have been taken up."

Auto Express carried out an impression drive in 2007 and wrote enthusiastically about the revised Aero 8 with comments like "Don't be fooled by the retro looks—there's nothing old-fashioned about the way Morgan's range-topper drives." Even though it cost over £60,000 they felt it offered far better value for money than Jaguar's XKR drop-top and BMW's M6 Convertible. They even expressed the opinion that Bentley could learn a lesson or two from Morgan's craftsmen by saying "the wood and turned aluminium dash is a work of art."

BBC Top Gear also reviewed the Aero 8 in 2007 and they also were similarly impressed. Their writer, Piers Ward, said of the car, "The highlight is still the BMW-sourced 4.4-litre V8. Morgan is rightly proud of the fact that it's managed to secure this engine—drive it and you'll understand why. The noise is simply fantastic. The side exit pipes mean that it burbles away just below you, so when you accelerate you get the full experience. I could accelerate and slow down all day, just to listen to it." It was not all roses according to Ward who criticised the steering—"could do with more accuracy on the initial turn-in"—and he felt the floor-mounted foot pedals took a little getting used to.

When the AeroMax was displayed at the Geneva Motor Show in 2005 the new front appearance drew international praise—"The media in particular were very quick to tell us how much they liked the new headlights," commented Humphries. The decision was made to transfer the change to the MINI Xenon lights across to the Aero 8 roadster. The change appeared from September 2004 and was incorporated as a running change, little else needing to be either changed or uprated.

As with the changes from Series I to Series II, so the change from Series III to Series IV would be significant insofar as Morgan would upgrade the engine to the latest N62 B48 version now with 4.8-litres capacity, DOUBLE VANOS and VALVETRONIC as part of its specifications. Cylinder bore and stroke dimensions were now 93.0 x 88.3 mm for

4,798cc and on a 10.0:1 compression the V8 developed 367bhp (274kW) at 6300rpm and 361 ft-lbs (490Nm) of torque at 3400rpm.

For the first time on a Morgan sports car the company offered an automatic gearbox as an option to the existing (and still available) Getrag six-speed manual. The automatic was the ZF 6HP 26. Matthew Parkin, then Morgan's congenial Sales and Marketing Director, commented, "Since we have had the automatic as an option the inquiry from potential buyers has been phenomenal to the point where I believe the majority of Aero 8 buyers will opt for the automatic option. Its performance is blistering and the ease of driving is increased significantly." At around the same time the Aero 8 steering specification was changed again, this time to a BMW ZF rack with the MINI electric power pump.

As a footnote to the Aero 8 story, Morgan has re-introduced in 2012 a sports car carrying the famous Plus 8 moniker. Ever since the release of the Aero 8 a decade ago Morgan enthusiasts have been suggesting to Charles and the dealers that while they appreciate the Aero 8 for what it is, what they would really like to buy was a reincarnated Plus 8 that would combine the benefits of the Aero's superb chassis and running gear with the traditional body styling of the old Plus 8. Morgan has relented and sanctioned the production of just such a sports car which intriguingly takes the Aero story full circle insofar as all the original prototypes (the P8000 series' cars) were Aero 8's under the disguise of the Plus 8 bodywork.

The new Plus 8 retained many of the old styling cues and added towering performance to the experience

Chapter Seven • The Evolution Begins

Standing back, looking at the new Plus 8 it looks remarkably like the original that had been discontinued in 2004 after a release in 1968 because Rover was unable to make the 3.5-litre alloy V8 meet forthcoming emission requirements. The similarity is especially evident from the front or from a front three-quarter view, where there is the traditional Morgan grille flanked by protruding headlights and small round indicator light below them. The long bonnet is there together with a row of louvres either side of the central hinge and the chromed bonnet latches, plus the flat windscreen with three wipers and the tight passenger compartment for two people. At the rear is the slab fuel tank, round tail/stop and indicator lights and under the lower skirt there are four exhaust pipes poking out. As an option buyers can specify a low restriction exhaust system with side exit pipes that boosts engine power up to 390bhp. Intriguingly no spare wheel is offered.

The interior again follows the style of the original with the two main dials placed in the centre of the dash—tachometer on the left, speedometer on the right (in right-hand drive Plus 8s)—with two smaller dials in front of the driver. Warning lights and switches are in the centre, too, including a "start" button. Seats are leather upholstered, there are two SRS airbags and buyers can even specify air conditioning and a premium sound system although why you would want to listen to that rather than the burble of the powerful V8 engine is beyond me!

Being built on the same aluminium bonded and riveted platform as the Aero 8, AeroMax and Aero SuperSports the new Plus 8 is wider than the original at 69-inches (1751mm), about 6-inches longer and 2-inches lower; kerb weight is higher by around 200kgs. Performance is superior, as you would expect, with the new model racing from 0-62mph (100km/h) in 4.5 seconds and having a top speed of around 150mph (250km/h) where the original ran to 124mph (200km/h) and took 6.7 seconds to run from 0-60mph (96km/h). As for the price, in 1968 a Plus 8 cost a mere £1477. 18s. 4d including all taxes where today's will cost more than £85,000 depending on what options are selected.

Morgan has successfully passed full European type approval with the Plus 8 which in the brochures is listed with the Classic range and not as a part of the Aero range. Interesting.

The new Plus 8 is an exhilarating car to drive with its massive power-to-weight ratio and it has been designed to meet international emission and safety requirements so Morgan traditionalists and enthusiasts all over the world can motor in the old style with wind in the hair and the burble of a lusty V8 engine providing a smile generating backdrop.

CHAPTER SEVEN • THE EVOLUTION BEGINS

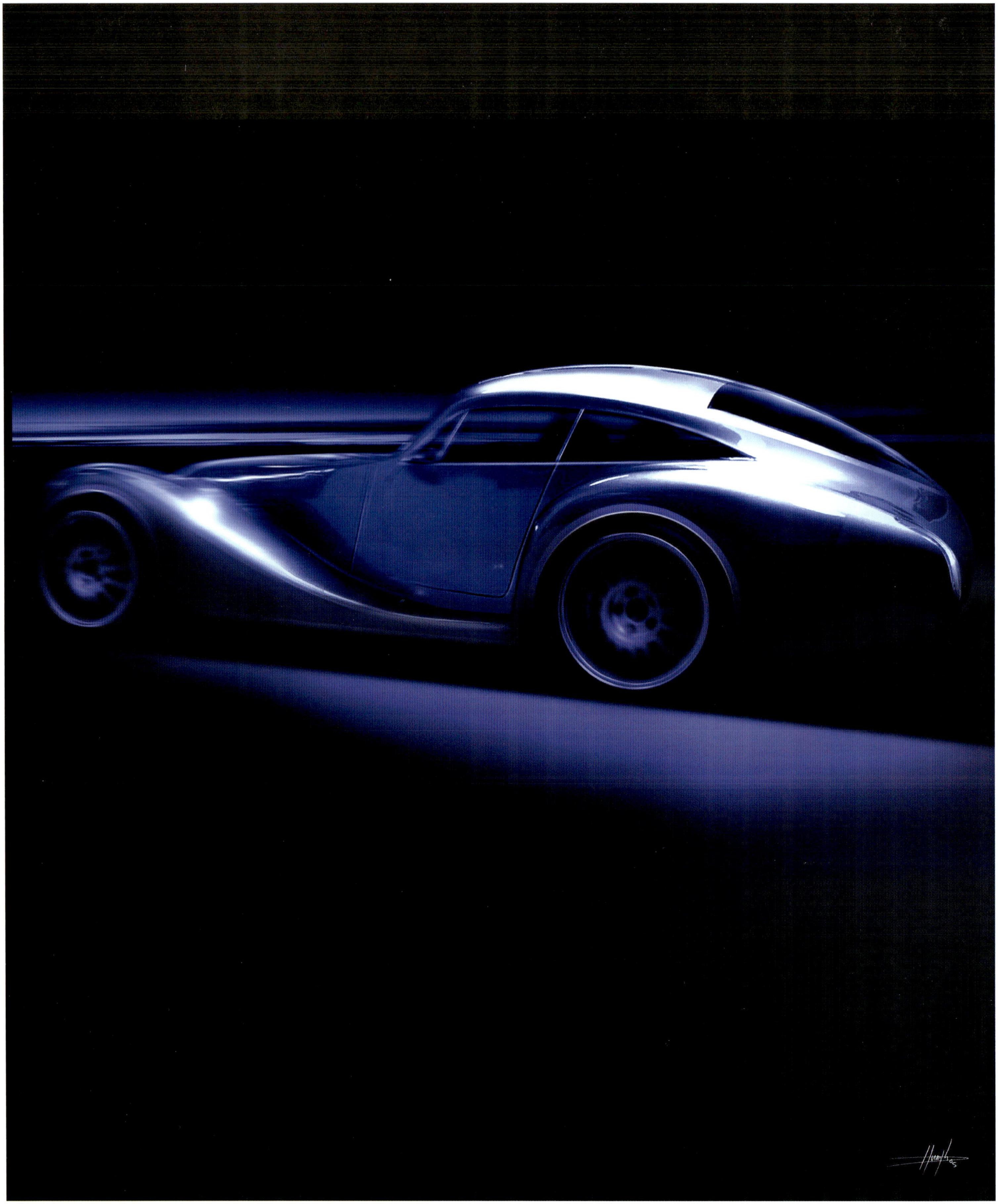

Chapter Eight

AERO 8 GAINS A ROOF

With the Aero 8 successfully launched and in limited production—between two and three cars a week—Charles Morgan was keen to explore other uses for the aluminium intensive chassis that the company had spent so much time and money developing.

Coincident with this thinking, Charles received a portfolio of styling sketches and ideas from a young stylist who was studying Automobile Design at the Coventry University, Matthew Humphries. Matthew, who was 21 years of age at the time, had compiled his art folio in collaboration with his mentor at Coventry, David Arbuckle, an ex-MG Rover stylist, in April 2004. Among the many companies to which he sent his folio was the Morgan Motor Company.

Soon after receiving it Charles called Matthew and invited him to Malvern for an informal chat at which his work and aspirations were discussed and, as Matthew commented, "I expected that would be the last I would hear from Charles." However, Charles was impressed by Matthew and arranged a second meeting at which he offered him two options to go away and work on—a variation on the traditional Morgan sports car theme, or an Aero 8 coupe.

The AeroMax undoubtedly will become a classic in its own time

"That decision was for me easy, it had to be the coupe," said Matthew when discussing what became the AeroMax. Matthew went back to Coventry and drew a number of sketches all of which exhibited styling influences from the 1930s, the era of the *Grand Routiers* in France and a time when carrozzeria such as Figoni and Falaschi and several other French coach builders were busy creating extravagant shapes on Delage, Delahaye, Talbot and other chassis.

CHAPTER EIGHT • AERO 8 GAINS A ROOF

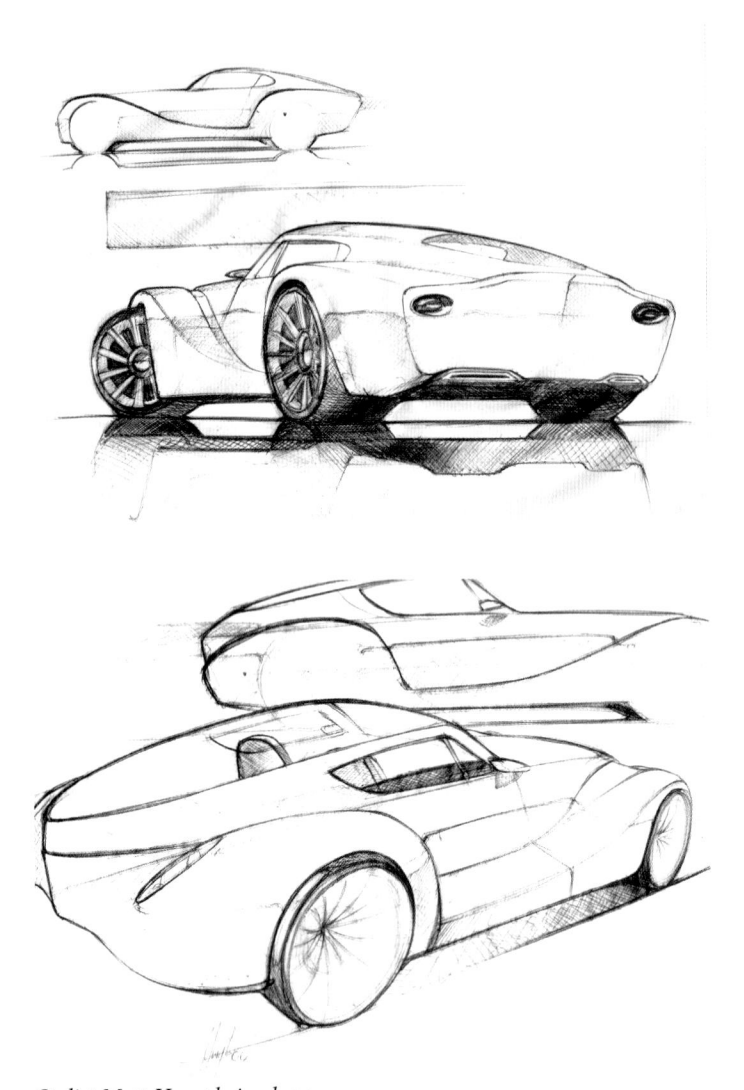

Stylist Matt Humphries drew many sketches all of which evoked a Bugatti-like style

"As well as these coupes there was also the Bugatti Atlantic which was one of the nicest shapes ever created," added Matthew.

He returned to Malvern a few weeks later, in May 2004, with a sheaf of sketches from which one was selected for further attention. In the meantime Charles Morgan had been in contact with his friend and Morgan enthusiast Prince Eric Sturdza, President of the Banque Baring Brothers Suisse in Geneva, who already owned an Aero 8 himself as well as a Roadster for his wife and a 4/4 for his daughter. He was interested in what Charles had said about the project and financed it to the tune of £100,000.

Matthew had returned to Coventry again and through July and August made a 1:4 scale model of his design. That was brought back to Malvern where Matthew did a presentation of it to both Charles Morgan and Eric Sturdza who at the end of it declared, "I must have it!"

From there the decision was taken to build it in a section of the factory well away from the daily production processes and away from the prying eyes of the staff. Two master craftsmen were assigned to the project by Charles— wood framer Nigel Hill and sheet metal worker Dave Cale. These two men took a Series II Aero 8 rolling chassis that incorporated a number of refinements and proceeded to hand craft the delicate shapes of the coupe body onto it, the work beginning in late November with the aim of having it completed in time for showing at the forthcoming Geneva Motor Show in March the following year. Hill made the wooden egg crate master over which Cale hand-formed the aluminium panels. It would be fair to say that the rest of the company's workforce was unaware of the creation of the new car. It was completed by late February just prior to being unveiled to the workers who stood and applauded and transported to Geneva.

In transforming the Aero 8 into the AeroMax, a name coined by Charles for the coupe after his son Maximus, a number of changes were made to the original shape. Possibly the most controversial aspect of the original Aero 8 was its headlights, Volkswagen New Beetle units set sideways in the wing that gave the roadster a slightly cross-eyed look. For the AeroMax the Beetle headlights were replaced by MINI units and positioned slightly higher on the wing, and the air splitter under the traditional Morgan grille was re-profiled. These, along with circular parking/indicator lenses, gave the AeroMax a sleek new look. An intriguing story surrounding the original headlights suggests that Morgan had wanted to use the MINI headlights from the start but the Aero 8 was released before the MINI and BMW was unwilling to allow the lights to be used on another car before the MINI was released.

The bonnet was altered slightly at the rear where it blended into new A-pillars making a roofline that swept gracefully up, back and down to the rear. The most controversial aspect of the rear styling was the two-piece rear window—it consisted of two almost triangular pieces of glass hinged on the central spine, which opened like the wings of a butterfly and were held open by two enormous holders fashioned out of metal and chromed—"We might have to make them smaller for production," quipped Matthew. Running down the spine of the roof of the AeroMax was the merest suggestion of a rib that ended at the lowest point of the slightly pointed rear.

On his sketches Matthew had drawn long slender taillight units that flowed down each of the rear wings. When the AeroMax was being built he had to find the lights and he did in the form of those from the Lancia Thesis that in Matthew's opinion were "just perfect."

Charles Morgan unveiled the Aeromax at the 2005 Geneva Salon where it caused a sensation. Not only was the media ecstatic about it but by the end of the show several well-heeled enthusiasts were keen to order one. Charles was non-committal about production possibilities but he did indicate that if there were 50 firm orders he would consider the possibility and suggested that the retail price would be of the order of £70,000. In truth Charles and others within the company were confident they could sell far more than that based on the reception to the car from the media and public at Geneva.

Chapter Eight • Aero 8 Gains A Roof

In the ensuing 18 months very little news crept out of Malvern about the AeroMax but behind the scenes much work had been going on, both at Board level where decisions on the viability of the coupe project were discussed in minute detail and with their suppliers, in particular Superform Aluminium who would be forming the complex shapes of the panels if a production sign-off was to eventuate. Technical director at Superform Aluminium, Dave Edwards, remembered an interesting detail that the original model did not have but would legally require—a Central High Mounted Stop Light (or CHIMSL, pronounced "chim-sell" in industry-speak)—and this created quite a stir with Humphries. The production car would have to have one so the two discussed the situation and came up with two alternatives: make a pod and site it above the rear windows which would look like an ugly after-thought, or design an arrow-shaped light that would fit on the spine at the base of the rear windows. The latter solution was chosen even though it required some very expensive tooling.

Those discussions led to the decision to go ahead with the AeroMax as a production car with the company making the following announcement in July 2006 on its website:

"The Morgan Motor Company is delighted to announce that following an exhaustive study into the viability of producing the stunning AeroMax Coupe, production is due to commence in January 2008.

A limited run of just 100 individually numbered coachbuilt coupes will be constructed at a rate of 1 – 2 cars per week, the final model leaving the production lines in our Centenary year, 2009.

Pricing is anticipated to be around £94,000 + VAT and will be supplied strictly on a first come first served basis."

Steve Cropley, managing editor at *Autocar* magazine and an ex-Australian motoring journalist visited Malvern soon after the AeroMax's showing at Geneva and was allowed a drive accompanied by Charles Morgan. He commented very favourably on the revisions to the car's styling and the latest modifications, saying, "They were immediately obvious, as

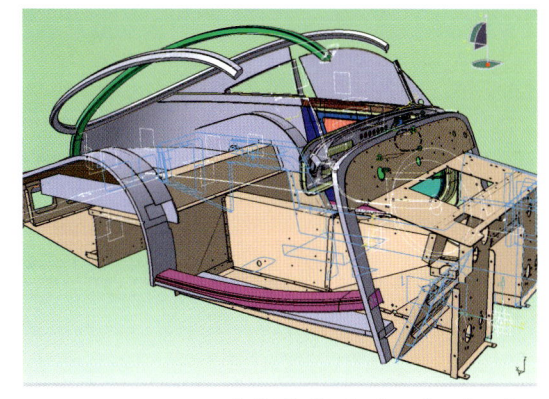

A CAD illustration showing the cabin structure (above); Matt Humphries seen below checking for form of a panel

CHAPTER EIGHT • AERO 8 GAINS A ROOF

Each AeroMax was hand built to special order

was the improved comfort. The cockpit is still snug, but there's no longer the feeling of being crowded by the right-hand door. The footwells are deep and generously wide, and the simple, machine-turned fascia is set somewhat higher and closer than most, which makes its ergonomics spectacularly good." He went on to say, "The Aeromax interior is truly a thing of beauty, especially if you love the wood and leather craftsmanship which the British have always been so good at." Few noticed or cared that there were BMW column stalks plus various buttons and trip computer, an off-the-shelf steering wheel with an airbag or that the door handles were from the MINI.

On the impression drive on the roads around Malvern Link Cropley was really impressed with the dynamics which resulted from the 335bhp coming from the BMW V8 engine powering a coupe that weighed less than 1300kgs; 0-60mph was despatched in less than 5 seconds putting the AeroMax in supercar territory. On its passing ability, he said "…provided the engine's turning at around 3000rpm, see a chance to overtake and you just squeeze the throttle, knowing that the car will erupt. And the long wheelbase-short overhang design gives the AeroMax great in-built stability."

EVO was also able to conduct an impression drive and wrote, "To drive the AeroMax feels exactly the same as the standard Aero 8. Same lovely rumble, same special feel." Again, as with their rivals at *Autocar*, the sheer beauty of the AeroMax's shape and the way in which Humphries had so evocatively blended so many styling influences from the 1930s famous French (in particular) carrozzeria drew many positive comments.

After the public showing at Geneva the AeroMax's shape was digitised so that the shape of its outer panels could be formed by the same special processes developed by Superform Aluminium. And as then marketing director Matthew Parkin proudly pointed out, "The roof panel of the AeroMax is the largest single aluminium pressing ever made for a car.

We're rather proud of our achievement there in collaboration with our colleagues at Superform."

Morgan issued a press release on February 27, 2008 with respect of the AeroMax that said, in part:

Just 2 years after its debut at the 2006 Geneva Autoshow as a one-off built to order for one of Morgan's discerning customers, the AeroMax coupe has entered series production at the Morgan factory.

Such was the interest surrounding this unique design that it was decided, with the kind permission of its owner, to make a limited production run of 100 cars, all of which were sold within a few weeks of its announcement.

Following a two-year intense period of production development, and a number of minor improvements to the overall design, the first customer AeroMax is shortly to be delivered.

The release went on to describe various aspects of the design and the revised specification of the engine—now the latest 4.8-litre BMW V8 developing 367bhp mated to the ZF 6HP 26 six-speed automatic gearbox with a lock-up clutch that enhanced gearchanges and improved fuel economy. Morgan claimed a maximum speed of 170mph for the AeroMax and a 0-60mph time of 4.2 seconds.

Chapter Eight • Aero 8 Gains A Roof

Through a number of articles in targeted magazines the company kept the AeroMax in the mind of potential clients to the point where all 100 cars for the European market were sold well in advance. A small number—thought to be 13—was built for US clients under a show and display exemption which meant the AeroMax did not have to undergo Federalisation and the owners could still register them for limited usage.

In conclusion the company said, "Morgan believes with the AeroMax it leads the way in exclusive bespoke low volume car construction using quality raw materials and advanced technologies that are not available to Morgan's competitors in the world of luxury car production. Owners of the Morgan AeroMax will have joined a very exclusive club with a unique opportunity to share their motoring dreams."

A stunning Matt Humphries sketch of the rear styling of the AeroMax

Chapter Eight • Aero 8 Gains A Roof

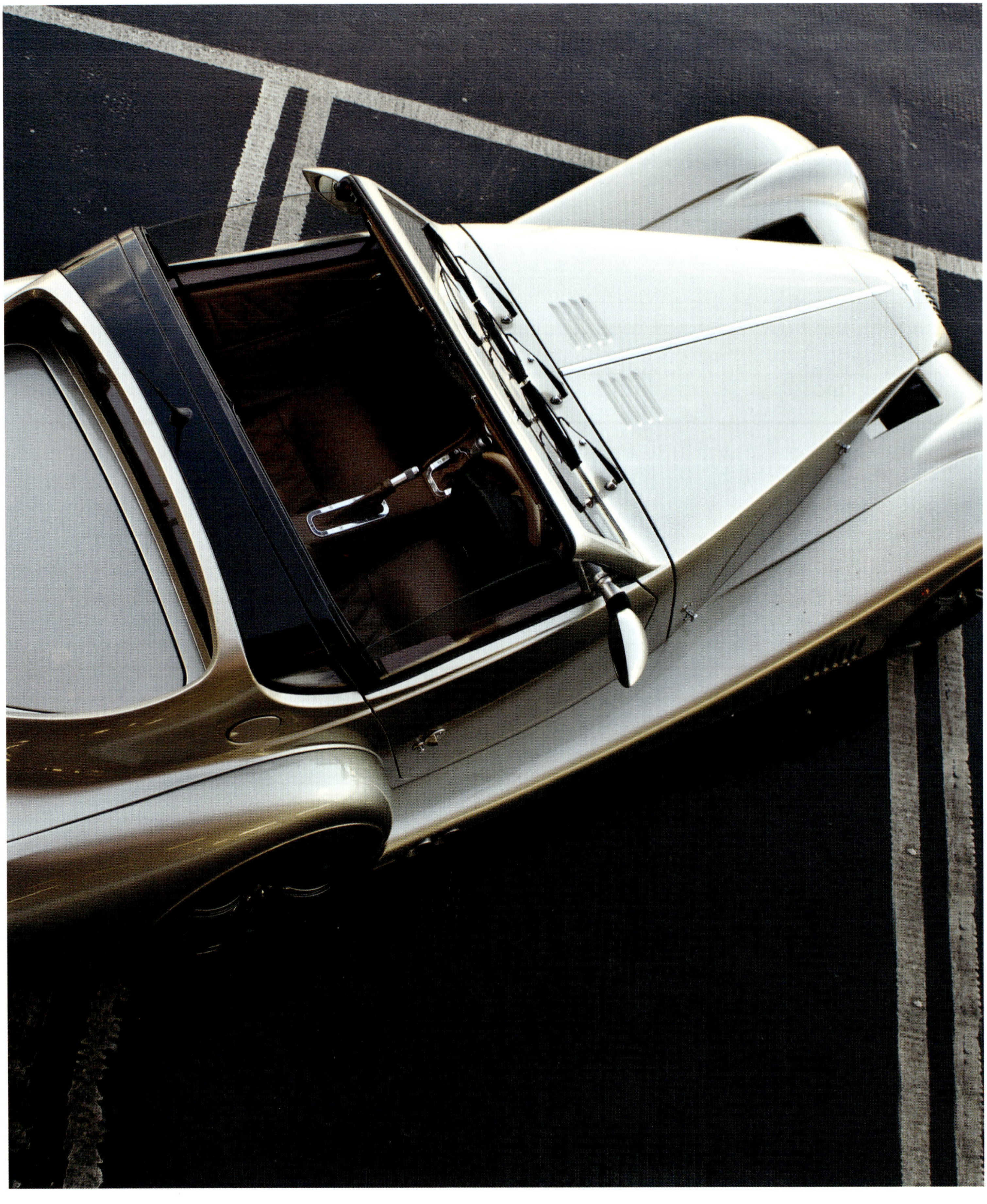

Chapter Nine

THE AEROMAX BECOMES THE SUPERSPORT

Change has come rather rapidly by Morgan's standards. Previously, and historically, where a model would enter production after some development by HFS Morgan or Peter Morgan and remain pretty much untouched for years, the past decade has seen mammoth changes in model development take place. A tiny fraction of this would be driven by the company responding to feedback from owners, but the majority has been driven in recent times by the need to comply with ever-increasing bureaucratic demands on car manufacturers. As well, there has been the desire to push the envelope a little.

The story about the evolution of the SuperSport is typically Morgan, that is, not straight forward and it could be said to have happened on a whim. Charles Morgan, accompanied by Matt Humphries, attended the Villa d'Este on the shores of Lake Como in April 2008 where the company displayed the production prototype of the AeroMax and the LIFECar. In addition, Eric Sturzda arrived in his personal AeroMax. As Humphries said, "After driving 2000 kilometres on the motorways to the Villa d'Este all you really want to do is drop the top and cruise around the lake in the sunshine. That got me thinking."

Matt Humphries concept sketch of how the SuperSport could look

Back at Morgan a week later he began sketching an AeroMax without its roof, the sketches all having the name "Speedster" on them. Three alternative roof styles were concepted and

Chapter Nine • The AeroMax Becomes The SuperSport

Building the first SuperSports

these were viewed by all the directors and the development team which included key people such as Charles Morgan, Mark Reeves and Steve Morris. Of the three, general agreement was gained for the one with a two-piece targa-style removable roof.

From there Humphries began working on a half-scale AeroMax where he cut off the roof and replaced it with clay and worked that into the shape from his sketch. In parallel to this colleague Jon Wells began working up the shape on ALIAS, a CAD computer program used for styling modelling that would allow them to visualise what the forthcoming SuperSport (as it was now known and was another name taken from the company's illustrious history) would look like in real life. A wooden egg box was made in the wood working shop and Dave Cale, the same man who hand beat the aluminium panels for the original AeroMax, rolled the panels that would be required for the new model. At the same time he rolled the panels for the LIFECar, a project that was running in parallel.

Where the SuperSport is different when compared with the Aero 8 is at the rear. The Aero 8 had a conventional flat rear with a full-width boot lid opening to a commodious luggage space but the SuperSport has a more pointed rear (like the AeroMax) and different roof and rear window line with a smaller triangular-shaped boot lid that gives restricted access to the luggage area. Like the AeroMax, it features the distinctive Lancia Thesis tail lights.

At the 2009 Villa d'Este Charles unveiled the first production SuperSport. It was painted an unusual colour, Zurallic blue, which appeared to the naked eye to be black in natural light but which became a deep blue in direct sunlight. The interior was upholstered in completely natural tan leather. "It looked stunning," commented Humphries who added, "Mr Zagato came over to see us and immediately fell in love with it!" Unusually for the time of year, the open-topped SuperSport was caught in a shower of rain…..

The SuperSport shared its dashboard with the AeroMax, the dash featuring a polished walnut dashtop with two raised shoulders over the two main dials—speedometer on the left with digital readout for total and trip mileage, tachometer on the right—with the minor gauges for fuel contents and engine coolant temperature plus a row of lights in the centre to monitor a wide range of functions and a parallel row of switches under them. Slightly below them was the premium audio system and integrated climate air conditioning controls. A console divided the interior and housed the lever for the selection of gears, manual or automatic depending on the buyer's choice.

The SuperSports interior was a most luxurious place to be for those long high speed Continental dashes

Following that success the car was further displayed at the Goodwood Festival of Speed in June 2009 where by now it had acquired the two-piece roof. Morgan was able to display it in the SuperCar paddock and drive it up the hillclimb. Charles was also able to show it at Pebble Beach in the USA in August that year where it gained a rapturous reception.

From there the company began planning the production process. Compared with the concept car, changes for production were subtle but necessary. The car was remodelled in ALIAS and then a full-sized foam model was cut from the bulkhead back in collaboration with Survirn Engineering who had also been involved with the original Aero 8. Humphries again, "We raised the roofline a fraction but when I stood back and viewed it I felt that the roofline was too crowned—it looked different in real life compared with the ALIAS version. Together with Jon (Wells) we ground the roof down by around 15mm to give it a lower profile and more 'speed' which transformed the sleekness of the whole car."

Craig Dollan was responsible for developing the A-class surfacing of the model in preparation for the manufacture of the tooling. Graham Chapman and his CAD team in collaboration with Steve Morris then took on the responsibility for production. Superform Aluminium was contracted to manufacture the new panels using their world-class vacuum forming system using dies made by Survirn. Compared with the Aero 8, only the front wings, splitter, bonnet and cowl were common; the lower part of the rear wings was the same but the rest of the body was new. To pass the strict US 50-mph crash safety requirements the aluminium chassis had to be changed in its details and the fuel tank repositioned from under

CHAPTER NINE • THE AEROMAX BECOMES THE SUPERSPORT

the floor to above the rear suspension. All models shared the structure, the difference being for the US versions where a V-shaped strengthening section was positioned between the bumper support and the rear bulkhead, a solution that was devised by Mark Reeves. While the chassis change was designed for the SuperSport, a small number of the last of the Series IV Aero 8s were built with it.

Production preparations were completed by March 2010 with the first car being displayed publicly at the Geneva Show a few days later. Customer cars followed soon afterwards.

Journalists from *Octane* magazine were permitted to drive the prototype SuperSport from Milan where it had been displayed at the Design Week exposition north to the Villa d'Este where it would participate in the events there. They wrote in glowing terms about the car, saying "Continuing from where the AeroMax coupe left off, this latest variation allows sunlight into the mix, the lift-off roof panels being storable within the surprisingly ample boot." Further, they said, "(t)his newest Morgan is an opinion-divider," and in a reference to its perhaps controversial styling said, "up close it works. More than any car that blends Lancia Thesis tail-lights, neo-Gothic buttresses and running boards has any right to. It's remarkable."

Morgan-owner Dennis Simanaitis writing in the American magazine *Road & Track* (July 2010) wrote a most positive introductory article about the car and published a set of performance figures that fitted well with its name—0-60mph in 4.5 seconds, standing quarter mile in 13.0 seconds at 107.2mph "with the SuperSport's quad side exhausts barking sharply from the running boards." He loved the interior—"the cowl contours have an Almost French exuberance of execution"—and his comments on the styling were interesting—"The latest pencil-beams fix this (the former cross-eyed look) admirably and from the A-pillar forward the SuperSports impresses one and all. Its rear deck, however, maintains the Aero controversy. The wing flanks are handsome, but I find a conflict of the targa top frame, vertical rear glass, deeply scalloped buttresses and embedded trunklid."

Autocar tested a SuperSports in August 2010 and was won over by the car's stunning looks—"You could park the SuperSports next to anything short of a gold-plated Bugatti and know that it would win the bulk of attention." On the performance side they talked in terms of 4.2 seconds for the classic 0-62mph sprint with an economy capability of 26mpg and a maximum speed in excess of 160mph. They loved the race-proved chassis saying, "The result is a very rigid chassis with excellent body control, agile responses and huge mechanical grip."

Only the targa roof system came in for any criticism. They wrote, "The targa roof system definitely isn't designed for making the most of a showery day. Removing the heavy panels and packing them in their protective bags takes a good ten minutes, and if you carry them with you they'll wipe out most of the otherwise generous boot space."

At £126,900 it was in company with the Bentley Continental GT and Aston Martin DB9 but as they commented, "The brand's success is that, experienced up close, it becomes impossible to deny that the SuperSports deserves its place in such rarefied company."

Morgan planned to manufacture only 150 SuperSports—shades of the AeroMax—and all but a handful are accounted for.

As a further addition to the range Morgan has added the Aero Coupe—not SuperSports Coupe, please note—where in place of the two roof panels there is an integral full and proper coupe roof. In all other aspects the Coupe is identical. This will bring the Aero 8 concept to a conclusion at Morgan.

Chapter Nine • The Aeromax Becomes The Supersport

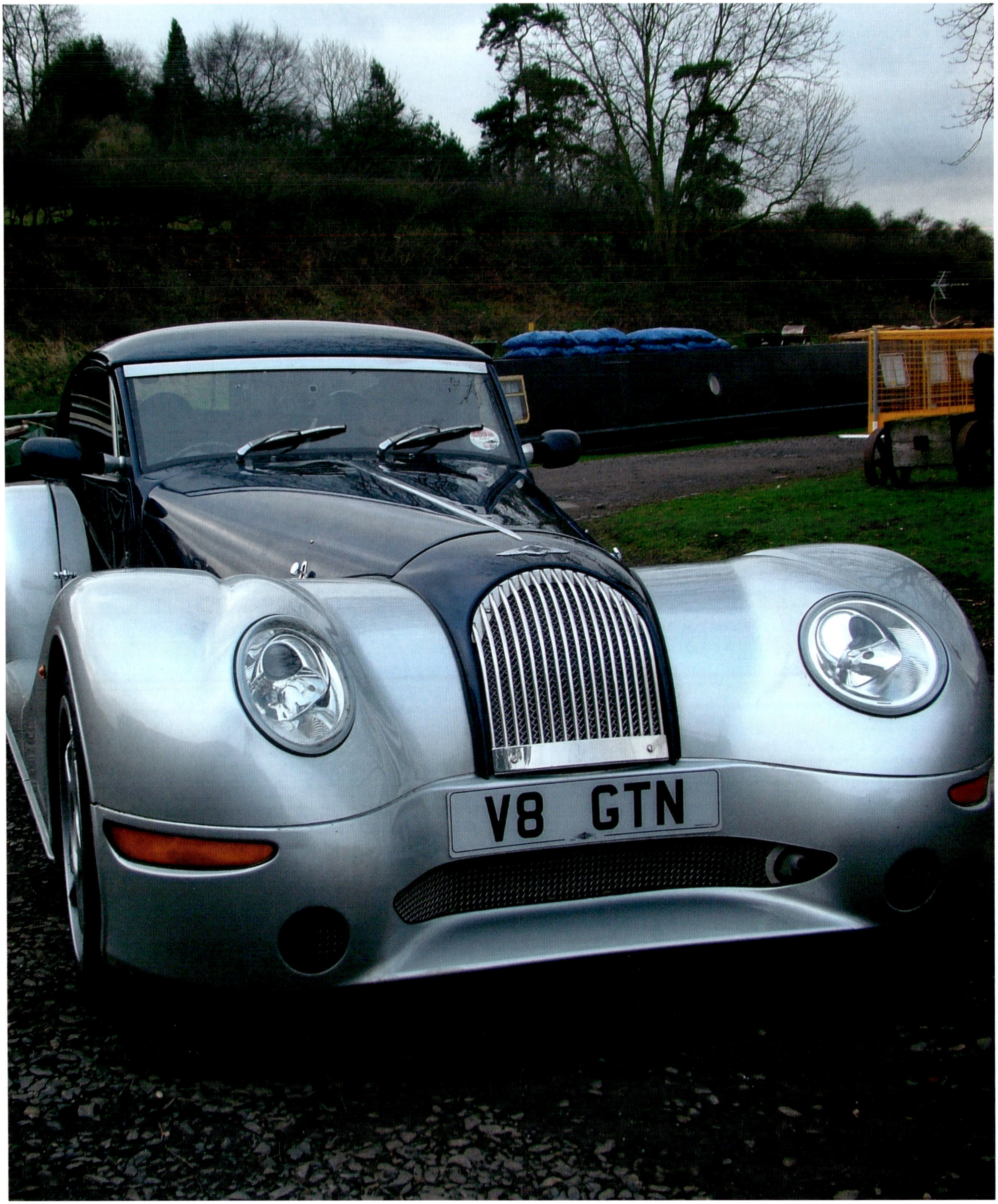
V8 GTN

Chapter Ten

RACING THE AERO 8

With the Aero 8 released and on the market Chris Lawrence continued development work and took it one step further with his Aero 8 GTN. His dream, although not necessarily the dream of the Morgan Motor Company, was to return to the scene of his great triumph in 1962, Le Mans. Charles Morgan was keen for the company to develop a car that met the requirements of the FIA's GTN regulations while Chris Lawrence wanted the car to meet the requirements of the French Automobile Club de l'Ouest (ACO) which were not the same.

Adrian van der Kroft saw the potential in the car as a Le Mans entry and competitor but was unable to broker a deal. In January 2002 the Aero 8 GTN was exhibited at the Autosport International Exhibition at the NEC in Birmingham where Marcos enthusiast Richard Stanton, well-known racing privateer in the British GT series, saw it and was enthusiastic about the idea of racing it at Le Mans now that the Marcos program had been cancelled. Stanton already had a major sponsor, the American tool company De Walt. A deal was agreed between Lawrence and Stanton for the sale of the car and after the show race preparations on it began in earnest. All preparations were carried out by Lawrence and the small band of assistants in the workshops at Malvern. A third GTN was prepared for Tom Hollfelder, the California-based Morgan dealer and race driver.

Lesoudier and Martin at Adria, 2009

To be successful at Le Mans a full commitment was needed and while Lawrence and Stanton fully understood this other parties did not and so the program was never able to achieve its full potential.

A Le Mans entry was secured for the car to everyone's amazement—Richard Thorne, Morgan dealer "We believe Chris might have pulled strings although he denies it." Once the car arrived at Le Mans it had to undergo scrutineering, a process whereby a group of officials go out of their way to

CHAPTER TEN • RACING THE AERO 8

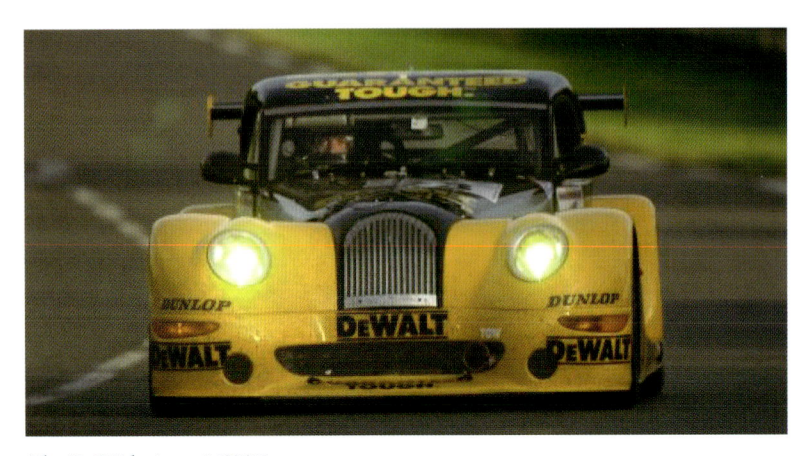

The DeWalt Aero 8 GTN racing at La Mans, 2002

find fault with the car's construction and to ensure that it complies with the absolute letter of the regulations and not the spirit of those regulations. When Steve Lawrence, Chris's son, came back all he said to the crew was that they had a "few issues" to attend to.

For Chris Lawrence, ostensibly the team leader, there were issues with Stanton's team manager Dennis Leach who wanted to make changes to the suspension system—"He wanted to fit anti-roll bars which I told him were unnecessary because of the geometry that I designed into the suspension but he was adamant so I let him," said Lawrence who was clearly aggrieved by this affront. But as Lawrence added, "Changes like that require hours of track testing to prove whether they will give you the benefits you want, but we didn't have that luxury; they were pure guesswork by Leach!"

The Morgan GTN was decked out in De Walt's yellow livery and powered by a Mäder-prepared BMW V8 engine of 4.4-litres capacity that produced 500bhp (373kW) at 6900rpm and 420 ft-lbs (569Nm) of torque at 6300rpm.

In practice further problems arose. In the first session lead driver Stanton drove lap after lap at 4 minutes 30 seconds (4:30) with a fastest lap of 4:27 which was far too slow. Relief drivers Steve Hyde and Richard Hay also turned in similar lap times much to Chris Lawrence's dismay. "We needed to get those times down by at least 10 seconds," remembered Lawrence, "If we were going to be assured of qualifying for the race." Late in the session excitement gripped the Morgan camp when the electronic screen monitoring their car flashed up 4 minutes 16 seconds! (4:16). To this day, Lawrence insists it was a glitch in the French timing system because his self-timed charts done with an old fashioned stop watch showed the laps to still be in the region of 4:25 to 4:27. "Never did trust those electronic systems!" quipped Lawrence. However, if that was the time the French said it was the team went along with it.

During the actual race the drivers consistently lapped at 4:27 for hour after hour. The daytime ambient temperature was a high 39° Celsius which placed inordinate stress on all components in the car and the pit crew. Around two o'clock in the morning, ten hours after the start of the race, Stanton came into the pits complaining of a vibration from the rear axle—a complete new axle was installed in just 14 minutes by the pit crew!

Several hours later the Aero 8 was still lapping consistently but then disaster struck at around nine o'clock in the morning when the engine suddenly and inexplicably went "off song." An engineer from the Mäder organization who built the race engine, examined it and pronounced the problem as terminal. Long time Morgan dealer and race driver Richard Thorne believes it to have been an ingested piece of an intake trumpet.

The volume of press generated by this "failure" at Le Mans was staggering and all ultimately good for the tiny Morgan Motor Company. Stanton and De Walt were keen to return to Le Mans for another try in 2003 but that was a year away and many events in the life of the car and company had yet to be played out.

Back at Malvern Lawrence drew up specifications for an Aero 8 GT "Cup" version that would allow the car to compete in national racing. Amazingly he received his first two orders for the Aero 8 Cup from America, the first English order coming from Keith Ahlers, a well-known Morgan client who was planning to return to British GT Championship racing as a privateer. A second local car was ordered by Richard Thorne, a Morgan dealer based in Grazely Green south of Reading in Berkshire.

The DeWalt Aero 8 GTN racing at La Mans, 2002

Interestingly, there was not a lot of modification required on the Aero 8 other than the requirements needed to cope with the demands of racing. Most people in the Morgan fraternity are proud to tell you that a Morgan Aero 8 was far more "standard" than a race prepared Porsche 911 GT3, Ferrari or Lotus Exige for example. The engine, for instance, was out to 4.6-litres capacity but was basically in standard tune with the exception that the VANOS system was rendered inoperative, it had no catalytic converters and ran with normal connecting rods although it did have a dry-sump engine lubrication system. In addition the engine's electronics had a "soft" cut-out at higher revs, six-pot brake calipers were fitted, a 120-litre fuel tank, a full roll cage and a rear wing for down force at maximum speed.

Although there would be no official "works" sponsorship—Morgan had already spent more than £2 million of its own money on the design and development of the Aero 8 plus a further £1-1.5 million on Federal Type Approval in preparation for selling the car on the American market—if the team was

Chapter Ten • Racing The Aero 8

Morgan wins an epic battle in the British GT class at Knockhill

Aero 8 GT2 driver change at a wet Spa circuit in the Ardenne

to go racing it would need to find sponsorship money from outside the company. Many companies were approached but no major sponsorship was secured.

The two cars, Ahlers' and Thorne's, were ready for their first race at Donington where drivers Neil Cunningham and Keith Robinson drove the Thorne-entered car to second in class and seventh outright while the Ahler's car, co-driven by Rob Wells, finished third in class.

Meanwhile an entry for the 2003 Le Mans 24-Hour race had been submitted and paid for. Some weeks later the team was disappointed to learn that their entry had been refused by the ACO committee and, despite the efforts of Chris Lawrence who knew people in high places within the ACO, no reason was given for the declining of their entry. Not to be defeated by the ACO decision, cars were entered for the Spa-Francorchamps 24-Hour race and the 1000Km at Donington.

In another blow for the team, there was a major misunderstanding between the FIA officials in Geneva and the race officials at Donington during scrutiny when it was discovered that the conditions of homologation of the Aero 8 had not been sent to the UK office. Despite frantic efforts the man concerned was not able to be contacted and so the Aero 8 did not race on British soil in that prestigious event. The car remained on display all weekend and so some PR benefit was gained.

Things were much brighter for the Spa event. Charles Morgan was a good friend of Prince Eric Sturzda, a wealthy Swiss banker and long time Morgan enthusiast; he was also a close friend of the French ex-Formula One driver Jacques Laffite who had retired and was available as a driver if the team felt that they could use his services. They certainly could, Laffite joining regular driver Neil Cunningham and newcomer, Paula Cook.

As part of the preparation of the car for the race BMW kindly allowed Morgan to carry out endurance testing at their Miramas facility in the south of France.

The race itself took place in torrential rain. With his greater experience Laffite started the race and very quickly had the Aero 8 well placed in its class; when his stint was over he handed over to Cunningham who continued the pace set by the Frenchman. However, on a particularly fast part of a very fast circuit the BMW engine cut out (it was a known problem but a cure could not be found) almost immediately after Cunningham had passed a GT3 Porsche. Under the dreadful conditions the Porsche driver had nowhere to go and unfortunately hit the rear of the slowing Morgan. The resultant collision spun the Morgan off the track into the barrier demolishing much of the rear of the car. It was the end of a promising race and the last the team would see of Laffite. Naturally the team was gutted by what had happened. Back at Malvern a freelance repairer and fabricator, Ben Coles, said he could repair the car despite most people believing that it was irrepairable.

Coles successfully repaired the Aero 8 and it was duly entered in the British GT race at Knockhill in Scotland where to everyone's amazement Neil Cunningham won, beating the many Porsche GT3s in the process

The GT2 at high speed in the wet at Spa prior to crashing

Chapter Ten • Racing The Aero 8

The final round of the British GT Championship was held at the Brands Hatch circuit, the car being driven by Cunningham and another newcomer to Morgan, the young Adam Sharpe. After a race dicing with Porsches in particular the Thorne team was able to pull off a stunning last lap class victory. After the race Adam's father, Robert, agreed to finance the team's entry at the 1000Km Le Mans on the Bugatti circuit and the 24-Hours race.

At the pre-race scrutineering it was found by the officials that the rear wheels were one-inch larger than the regulations allowed and so were not passed. Frantic calls back to the factory were made and Steve Morris was coerced into going back and finding the correct sized wheels. This he did and made sure they were despatched immediately to Le Mans. In the meantime, an electronics expert and a suspension expert were brought in by Sharpe to ensure that debacles like that at Spa could not be repeated. In the event, and running in the LMGT class, the Aero 8 was able to compete on a much more level playing field with the hordes of Porsche GT3s to the point where at the end of the race it finished eighth in its class and eighteenth overall.

For the Aero 8's next race Robert Sharpe took the team half way around the world, to Bathurst in the western rural districts of New South Wales, Australia, to compete in the 24-Hour race on the infamous Mount Panorama circuit. The car was the Richard Thorne Aero 8 Cup car with the drivers being Adam Sharpe, Neil Cunningham, Keith Ahlers and Tom Shrimpton. Throughout practice the car had been excitingly quick as the drivers learned their way around the demanding circuit that was 6.172 kms long that climbs some 200 metres from the start-finish line, up Mountain Straight, through the Cutting to what is known as Skyline at McPhillamy Park before dropping down through the Dipper and the Esses to the sharp left-hand corner known as Forest Elbow and then down Conrod Straight to Murray's Corner and back to the start. Conrod Straight used to be 1.86km long with a hump mid-way that often caused cars to lift and flip. Today the hump has been reduced and there is now a long chicane before entry to Murray's in an effort to slow cars down but speeds in excess of 250km/h are common in the V8 Supercars.

Rain had been forecast, the first storm hitting just hours before the start. When the race started it was in dry conditions but all through the race rain storms created difficult conditions for the drivers. After two hours racing the Aero 8 came into the pits with overheating problems that was believed to have been caused by the bottom radiator hose. Race officials stopped the race at one stage because the track surface was awash and a danger to all competitors. Six hours into the race and disaster struck, a conrod let go and the engine blew in a big cloud of smoke. It was a disappointing end to a valiant effort.

After Christmas 2003 Morgan launched a US-spec Aero 8 in Los Angeles with local dealer Tom Hollfelder making the arrangements. It was a big success. Discussions took place during the event with regards to racing an Aero 8 at Sebring as a pre-cursor to lodging an entry for the 2004 24 Hour at Le Mans. The logic was that Sebring was run under license from the French ACO as a part of the American Le Mans Series which meant that the Aero would be scrutinised under the same regulations as for Le Mans.

The team drivers for the race would be Adam Sharpe, Neil Cunningham and Keith Ahlers. The Aero 8 was despatched to Sebring in plenty of time and preparations to race began. However, scrutineering did not go as simply as thought because of the efforts of an over-zealous official but eventually the issues were satisfactorily resolved and the car was allowed to race.

Practice went well with all three drivers coming to terms with the rough track surface and posting competitive times. During the race the Aero circulated quickly and reliably stopping only for fuel and to change drivers; the only "repair" was a stop to replace a blown headlight bulb. At the end of 12 hours of tough racing the Aero 8 finished in 10th place out of 22 in the GT class and in 20th place overall out of a field of 44 starters having beaten the TVR team and many of the Porsche teams. The team had completed 281 laps while the winning Audi R8 completed 350 laps!

Several days after returning to the UK the Morgan team learned that their entry for the 2004 Le Mans had been accepted.

In pre-qualifying two of the three team drivers—Sharpe and Cunningham—completed the requisite 10 laps but unfortunately for Keith Ahlers he did not. He had completed 8 laps when he had an "off" and damaged the car, the damage being too much to repair in the time available. He was subsequently not accepted by the French authorities. This meant the team had to find a replacement driver—preferably one who could contribute sponsorship money—and get the car repaired.

The car was returned to Malvern where it was repaired; indeed the actual damage was far less severe than it appeared thanks to the strength of the Lawrence chassis. During this time Steve Hyde was signed as the third driver—he was well-known to the factory people and had been a member of the 2002 De Walt Morgan Team.

Club racing with the Aero 8 GT has always been popular

Unlike Le Mans 2002 where scrutineering was a nightmare for the small team, that for 2004 was accomplished with a 100 per cent result from the scrutineers. Obviously the team's experience at Sebring had stood them in good stead.

In the practice sessions the car's speed was slower than expected but the car was running smoothly and reliably. Sunday 1600 hours arrived, the cars set off from the grid and the race for 2004 was underway. For the first six hours everything went to plan, there were no incidents to worry about and the car was circulating consistently at around the 4:23 mark, stops only being made for scheduled fuel, tyres and driver changes. And then at 2200 hours the team's rhythm was blown by the alarming news from Neil Cunningham who called in over the radio, "I've run out of gas!" The rules at Le Mans are unequivocal insofar if a race car breaks down out on the circuit it is the responsibility of the driver alone to get it going or back to the pits. On checking the data in the computer it showed that there should have been fuel for at least another two laps with more for a margin of error.

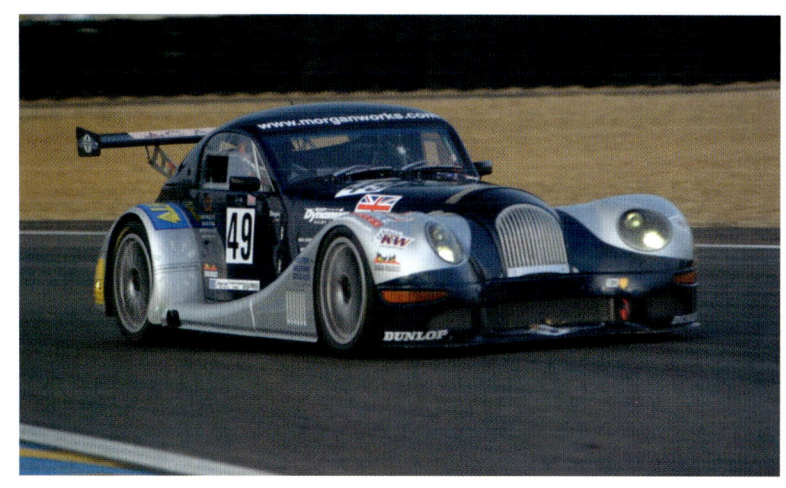

Aero 8 GT3 racing in the British GT Championship

Over an hour went by without success. Midnight came and went. The team realised that they were in danger of being unclassified at the end of the race if something could not be resolved quickly. At the scene, Cunningham had tried everything he could under instructions from the pits and in frustration decided to hit the green start button one more time—it worked! The engine roared into life and he quickly returned to the pits where the fuel pump was replaced and the fuel tank filled.

Six hours later the car came back into the pits with a broken accelerator cable—it had snapped on the approach to the pits luckily—and was quickly replaced and the car sent back out. At 0930 hours there was further drama when the car came in with a broken radiator. Soon afterwards the computer data showed the engine to be using rather a lot of oil and rather than replace the engine it was decided to soldier on at a reduced speed and keep filling it with oil. The engine coolant temperature, too, was running at a higher than desirable level but there was little that could be done other than keep their fingers crossed—the stage was set for an expensive engine failure. And then at 1330 hours another blown radiator added to the team's woes, this one being caused by a rock thrown up by another car. It was replaced and the Aero 8 kept circulating in a cloud of steam and oil smoke.

At the final pit stop Adam Sharpe took over for the final stint and at a few moments after 1600 hours he crossed the start/finish line to accept the chequered flag after 222 laps; they were ranked 27th at the end and sadly were not classified. The tiny team from Malvern had made it! They had competed and completed Le Mans!

As a bonus the team was selected by the OCA to be the recipient of the prestigious and coveted ESCRA award for the best technical crew in the race.

There was no official Morgan racing team for the 2005 and 2006 seasons but the bar was raised somewhat starting with the 2007 European GT3 season. The two key people were Jacques Laffite and Jean-Pierre Jabouille. Besides being good friends both had enjoyed stellar careers as Formula One drivers and Jabouille also had experience on the management side of the business with the Renault team. He was one who pushed strongly for the turbocharged engine with which Renault won the Championship. He also had worked for Peugeot during their successful Le Mans years as well as with Ligier and Matra and had connections throughout the French industry.

Jacques Laffite was a friend of Prince Eric Sturdza and with Charles Morgan decided to establish an organisation to once again race the Morgan Aero 8. Laffite argued persuasively with Sturdza for Jabouille to join them and once he was familiar with his success in racing Sturdza invited him to join the project. Before launching the project many meetings were held and in July 2006 a new company was formed called AutoGT Racing France with its two principal operators being famous French racing drivers Laffite and Jabouille in a 50:50 partnership between them and Baring Brothers Banque in Geneva, Switzerland. Charles Morgan was included and he agreed to provide materials for the team. The company was registered in Paris in July 2006 and for the first six months of operations was based in a garage in Pontchartrain, 30 kilometres south of Paris. From January 2007 a new facility was established in Dannemarie a further 40 kilometres south with the company registration details being moved to Chartres. Initially it consisted of a staff of five plus Laffite and Jabouille, Sturdza and Charles Morgan. In overall charge of the business on a day-to-day basis was Frédéric O'Neill with Frédéric Ducastel looking after the car's electronics systems, Lionel De Oliviera, who had been the technical chief with the Alain Prost racing team, was recruited as the chief mechanic responsible for the engine and chassis with three mechanics reporting to him—José Dos Santos, Christian Weisse and Nicolas Magnin.

Aero 8 GT3 racing in the FIA Championship 2007

The terms of the three-year plan were quite simple. Over a the first half the aim was to be competitive and in the second half to win races. Sturdza agreed a budget that was considerable for a small team but as O'Neill said, "It was only a tenth of that available to the factory teams like BMW and Porsche." Jabouille spent a considerable amount of time driving a Morgan Aero 8 in England and France, and also in 2004 Le Mans car which was owned by Sturdza.

Morgan delivered the first rolling chassis late in 2006 and to the experienced team members it was obvious that apart from the basic structure the rest of the car would have to be significantly modified to be competitive. Initially they dismantled the 2004 Le Mans car so that a bench-mark could be established. The aim at that point was to have a car running by the end of March 2007 at the latest and to be ready for the first race of the season at Silverstone in May.

The strategy decided upon was for the first car to be state-of-the-art having benefitted from all the developments while the second car would be a development car for potentially new solutions. Laffite, Jabouille and Sturdza selected the drivers and for the lead car they were Johan Boris Scheier and Jean-Francois La Roch while those for the second car were two experienced (and older!) drivers, Laffite and Frederic O'Neill. A third car was prepared for Margot Laffite and Georges-Alexandre Sturdza, nephew of the team's sponsor.

The first car was completed in April 2007 and driven with generally good results although it was obvious that there was a major aerodynamic issue that as O'Neill recollected "promoted roadholding and instability problems during braking and limited maximum speed." Power output from the BMW V8 engine was 440bhp and torque was 540Nm while the top speed was only 230km/h.

Aero 8 GT3 racing on the Bucharest circuit 2007, this is the Laffite/O'Neill car

At first the team continued to run with the Mäder-prepared BMW V8 engines but it was clear to O'Neill in particular that another engine tuner was needed. Ducastel was learning the engine's Bosch electronics and was finding ways to liberate more power by finessing and refining the processes of the ECU.

The first round of the European GT3 Championship was held at Silverstone in early May. However, the AutoGT cars were not ready and the FIA would not approve of them and therefore did not compete. Three laps behind the pace car was all they managed.

Two weeks later, however, in Bucharest, Romania, they made their racing debut. Numbered #49 and #50 the cars were driven by Jacques Laffite/Frédéric O'Neill and Jean-Francois Le Roch/Georges-Alexandre Sturdza respectively. Again the team had trouble with the FIA, this time because the exhaust noise level from the cars at 110dB was above the 100dB limit! As if that was not enough, because the car's qualifying times were slower than everybody else the track officials wanted to ban them from the race. Laffite and O'Neill found themselves having to front the senior track marshall where Laffite explained that he was a former Formula One driver and that O'Neill had just beaten Vammelet, the leader of the GT3 championship, in a feature race where both were driving Ferrari 430s! Car #49 finished 29th in the first race on a wet and oily track but the #50 car DNF because of an accident in which it was not too badly damaged. The second race was a complete disaster with both cars retiring with electrical problems.

Meanwhile the team continued their test and development program using the Magny-Cours circuit which is around 160 miles from Paris and which hosted the French Formula One Grand Prix from 1991-through-2008, the intention being to find ways of improving braking performance—

The team cars and transporter for the 2007 season

there was ample "bite" but the front-to-rear balance was not satisfactory. And the electrical problems they had experienced with the cars was traced back to the alternator which was not providing the required power and was replaced by a much higher output unit.

In late June the team headed for the famous Monza circuit in northern Italy where three cars were entered. #49 continued with the Laffite/O'Neill pairing while Margueritte Laffite (Jacques' daughter) joined Georges-Alexandre Sturdza in car #50 and the third car, #51, was driven by Johan-Boris Scheier and Jean-Francois Le Roch. None of the cars were competitive and the results were disappointing for all concerned, #49 and #50 finishing in 24th and 25th places two laps in arrears of the winner respectively in race 1 (#51 DNF'd) and in the second race only #50 finished in 24th place four laps down. According to O'Neill Monza with its long straight and the need for power did not suit the Aero 8 at all.

Aero 8 GT3 competing in the 2007 season

The next meeting in the Championship was in September in Brno, Czech Republic on the famous Masarych Ring circuit on the outskirts of the city. Again three cars were entered and all had very similar settings. Scheier and La Roch qualified the fastest of the three Morgans in 11th place, a mere 0.3 seconds slower than the car on pole! A lack of track knowledge and to some degree the car's preparation counted against them. The race start was marred by an accident which eliminated the Scheier/La Roch car while Margot Laffite/Sturdza in car #50 finished in 25th place and Laffite/O'Neill in 27th place. A lack of power and issues with the Aero 8's aerodynamics still needed to be sorted. Race 2 was almost a carbon copy of Monza with only #50 finishing, #49 DNF'd and #51 did not start. One of the problems identified by O'Neill and Jabouille at this point was the comparative lack of race driving of the Morgan team members—almost all the other GT3 drivers also raced in other championships which assisted their efforts in GT3.

The last race meeting for the season was held in Dubai, in the United Arab Emirates but the AutoGT team opted not to compete. The race organisers had demanded that the cars be sent a month before the race which was unacceptable to the team management. Sturdza, Jabouille and Laffite, therefore, decided to invest the budget in further developing the cars in preparation for the 2008 season. A meeting between the three team principals and Charles Morgan made the decision to base the 2008 cars on the existing chassis of which three were delivered by Morgan early in October.

At this time there was some re-arranging of roles within the AutoGT team. Sturdza remained as the owner and financier of the team, Jean-Pierre Jabouille was made the general director and team manager, Frederic O'Neill became the administrative director, Lionel De Oliviera was the chassis and engine manager, Frédéric Ducastel the electronics manager, Philippe Guyoy the track manager, and the mechanics were Oliver Potiron, Emmanuel Landreau, Christian Weisse, Nicolas Magnin, Jean-Luc Grasser and William Lormeteall.

Over the winter of 2007/2008 every aspect of the car's performance was examined, assemblies were redesigned to lower the centre of gravity or reduce weight and to provide a better front-to-rear balance in the car. The wheels were changed to sets made from titanium which were lighter, the spring/damper settings were altered to improve roadholding and the engine's performance was reviewed. At this point in time the decision was made to change from Mäder to a French company, PIPO Motors, who had many years experience in Formula One (in the 70s) and at that time were preparing engines for the successful Ford rally cars. The result of PIPO's work was an increase in power to 490bhp and torque to 560Nm—the first engine is in the Morgan Aero 8 GT3 that belongs to the Sturdza Collection.

The overall effect of this program was a car weighing less—down to 1050kgs—with considerably more power and torque.

Testing of the cars took place at the Adria circuit in northern Italy where it was found that the top speed had risen to 250km/h, acceleration was improved because of the higher torque output and the engine was more easily managed at lower revs.

This is the Laffite/Sturdza GT3 at Silverstone, 2008

With new developments incorporated into the Morgan Aero 8s the team began the 2008 FIA European GT3 Championship season with renewed confidence. Three cars were entered at Silverstone—#29 for Johan-Boris Scheier and Gael Lesoudier (La Roch had been replaced following a number of crashes and other errors of driving judgement), #30 for Jacques Laffite and Frédéric O'Neill, and #31 for Margueritte Laffite and Georges-Alexandre Sturdza. Scheier/Lesoudier would drive the lead car while the other four drivers would drive the "laboratory" cars.

As in the previous year and despite the improvements the Aero 8's were proving to be off the pace and also unreliable. Weather conditions were dreadful for racing because it teemed with rain all weekend. In practice Scheier had qualified in 20th place just 1.2 seconds behind the pole sitting car but in free practice he spun at Copse at 170km/h and hit the bank destroying the car, fortunately not injuring him too badly. In the same free practice session O'Neill had the rear suspension collapse while going through Stowe corner at 180km/h which caused the car to spin uncontrollably, again fortunately without suffering too much damage.

Only one car finished the first race, in 26th place—it was a race that the team would rather forget! Things improved dramatically for race two where Scheier qualified in 4th place (1.8 seconds in arrears of the pole car), Jacques Laffite qualified 24th and Margot Laffite in 34th place on the grid. Scheier got away very quickly and for most of the race was in 3rd or 4th place and eventually finished 4th. Jacques Laffite, however, was not so fortunate because as he was accelerating away from the line he was shunted from behind and lost control, the car hitting the bank with considerable force and being totally wrecked. Laffite said afterwards that he would never ever race again in England!

At Monza three weeks later (mid-May) the same driver pairings achieved similar results in similar (wet) conditions. All three cars found themselves starting from pit lane because of a major blunder by the starting official but nevertheless they finished the first race, Scheier and Lesoudier finishing 5th despite the early handicap 31.6 seconds adrift of the winner while car #31 finished in 22nd position and #30 was 25th. Sadly the good work was not repeated in the second race with only #30 finishing way down in 26th place, the two other cars DNF'd.

From Monza the teams travelled north to Oschersleben, a relatively new circuit near Magdeburg in the east of Germany. It is a tight track with many corners and again the weather is against them—it rained all weekend!

This is the Scheier/Lesoudier GT3 at Silverstone, 2008

In qualifying for race 1 Lesoudier put his car in 14th place on the grid, O'Neill was in 24th place and Margot Laffite in 29th place. The weekend was to prove to be a disaster for the team with only the #29 (Scheier/Lesoudier) car finishing both races, in 14th place in race 1 and 31st in race 2, 11 laps in arrears. Interestingly, for this meeting car #30 was driven by a

Chapter Ten • Racing The Aero 8

new pairing, Frédéric O'Neill with Charles Morgan, but they DNF'd in race 1 with electrical problems and the Laffite/Sturdza car was involved in a race incident which put it out.

In September, the Masarych circuit near Brno was the scene for the next contests with the Morgan driver pairings remaining the same. Improvements had been made although the results still were disappointing to the team's principals. Car #29 finished 11th in race 1 51.08 seconds in arrears and 5th in race 2 at an average speed of 149.72km/h and 19.39 seconds behind the winner. Car #30 also finished but in 31st place in the first race and 21st place in the second.

Then in early October the scene was the Nogaro circuit in the Armagnac region in the south of France where Jacques Laffite replaced Charles Morgan in car #30 but it made little difference to the results. It was a circuit that was well-known to the team members, Jabouille and Laffite having won races there since the late 60s and Lesoudier and O'Neill since the mid-90s.

Sadly practice did not go as planned even though Scheier found himself in the top five qualifiers. Laffite crashed while exiting a corner too wide and too fast and wrote his car off—that was the end of racing for weekend for Laffite and O'Neill. The car Laffite hit was the Scheier/Lesoudier car! It had spun on the same corner and had briefly stopped facing the wrong way on the side of the track when Laffite suddenly appeared…. Car #29 was repaired using all the available parts but #30 could not be repaired.

Only the #29 car upheld the honour for Morgan with a 13th place finish in race 1 and a strong second in race 2 being 27.31 seconds behind the winner having averaged 135.25km/h for the race distance. Margot Laffite and Georges-Alexandre Sturdza in car #31 did not finish race 1—it was shunted at the start and suffered minor damage—and was in 22nd position in race 2 when the chequered flag fell.

In the final race for the season, held in Dubai, the AutoGT team entered two cars, #29 for Scheier and Lesoudier and #31 for new Belgian driver Maxime Martin teamed with Jacques Laffite. Both cars finished the race in 13th and 19th positions respectively. It was a better finish to the year than 2007 had been but clearly further improvements were needed. Martin was a driver whom O'Neill had seen racing in other classes and was highly impressed by his professional manner, his focus and importantly, his consistent speed. Jabouille was at first sceptical of the young Belgian but relented when he saw him race.

CHAPTER TEN • RACING THE AERO 8

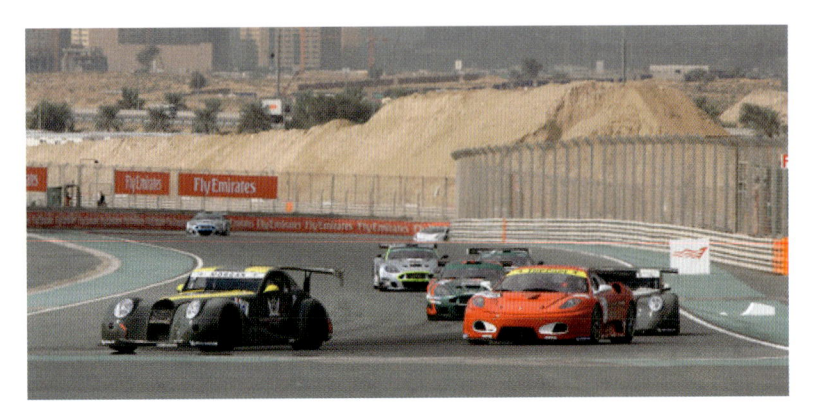

This is the Scheier/Lesoudier GT3 in the final race of the 2008 year at Dubai

Over the winter of 2008/2009 Jabouille and O'Neill planned and implemented a number of innovations for the new season's racing. Probably the most significant was the change from the Aero 8 roadster body to the more aerodynamic Aero SuperSport body that evolved out of the AeroMax. Its superior aerodynamics added a further 17km/h to the car's maximum speed which made it competitive with rival cars for outright speed, and the engineers at PIPO had extracted more power—now 550bhp—from the BMW engine. The team would not have known it at the time but that extra power from the engine would come at a price. The aerodynamic work was carried out in the Peugeot wind tunnel located 100 kilometres south of Paris and was arranged through Jabouille and his connections.

Also at this time Car #29 from the 2008 racing season was rebuilt and is now a part of the Eric Sturdza Collection.

The opening round of the 2009 FIA GT3 European Championship was held as usual at the Northants circuit of Silverstone. AutoGT Racing entered two new cars, #100—the race number was in celebration of Morgan's centenary—for Johan-Boris Scheier paired with a new driver Dimitri Enjalbert and car #101 to be driven by Maxime Martin and Gael Lesoudier. To the absolute joy of all team members Scheier and Enjalbert took the chequered flag having won race one at 157.56km/h and Martin/Lesoudier came home in 6th place! Their joy continued with race two the next day when Martin and Lesoudier won that at 158.56 km/h, the joy of the victory being tempered by the sister car expiring after only 16 laps. For some inexplicable reason when Enjalbert treid to restart the engine after taking over from Scheier at the compulsory pit stop it refused to start. Lesoudier, meanwhile, continued lapping with a 1.7 second lead over an Audi R8 but he held on to win.

As was written in a race report at the time, "In a perfect display of Anglo-French relations the Morgan Aero SuperSports of Maxime Martin and Gael Lesoudier scored a lights to flag victory in the 2009 FIA GT3 Championship at Silverstone. The British car, prepared and run by the French AutoGT Racing team, dominated the opening weekend of the championship."

From there the team travelled to Adria full of hope and expectation because at last the Morgans were competitive with their rivals from Audi, Aston Martin and Chevrolet. However, the Scheier/

Enjalbert car (#100) failed to finish the first race and was a non-starter for the second race which was a huge disappointment through engine reliability problems. Against that, the Martin/Lesoudier car (#101) had a reasonable weekend by finishing 18th nine laps in arrears in race one and came home a strong second just 0.979 seconds behind the winning car in race 2.

North to Oschersleben and again it was a weekend of mixed results. Car #100 did not start in the first race—engine problems again—while its sister car finished 15th 1:09.169 behind the winner. The second race the next day was a little better with Scheier and Enjalbert coming home in 8th place 40.56 seconds behind while the Martin/Lesoudier car suffered another engine malady. As O'Neill, who was now only involved in the team's administration and no longer as a driver, remembered, "The 2009 season was marred by engine problems with more than 5 being destroyed, and they were very expensive engines!"

The Algarve weekend in Portugal proved to be a complete disaster for the AutoGT Racing team. Both cars completed only 3 laps in both races for the weekend because of engine reliability issues and the team was reduced to the role of spectating, not what they were in the business for! Paul Ricard three weeks later was better but not by much. Scheier/Enjalbert finished 4th on the Saturday with Martin/Lesoudier coming home in 19th place but the second race the next day saw both cars fail, car #101 after only 8 laps and car #100 pulled out on the following lap.

This is the Scheier/Enjalbert GT3 taking the chequred flag at Silverstone, 2009

145

Chapter Ten • Racing The Aero 8

The last round of the championship was held at the Dutch seaside circuit of Zolder, once famous for its Formula One races back in the Fifties and Sixties. For this round car #100 was driven by a new pairing, Julien Briche and Johan-Boris Scheier while Martin and Lesoudier continued with car #101. While the results for the round were not outstanding at least both cars finished both races which was a big shot in the arm for the team and a good note on which to finish the season. Briche/Scheier came home 8th and 10th for their two races and Martin/Lesoudier came home 7th and 15th.

At the end of the season Eric Sturdza made the decision not to continue his financial support of the AutoGT Racing team. His decision was partly precipitated by the comparatively poor results achieved with the not insignificant investment on his part and a certain disaffection with the way the GT3 series was administered. Car #100 was added to his Morgan Collection.

Jean-Pierre Jabouille, however, wanted to continue racing the Morgan and he took Car #101 and raced on a very limited budget for part of the 2010 season having won at Dijon before calling it a day. The car was sold to an Austrian driver who raced it without success.

Car 101 driven by Martin/Lesoudier leading team mate Scheier/Enjalbert at the Adria circuit 2009

146

Chapter Ten • Racing The Aero 8

INITIAL SKETCHES.
THE CAR IS BASED ON A NARROWED AERO 8 CHASSIS TO REDUCE
FRONTAL AERIE FOR AERODYNAMIC REASONS.

Chapter Eleven

THE LIFECAR PROJECT

Ever since the acceptance of the motor car in the late 19th century people have been experimenting with the notion that a much cleaner and quieter system of propulsion could be developed. After all, the very early examples of the motor car were noisy, smoky and downright dangerous to all and sundry. But the engineers learned very quickly and by the 1920s the car was vastly more refined and offering people the possibilities of long distance travel in relative comfort and safety.

Running in parallel with developments of the internal combustion engine were efforts to prove that electric vehicles could be a viable alternative. However, battery technology, or lack of it, was the stumbling block as the cars required constant and expensive recharging after comparatively short distances. As a result of these shortcomings electric powered vehicles quietly faded from the motoring scene but not before some impressive speed records had been established.

The LIFECar project broke new ground for Morgan, the styling being obviously based on the Aero 8

Another fuel that has been actively investigated in more recent times is hydrogen. Perhaps the biggest issue with hydrogen powered cars is not their own emissions—it is pure, clean water vapour—but the CO_2 released when hydrogen is extracted from natural gas and whether hydrogen makes sense depends entirely on how efficiently the hydrogen is used. At 40 miles per kilogram it is bad news but at 144 miles per kilogram (LIFECar test figures) it is far better than anything currently available. The other major issue is the lack of commitment from Governments around the world,

CHAPTER ELEVEN • A LIFECAR PROJECT

Many manufacturers have entered the market with hybrid cars which have incredibly complex onboard systems. Is this the way?

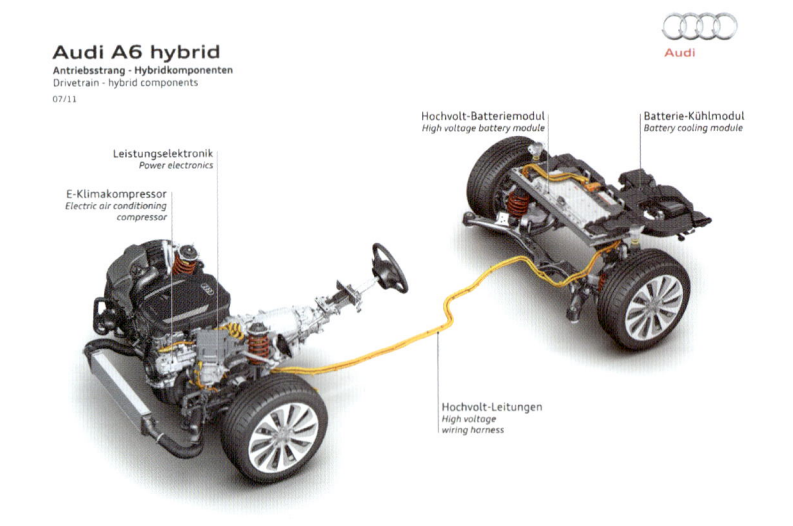

none of whom seem willing to embrace hydrogen as a fuel for motoring even though the resource itself is renewable and has no emissions.

Japanese rivals Toyota and Honda have gone down the hybrid path by combining a small capacity internal combustion—around 1.5-litres—with an electric motor that draws its power from nickel-hydride batteries that are kept on charge by the automatic cutting-in and cutting-out of the engine. Both companies boast of huge reductions in fuel consumption and emissions. Hybrid automobiles have proliferated in recent years with Toyota adding the Camry Hybrid to supplement the Prius while its luxury stablemate, Lexus, has introduced a range of vehicles—CT200h, HS250h, GS450h and LS600h—that are also hybrids. Their system comprises an internal combustion engine, high output electric motor with regenerative braking, a nickel-metal hydride (Ni-MH) battery and a powerful electronic Power Control Unit (PCU). It is a complex system that is heavy and undoubtedly expensive to manufacture with future (possibly unknown at the moment) costs to the owner when things inevitably wear or go wrong.

Ford now markets the Fusion as a hybrid and there is the Lincoln MKZ Hybrid on sale while Mercedes-Benz markets its E320 Bluetec and S400 BlueHybrid saloons, BMW has its ActiveHybrid 3 and 5 Series which have drawn rave reviews from the world's media, and Porsche now has its Panamera S hybrid in production.

Besides these cars there are several other manufacturers actively promoting battery electric cars with many having been displayed at motor shows in the last four years. For example, BMW has planned to release the i3 pure electric car in 2013, rival Daimler is readying electric cars based on their A-Class platform and the tiny smart cars badged BlueZero, Nissan has released the Leaf as a pure electric car along with Mitsubishi and the iMiEV and we should not forget the Chevrolet Volt and Tesla models that are gaining huge reviews internationally.

One of the dreams of sports car enthusiasts in these globally pollution conscious times has been the 100-mph zero-emission car. It has taken one of the minnows of the automobile industry to come up with a realistic response to the issues in the form of the Morgan LIFECar—Lightweight Integrated Fuel Efficient Car. Based loosely on the Morgan AeroMax coupe, it replaces the BMW V8 engine and associated gearbox with an advanced fuel cell system that is hydrogen powered and releases only water vapour into the atmosphere.

The LIFECar project is one of the most innovative ideas to spring from the British motor industry, or what is now left of it. As Charles was quoted saying in *The Sunday Times* way back in April 2007, "The LIFECar's purpose is to demonstrate that a zero-emissions vehicle can also be fun to drive."

In simple terms the LIFECar is an electric sports car powered by a hydrogen fuel cell. The basis of the car is the relatively new and very innovative Morgan Aero 8; Morgan collaborated with defence contractor QinetiQ, the University of Oxford, Cranfield University and BOC a supplier of industrial hydrogen, Oscar Automotive later renamed Riversimple, and the British Government through the Technology Strategy Board. Around £1.9 million Pounds was invested over a three year period from May 2005 until July 2008 to make the LIFECar a reality

The Riversimple Mark I Local Car designed for city commuting

The idea for such a collaboration came from a conversation between Hugo Spowers, head of Riversimple, and Charles Morgan (the two men have been friends for many years) to investigate new concepts in environmentally superior transport solutions. Announced shortly after the LIFECar was the Hyrban project that led to the Riversimple Mark I Local Car that was designed at Riversimple with finance coming from the powerful and influential Piëch family. Weighing just 380kgs,

151

the Riversimple Mk I is similar in many respects to the Smart car apart from its power unit which is a tiny 6kW fuel cell that allows better performance than the Smart up to 50mph, also the maximum speed and a range of 200 plus miles. Like the Morgan it has ultra-capacitors that provide most of the power for acceleration and four electric motors that double as brakes and electricity generators; unlike the LIFECar it also has a lightweight composite body. The shires of Herefordshire and Shropshire as well as the city of Leicester have agreed with Riversimple to carry out an extended test program using 30 Local cars each.

Hydrogen was the fuel of most interest because the only emission from its combustion is pure water vapour and an efficient hydrogen car is more efficient than any other powertrain for a car with a reasonable range. It can also be generated from any energy source so that investment in hydrogen vehicle technology and infrastructure is a long term investment allowing a seamless transition from fossil fuels to renewable fuels at any rate we like. BOC was brought into the project because of its experience in producing the gas and distributing it while QinteQ came on board because of their fuel cell expertise, their cell working at 45 per cent efficiency.

This is the driving end of the Morgan LIFECar

Basically, the LIFECar propulsion system works by converting the hydrogen to electricity using a 4-stack PEM—Proton Exchange Membrane—fuel cell which produces heat and water as by-products. The electricity is directed to four electric motors/generators each connected directly to a wheel and each has in-built regenerative capabilities that captures kinetic energy for when acceleration is required. Not only do the fuel cells work at a far higher efficiency than an internal combustion engine but the driving motors operate at an average of 92-94 per cent across their range. Regenerative braking is not new, but the system employed by Morgan raises the bar considerably by recovering more than 50 per cent of the vehicle's kinetic energy to be re-used where conventional systems operate at around 10 per cent. Furthermore, this powertrain layout lends itself to dynamic control far better than any mechanical drivetrain; with 4-wheel drive it is only a matter of software upgrades to install ABS, traction control, yaw control or variable slip differential profiles.

Like the Aero 8 and AeroMax, the LIFECar has an aluminium body.

In other applications the energy from regeneration would have been stored in batteries that as is well known are heavy in weight and contained heavy metals. They were also limited in their ability to store electricity. As Dr P D van der Koogh from Delft University noted, "Battery electric vehicles are vehicles built mainly for carrying batteries, not very far and not very fast—otherwise they would need to carry more batteries."

This is the LIFECar chassis with a clear view of the hydrogen fuel tank

For the LIFECar a more sophisticated approach was deemed necessary to fit with the overall philosophy of the project, in this case a bank of ultra-capacitors that have the ability to shuffle up to 1000 amps back and forth at a round trip efficiency of over 95 per cent maximising energy storage during braking and being able to deliver the power instantly when required for acceleration.

Cranfield University had developed expertise in electronic management systems beginning in the days of the "wedge" Lagonda V8 in the mid-1970s when Aston Martin came to them for assistance with that car's electronic dashboard. For the LIFECar Cranfield has developed electronic control systems for the ultra-capacitors, hydrogen supply, the fuel cell and the driving motors that allows them to be either driving or braking the car. Included in this latter development is the ability for the braking system to seamlessly switch from electronic to conventional hydraulic operation without the driver ever knowing.

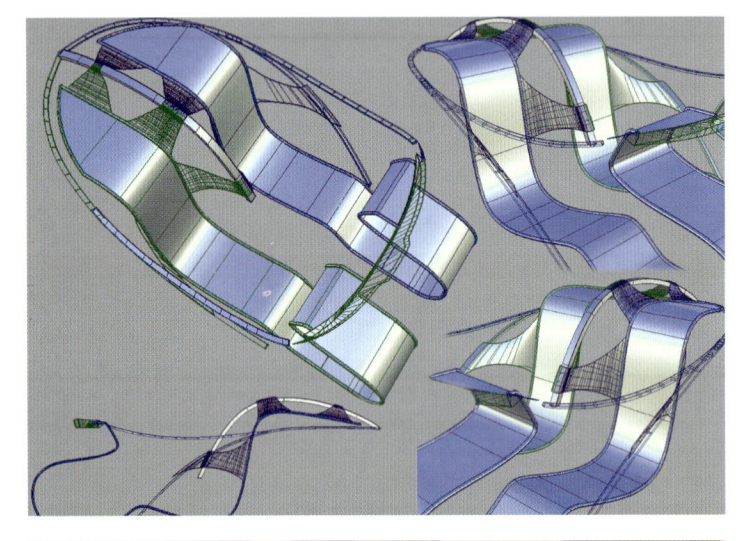

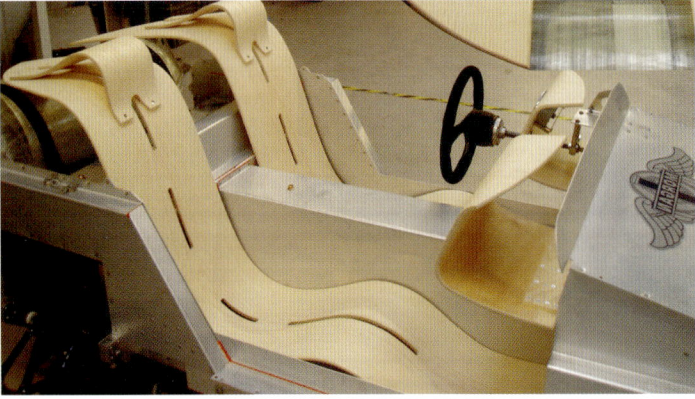

Having set a number of objectives which included learning how to integrate the advanced hybrid fuel cell components by going beyond the adaptation of traditional designs and develop an innovative architecture around a fuel cell hybrid drivetrain, to demonstrate a fuel economy for a 300 mile range at between 200-and-300 per cent superior to conventional cars and with well to wheel CO_2 emissions well below 60g/km, even if using hydrogen from natural gas. Other aims were to use a 20kW fuel cell system together with a novel control strategy, six phase motors as well as the development of a 700 bar hydrogen tank. Uppermost in the designer's minds was to ensure that the LIFECar would be exciting to drive, just like any other Morgan.

The basis of the LIFECar was the aluminium chassis manufactured for the Aero 8 but with modifications made to suit the needs of the new vehicle. Beginning in May 2005 Mark Reeves and his small team started out on a new adventure that would lead them from the Aero 8 to the LIFECar. The tub of the Aero 8 weighs only 80kgs but even that was considered to be too heavy and so it was re-made using thinner aluminium material, reduced in thickness from 2.5mm to 2.0mm and in some places it was as thin as 1.5mm. In addition the chassis was cut behind where the rear sub-frame bolted up without apparently compromising rigidity; these modifications reduced the chassis weight to just 50kgs.

Part of the cleverness of the LIFECar is the interior where occupants sit on wooden seats shaped to the body

In the space now available (behind the rear suspension) the circular hydrogen tank was secured in place and the 400V bank of ultra capacitors was housed in a revised transmission tunnel. A simpler, and lighter, independent suspension system was designed by Oscar Automotive—actually Andy Thorby, a well-known racing car designer who subsequently joined the Wirth F1 Team and was chief designer of the McLaren MP4-12C GT3 car—where the front consisted of upper and lower wishbones mounted to a box sub-frame bolted to the front longeron, the suspension medium being coil springs-over-dampers. At the rear a sub-frame system was retained although considerably modified. Half frames were designed by Thorby that remotely held the electric motor-and-gearbox, suspension upright, wishbone and coil springs-over-dampers as a unit, one each side. Short drive shafts connected the gearbox to the wheel hubs. Each sub-frame—front and rear—was held in place by four bolts which facilitated easy removal for servicing and repair.

Front suspension of the LIFECar, quiet different from the Aero 8

The electric motors were mounted in metalastic bushes in the sub-frame, two on one side and one on the other to minimise torque reaction. The actual motor housing was shaped like the head of a tennis racquet. Conceived by Oxford University, the mechanical design was done by Oscar, again principally by Andy Thorby, and incorporated a 3:1 reduction drive engineered by Hewland.

QinetiQ manufactured the fuel cells in four stacks which were reasonably heavy and so were mounted in the centre of the chassis across the front bulkhead which necessitated modifying the front longerons slightly. Once they had been placed the team then had to route the necessary pipe work for the hydrogen, air and water. A complete rolling chassis was weighed and it came in at 270kgs—remarkable.

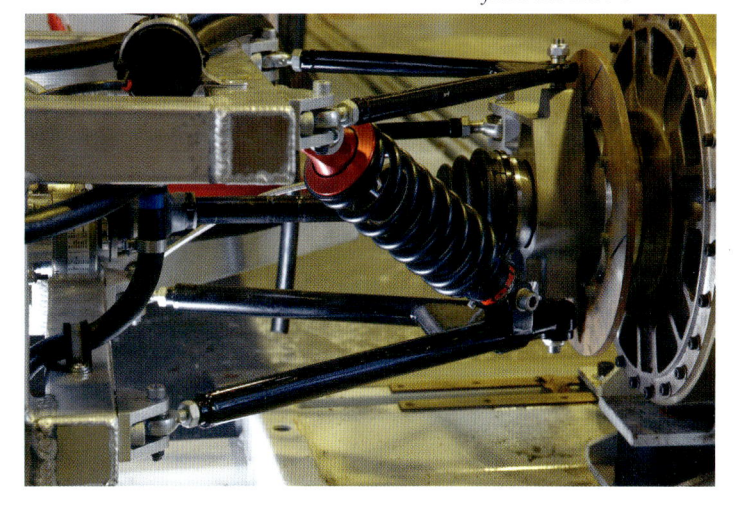

Meanwhile, Matthew Humphries had been busy developing the body's styling that would have a clear link to the Aero 8 but at the same time be able to dramatically show this new technology. With the chassis in the company's sophisticated computer system he was able to refine his sketches and create a clay scale model where the exterior surface would be refined in preparation for digitising, the data being then imported to a program called ALIAS which enabled an egg box structure to be made in 1:1 scale from which the aluminium panels were made.

For the interior Humphries conceived the rather unusual sprung ash wooden seats together with wooden-framed doors and the polished ash wood dashboard. With the aim of reducing the car's weight to 700kgs it was decided to not fit such luxuries as air conditioning, audio system, air bags or central locking.

While a rolling chassis was displayed at the Grove Fuel Cell Show at the Queen Elizabeth II Conference Centre in Parliament Square, London, in September 2007, the real aim was to have a completed LIFECar ready for display at the Geneva Motor Show in March 2008. It was unveiled by Charles Morgan in front of the world's media who were amazed by what they saw—it was certainly one of the stars of the show. Morgan claimed a working range of 250 miles from the tank of hydrogen and suggested a time of 7 seconds for the classic 0-60mph sprint with a cruising speed of 80mph.

Morgan was invited to attend the Villa d'Este show on the shores of the beautiful Lake Como the following month where it was entered in the concept class.

Upon its return to England development continued with the rolling chassis going to Cranfield where dynamometer testing of the drive system commenced.

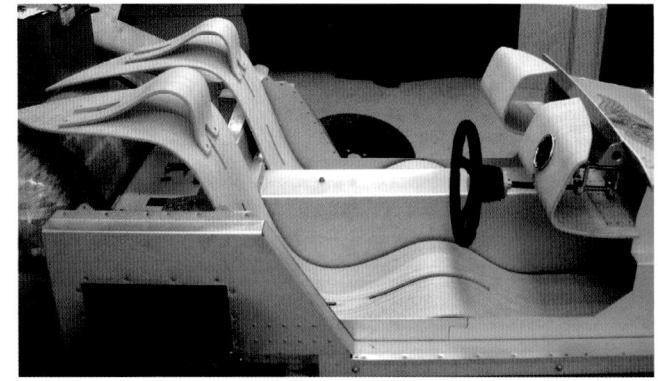

Two technical highlights need mentioning where LIFECar is concerned; the first is the Yokeless And Segmented Armature (YASA) electric motors developed at Oxford University by a team led by Malcolm McCulloch and a PhD student Tim Woolmer which have achieved an unparalleled torque density for a traction motor; and secondly the fuel cell system itself which was initially designed to run at 400-500mbar over ambient pressure but which in their final development achieved the required performance at only 125mbar which significantly reduced losses and increased efficiency.

As the Morgan Motor Company said in a statement to the media, "As a research project, LIFECar set exciting and ambitious goals from the very beginning. Not only were the specific performance targets challenging in the extreme, but achieving these objectives was premised on integrating a wide range of disciplines. The data acquired from the rolling road at Cranfield has been integrated with data from the fuel cell test facility at Qinetiq. The fuel cell system was a major development exercise in its own right and it has now achieved the specified output; unfortunately, this work was completed after the project finished, so it has not yet been run in the vehicle. Nonetheless, the heart of the project is in systems integration; this system has been modelled, built, tested and validated and the data demonstrates the power of the architecture and control system and the potential gains it can yield."

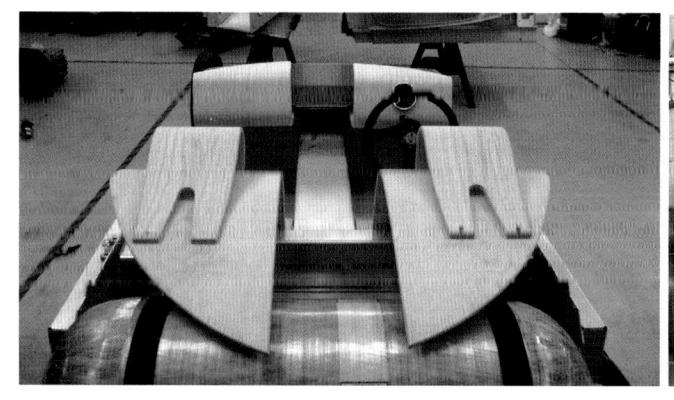

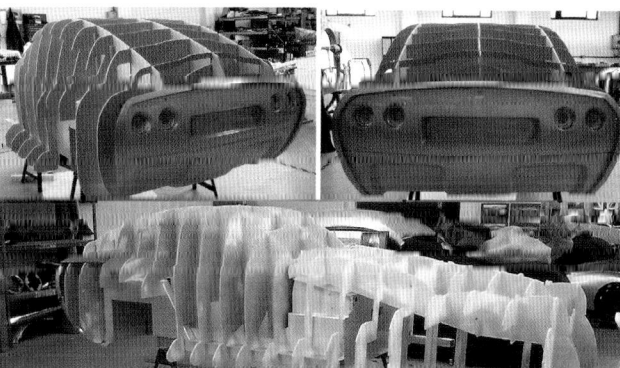

Power comes from a bank of lightweight hydrogen fuel cells that were developed by the UK defence company Qinetiq. The fuel cells produce about 22 kilowatts—roughly twenty per cent of the power of a typical combustion engine—and with that can provide all the cruising capability that is required. When power to accelerate or climb a hill is needed it is drawn from a bank of ultra-capacitors that are aligned down the central spine of the car. These units are like batteries but they do not store quite as much energy, they permit it to flow in and out far quicker than a battery can and are charged primarily by the regenerative braking system. As Mark Reeves from Morgan said, "Most hybrid cars use regenerative braking already but it only restores about 10 per cent of the energy but the new system in the LIFECar can reach up to 50 per cent."

The big issue with any sports car, and the Aero 8 is no exception, is weight—design engineer Chris Lawrence aimed at a maximum of 1000kg and achieved it through the use of an aluminium intensive chassis and running gear. The LIFECar takes that one step further with a lightweight wooden interior and by removing such luxury items as the complex audio system, air conditioning, central locking and airbags and has been able to keep the weight down to around 750kgs.

As far as Hugo Spowers is aware the technology embodied in the Morgan LIFECar and the Riversimple Mk I is unique; the concepts were first proposed by the Rocky Mountains Institute in the Hypercar project but they have yet to be implemented in any other car that they know about. Both cars are light in weight—"Weight is the curse of automobile engineering," according to Spowers who continued saying, "Engineers want more power which requires a larger (and heavier) engine which requires a heavier transmission which requires a heavier body structure. It is a problem which compounds itself and the industry seems incapable of breaking that cycle. It is very hard to make significant weight reductions by increments in all areas of the car's construction whereras we have achieved reduced weight by reconsidering the whole system, as it is inherent in this new architecture without any significant compromises in convenience or performance."

CHAPTER ELEVEN • A LIFECAR PROJECT

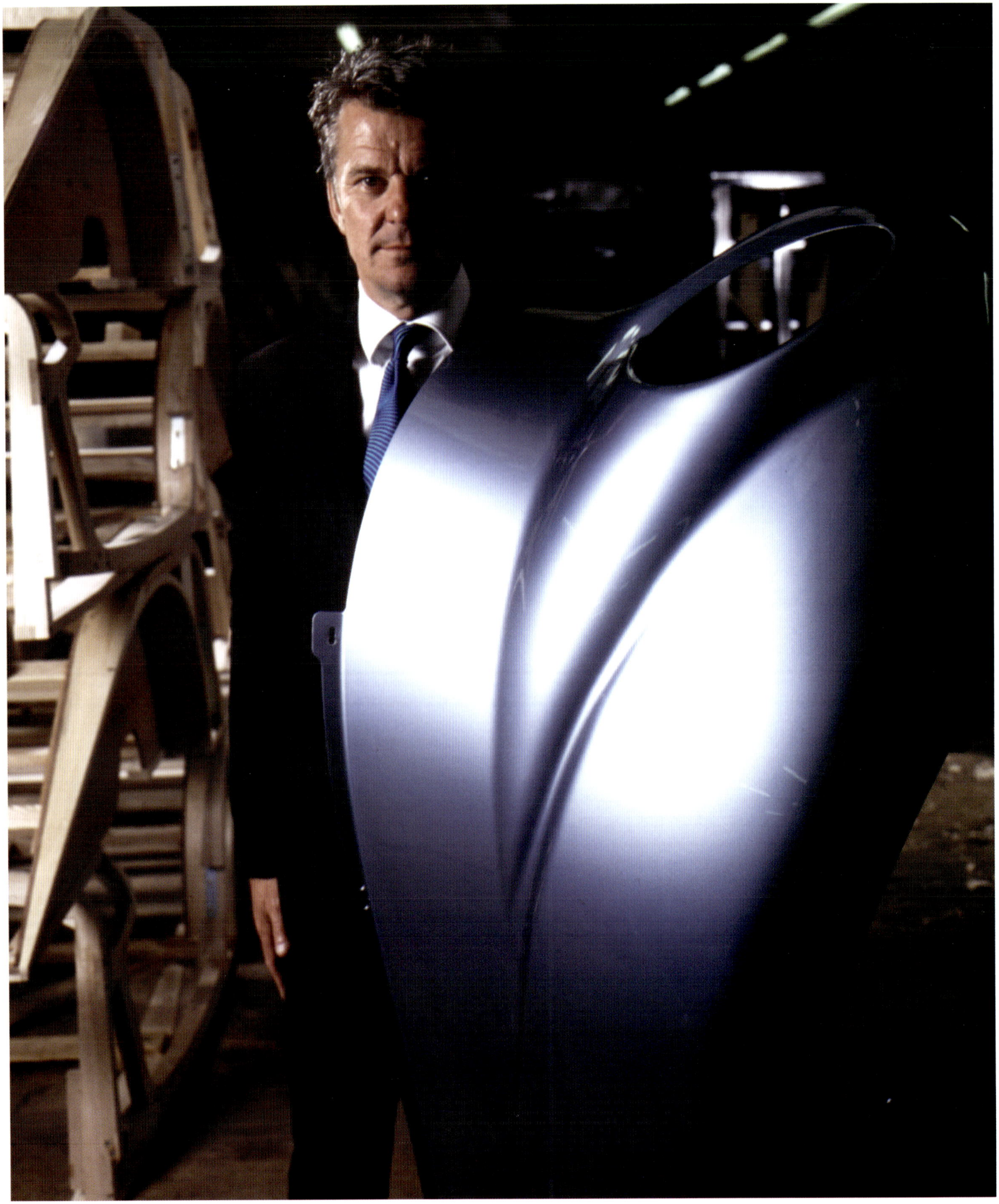

Chapter Twelve

CHARLES MORGAN: VISIONARY INHERITOR

Charles Morgan has had an amazing career that has been full of highlights. Born Charles Peter Henry Morgan on July 29, 1951, he was the only son of Peter and Jane Morgan (nee Christie) who had three other children, all girls. From an early age he showed distinctly artistic leanings in his interests and seemed not to be all that interested in things mechanical.

He enjoyed a well rounded education that included The Elms School in Colwall, Malvern where the family lived followed by six enjoyable years (1963-68) at Oundle School in Oundle, Northants before going to the Sussex University from 1969 through 1971 where he graduated with a Bachelor of Arts degree with Honours in the History and Theory of Art. "I enjoyed my years at Oundle because it was a practical education and very hands-on," said Charles

After his studies he worked for two years as the assistant to the managing director of Ideas Books Limited, a company that specialised in publishing art books. In 1973 Charles attended the London University where he gained a Diploma in Film Studies, these studies taking place while he was employed by Independent Television News Limited of Wells Street, London, where he was an assistant in the news film library. It was a seemingly inauspicious beginning to a brilliant career within the industry. From 1974 until 1982 he worked for ITN Newsfilm as a cameraman and then from 1982 to 1985 for Television News Team Limited making documentaries and news programs. During this period he was co-founder of a TV production and facilities company.

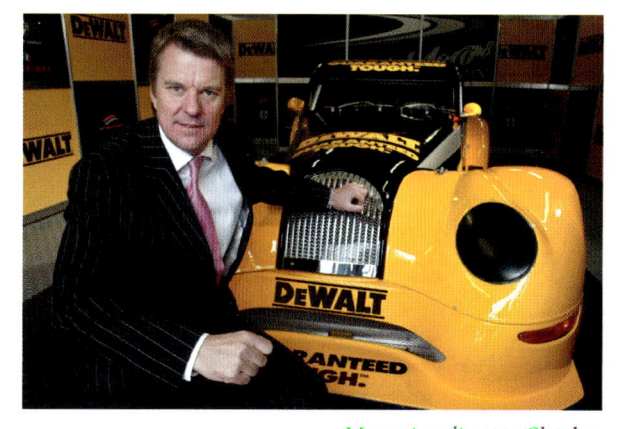

Managing director Charles Morgan posing with the DeWalt racing car

161

Charles travelled the world as a cameraman for ITN covering such sensitive international events as the departure of the Shah from Iran and the takeover of government in Teheran by the Ayatollah Khomenei that led to a period of isolation of the country while it underwent many social and political changes; the aborted rescue attempt by US forces of hostages who were being held in Iran, the conflict in Beirut in 1976 and the Israeli invasion of southern Lebanon two years later. In addition he covered the transfer of political power and the first free elections in Zimbabwe (formerly Rhodesia) with Ian Smith ceding power to Robert Mugabe and, for a change of scenery, the collision between the Icelandic gunboat *Baldur* and HMS *Diomedes*, a Royal Navy frigate, in the sea off Iceland during the "Cod War." For this he was awarded the Silver Nymph at the Cannes Film Festival, an award of which he is extremely proud.

At Television News Team Limited he directed and filmed with Sandy Gall the first documentary from a crew that had gone behind the Russian lines in Afghanistan in 1982. It depicted the bloody conflict between Ahmed Shah Massud and his mujahedeen against the well-equipped (but dis-spirited) Russian army in the Panjshir Valley.

In between all this dashing around the world with a camera, Charles found time to marry, sire four children (Xan, Harriet, Kate and Maximus) and race Morgan sports cars. He won the British Racing and Sports Car Club and British Racing Drivers Club production sports car championships in 1978 and 1979 driving a Morgan Plus Eight. In 1997 and 1998 he drove a works Plus Eight GTR in the FIA International GT series

In 1985 he left the glamour and fame of the television news world and began working for the family firm in Malvern Link where he was appointed Production Manager. In addition to these responsibilities Charles undertook a three-year part time MBA course in Manufacturing Management at the Coventry University beginning in 1994 with further studies resulting in honorary doctorates in Business Administration from the Coventry University (2003), honorary degree of Master of Arts from the University of Worcester (2008), an honorary doctorate from Loughborough University (2009), and in 2010 he was appointed a

During the 80's and 90's Charles enjoyed racing his own product, often with success

Deputy Lieutenant of Worcester, awarded an honorary Doctor of Business by the Southampton Solent University and an honorary degree from the City of Birmingham.

Charles assumed the position of Managing Director of the Morgan Motor Company in 1999 at the time when his father was in poor health and had retired even though he visited the factory several times a week. In 2005 he was appointed Chief Executive Director of the company and in 2007 added AeroRacing Limited to his directorships.

Improving product quality had been uppermost in Charles's mind during his years in charge, having personally initiated many quality improvements to the range of cars and services offered by the company. That is an on-going process as is continual training of the staff. The introduction of new technology, notably in the Aero 8, has been an integral part of the development of the company, Charles having been the team leader during the design and development of the Aero 8. However, as he stressed to the author, "My father was a key man in the P8000 project and shared my view that it was important to the future of the company." He continued by saying, "We both knew our long term future did not include the Rover V8 nor the galvanised chassis as it was getting more and more difficult to get it through Type Approval. We had to come up with a product that would give the company some length, otherwise we would be legislated out of business and neither of us wanted that!"

With respect to BMW, Charles was full of praise for the company and the people with whom he has dealt. As he said, "BMW has been a great partner for us and has given us access to everything including Miramas. MIRA is on our doorstep but they are difficult to deal with and, in any case, Miramas is vastly superior as a test facility and we had the use of it all. Marvellous!" He further commented, "BMW was good for the Morgan Motor Company insofar as when they said they would do something it was done—they charged a lot of money but it was done and it was done extremely well. They provided a German rigour to our development program which was really good for us. Interestingly, they benchmarked our P8000 against their Z8."

Continuing his comments, he added, "The Aero 8 program was a team effort and for me driving it forward was sometimes a challenge but one that I enjoyed. The car is still 20 per cent lighter than any comparable sports car on the market even though it's been out there for several years. It was the first aluminium intensive vehicle in Europe and I still think it is ahead of its time!"

Away from the demands of the Morgan Motor Company, Charles is a member of the Worshipful Company of Coachmakers and Coach Harness makers, the British Racing Drivers Club, the Royal Society of Arts, the Academy Club, the St Moritz Tobogganing Club and he is President of the Morgan Sports Car Club. His interests in life include skiing, studying art and architecture as well as casual painting and sketching.

In preparing the Morgan Motor Company for the future, Charles has focused on a number of challenges that involve using the company's superb human resources to facilitate new model design and development; introducing and utilising new technologies for the benefit of the company; and to broaden the appeal of Morgan sports cars across a wider spectrum of the international market. This means establishing Morgan in such diverse markets as China and the Middle East as well as ensuring that North America once again becomes a major marketplace for the company.

As well as these initiatives Charles has actively fostered collaborations between the Morgan Motor Company and many universities and other centres of technical excellence where ideas can be created and shared to the mutual benefit of all involved.

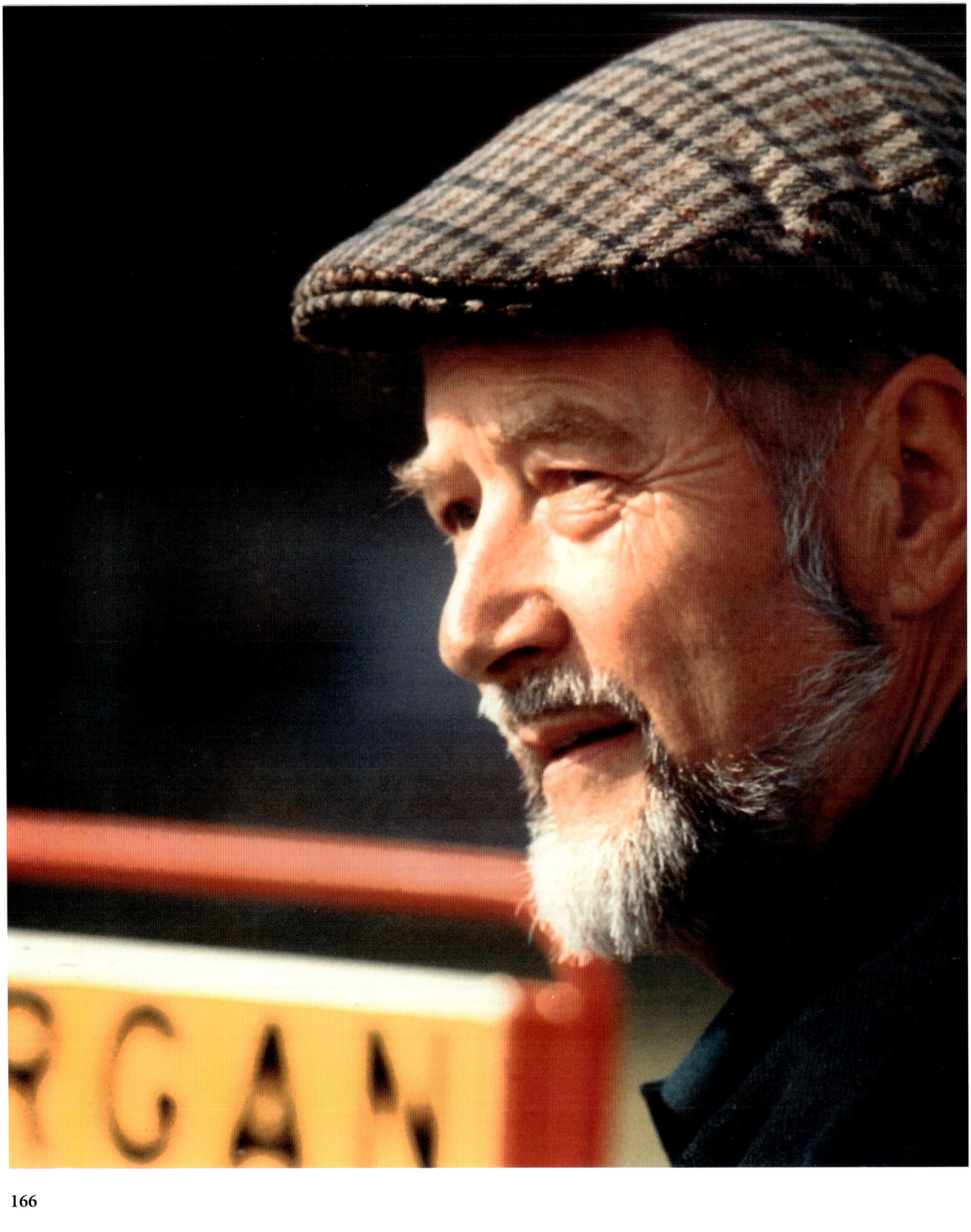

Chapter Thirteen

CHRIS LAWRENCE: LIFETIME MAVERICK

The man with the vision of what a future Morgan ought to be, and the man who made it happen, was Christopher Lawrence working in collaboration with the company's managing director Charles Morgan. All of Lawrence's considerable engineering experience and expertise came to bear when he sat down and thought about the specification that would eventually become the Morgan Aero 8.

Lawrence and Morgan (the company as well as the people) have been associated for the better part of the past half century but that is getting a little ahead of the story. Chris Lawrence had been something of a maverick thinker and doer for his entire engineering career. Sure he had made some mistakes and some of his good ideas did not work out as well commercially as he had hoped but as they say in the classics, "Nothing ventured, nothing gained." As one former associate said of him, "A fence sitter he definitely was not!"

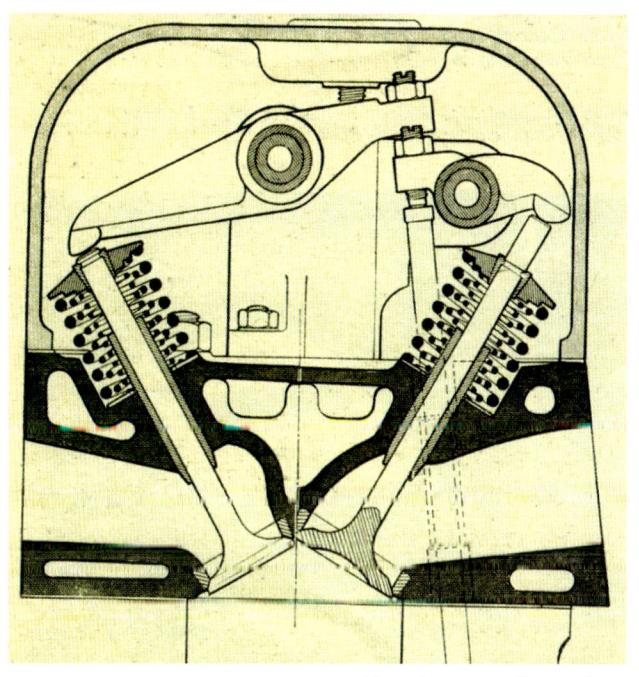

He has been a tuner of engines, a constructor of racing cars, designer and constructor of road cars, racing driver and race team manager all with varying degrees of success. Some critics, most of whom have achieved little in their own lives apart from being critical of others who tried, regard Lawrence as something of a villain while others regard him as a hero.

Chris Lawrence designed a cross flow cylinder head for the Triumph sports cars as well as the Morgan

The clone-like world of automobiles today desperately needs people of Lawrence's ilk, people who are prepared to have an opinion and stand by it, not be persuaded that their opinion is wrong when all it is, is not what the rest of the world thinks. Throughout his long and illustrious career Lawrence has held true to his convictions regardless of the outcome. That takes balls.

Christopher John Lawrence was born in 1933 in Acton, East London, the only child of William John Lawrence and Joan Winifred Sanderson. His father was a chartered accountant and had his own practice; for recreation he raced motorcycles, a hobby that Chris believes he inherited from his grandfather who owned many motorcycles over the years. The genes were passed on for the first motor sport activities undertaken by a young Chris Lawrence also involved motorcycles. His father had purchased an AJS 350 after the war that was offered to him by Associated Motor Cycles, manufacturers of AJS, Matchless and Villiers motorcycles—he knew the company's famous sales executive Jock West—as well as Herbert Le Vak's Pendine Sands record breaker. His father was one of the five original people who met and formed the Vintage Motor Cycle Club back in 1945.

In 1951 his mother bought him a Morgan three-wheeler. As Chris remembered, "It had an 1100cc JAP engine and was very fast. It had no brakes to speak of and no lights but that just made it more exciting!" The Morgan proved to be the perfect vehicle for a young man who wanted to go racing even if the family disapproved.

Lawrence entered the Royal Navy Engineering College, HMS Thunderer, Crown Hill, Manadon, in Plymouth where he began studying for his naval engineering degree. Interestingly, he went there because of his mother's wishes—"She had a brother, Tony Sanderson, who became the youngest commander there had ever been in the Royal Navy and she was adamant that I should follow in his footsteps," commented Lawrence; for his part, he wanted to fly but she felt the Navy was safer.

Motorcycles were not entirely out of the system either with Lawrence buying a Norton ES2 (the last one made) that he raced with mixed fortunes. In one race he fell off damaging the bike and injuring himself and, in Lawrence's words, "This two-wheel lark was a bit dangerous, I thought I would stick with four wheels from then on!"

During his time at the College, he owned and raced the Hillwood MG that had been designed by Norman Hillwood (a jeweller by profession) based on the 750cc MG NE/K3 that was one of the ex-factory "Three Musketeers" trials team cars. This car was built up out of two of the team cars: "Athos" that had been heavily damaged in a head-on collision with a bus and "Porthos" that had not been completed. The car was registered JB6866 and carried the name "Porthos." While still at College he bought a Bugatti T38 that he and some colleagues rebuilt and in which he won the Torbay/Torquay hillclimb that was run by the Plymouth Car Club. This was followed by a rare BMW 328-powered AFM, an early post-war racing car designed around the engine and transmission of the legendary BMW 328 roadster by the equally legendary engine designer Alex von Falkenhausen. The trouble was the 1.5-litre engine proved to be a little fragile and as Lawrence said, "I did not have the money to be constantly rebuilding the engine so I sold it on. It was, however, a beautiful car to drive because it handled brilliantly." Apparently the AFM has survived and is reportedly in England in private ownership.

Upon graduation from the Navy, Lawrence found himself on NATO exercises north of the Arctic Circle. For a man who really wanted to go racing this was definitely not the direction he saw his career path taking. However, he never really made a name for himself until 1959 after he had concentrated his efforts on Morgans. "I learned a few tricks about tuning the Triumph four-cylinder engine that they used and I guess I got lucky," he commented in his self-deprecating style. Lucky indeed. In 1959 he won the Freddie Dixon Trophy for his performances at Goodwood and other circuits and he enjoyed a class win in the GT race at Silverstone International Trophy.

He formed Lawrencetune Engines Ltd in September 1959 in partnership with Leslie Fagg, John Harvey and Len Bridge with the intention of earning enough money to enjoy life, to continue racing Morgans and tune TR engines. Other projects soon followed; three Formula Junior racing cars in 1960 followed a year later by the first Deep Sanderson. Initially this was not a success on the track but gradually Lawrence refined and improved it to the point where in 1963 and 1964 he competed at Le Mans with the Mini-based Deep Sanderson 301. Various versions of the design were produced with Mini power packs and, later, there was a version (the 302) with the Ford Cortina 1600GT engine and Hewland FT200 gearbox mounted longitudinally. At least one car had the Martin V8 engine

CHAPTER THIRTEEN • CHRIS LAWRENCE: LIFETIME MAVERICK

installed, this engine being a compact, light weight 3-litre SOHC per bank V8 designed by well-known designer/engineer Ted Martin who was an associate of Lawrence. This car was built for Le Mans 1969 but the team was denied an entry despite Lawrence's race record.

The derivation of the Deep Sanderson name showed a softer side to Lawrence's personality. His father had been in a jazz band during the 20s and one of their best songs was called Deep Henderson. As Lawrence related, "I loved that song, it was one of the best pieces of music I have ever heard and over the years I vowed that I would name something I did after it. My mother's maiden name was Sanderson and as she'd helped me enormously financially when I started building cars it seemed natural to join the two names. And that was how the name Deep Sanderson came about."

Around 30 of the Mini-powered model 301 were made in collaboration with John Pearce who had earlier worked at Coopers in Surbiton and was familiar with the Cooper Formula One cars that

Chris with his final creation, the Morgan Aero 8 at Goodwood 2005

were raced by Jack Brabham and Bruce McLaren. Lawrence and Pearce teamed up to build a 3-litre Formula One car when the formula changed from 1.5- to 3-litres in 1966.

"We bought the ex-Bruce McLaren Cooper T73 that had won at Monaco in 1964 and the 3-litre V12 engine out of the famous Ferrari 250 'Breadvan' that had been demolished at Paddock Bend, Brands Hatch, by Chris Kerrison and we put them together. It wasn't the fastest car on the grid but I did finish fifth in the Oulton Park Gold Cup and for a while was competitive in the German GP on the Nürburgring. It was fun while it lasted!" commented Lawrence.

Lawrence continued racing with his famous Morgan Plus 4 (registered TOK 258) with some success and international recognition. In 1962 he finished 13th overall and won his class at Le Mans while at the demanding Spa-Francorchamps race he finished 4th, took 8th and second-in-class at the Tourist Trophy race and was 27th overall in the Nürburgring 1000 kms that year.

Further recognition came from Morgan, who offered the Lawrencetune 2.0-liter Triumph engine as standard in their Morgan Plus 4 Super Sport. His work with Triumphs and Morgans saw the development of the aerodynamic SLR bodyshell that could be fitted to the chassis of either make, but only four were built—one on a Triumph TR4 chassis and three on a Morgan chassis. The SLR—Sprinzel Lawrencetune Racing—was styled by Lawrence and bodied in aluminium by Williams and Pritchard at the urging of John Sprinzel and Neil Dangerfield. Lawrence finished fifth in the 1964 Spa 3-Hour race in his SLR in a race that was dominated by Porsche 904s. In 1965 he drove his SLR (now powered by a 2.6-litre Triumph engine fitted with a cross flow alloy cylinder head designed and machined by Lawrencetune) to fourth overall and first in class in the BOAC Double 500 weekend. In the Whitsun Trophy meeting at Goodwood the following year Lawrence finished first in his last outing in the SLR.

In mid-1967 work began on a luxury sporting saloon called the Monica, named after Madame Tastevin, wife of Jean Tastevin, a self-made wealthy industrialist from Balbigny near Lyon in France who wanted to diversify his business away from railway rolling stock to include a modern era Grand Routier. Tastevin had tracked Lawrence down through the French journalist Jabby Crombac who knew him and recommended him. A working prototype was running less than a year later with a 3-litre version of the Martin V8 for which Tastevin bought the design and manufacturing rights. Although light and powerful, it was no match for the comparatively heavy Monica and so an enlarged 3.5-litre version was built but it, too, was not able to provide the level of performance that both Lawrence and Tastevin desired. A Chrysler 340 V8 was substituted and there were immediate gains in both weight and performance. Development continued through to February 1975 when, after the fuel crisis precipitated by the Yom Kippur war, Tastevin closed the project down. "I was gutted. I'd put my heart and soul into that car as did several loyal employees. That car deserved a better fate because it was a very, very good car even if I do say so myself. I walked away from the car business after that," said an emotional Lawrence.

He tried to keep the Monica team together with contract engineering work, the most successful of which was the building of portable generator sets for refrigeration boxes. He also designed and built a regenerative braking system and a straddle carrier for use on docks but neither were commercialised. He then moved to California for 12 years where he busied himself with maintaining other people's historic racing cars.

Returning to England in late 1995, he worked for Marcos for a year managing their LM600 racing car team before returning to his first love, Morgan, where he was responsible for the engineering of the acclaimed Morgan Aero 8 sports car.

He lived in retirement with his wife Carrie in Herefordshire and after several years of ill-health passed away peacefully on August 13, 2011.

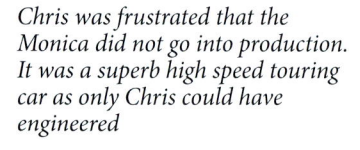

Chris was frustrated that the Monica did not go into production. It was a superb high speed touring car as only Chris could have engineered

CHAPTER THIRTEEN • CHRIS LAWRENCE: LIFETIME MAVERICK

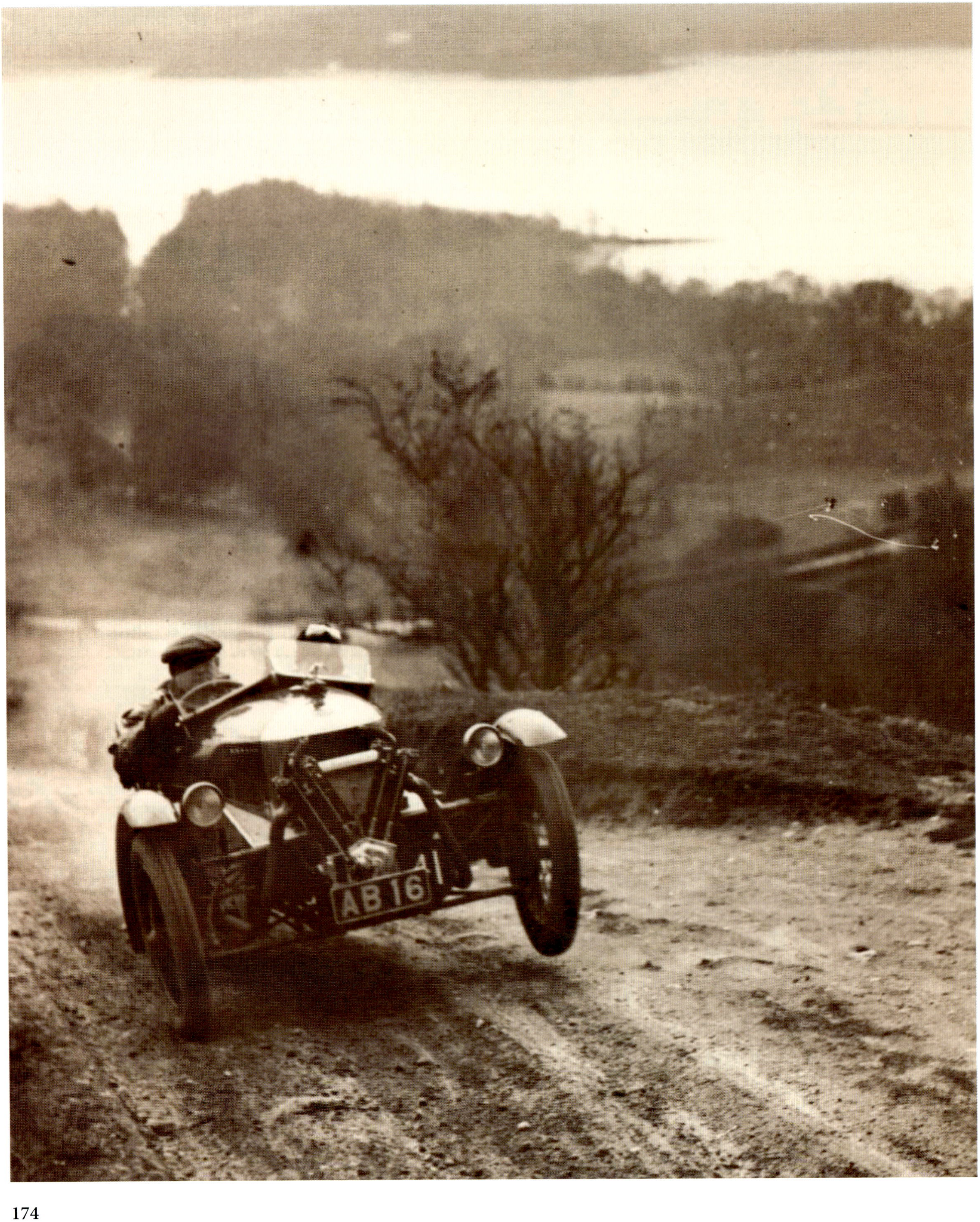
AB 16

Chapter Fourteen

A LITTLE COMPANY HISTORY

Morgan is a quite remarkable company in an industry that is renowned for swallowing the smaller fry and spitting them out when it suits. That the company has survived for a century in such a cut-throat business environment is truly amazing; that it is still owned and controlled by the same family is an even more remarkable achievement.

Good and bad times have visited upon the Morgan Motor Company tucked away as it is in the Malvern Hills in Worcestershire—quite a long way off the beaten path in terms of location vis-à-vis the rest of what was the British automobile industry and its suppliers—but it has survived all that has been thrown at it. In fact it has prospered at times when larger companies have fallen by the wayside.

The history of Morgan began with Henry Frederick Stanley Morgan, generally known as "HFS," who began by building what were in effect motorised tricycles in response to a unique set of conditions that existed in England in the early years of the 20th century.

HFS was the eldest child of Henry and Florence Morgan and was born at Morcton Jeffries, Herefordshire on August 11, 1881. His childhood was spent at Stoke Lacy where his father was the rector. However, when it came to schooling he was sent to the Stone House preparatory school at Broadstairs in Kent followed by Marlborough College public school a little closer to home in Wiltshire. He was enthusiastic about all things mechanical and enjoyed a technical education at the Crystal Palace Engineering College at Sydenham, South London.

HFS Morgan, founder of the company

175

Chapter Fourteen · A Little Company History

In 1899 he had the good fortune to be apprenticed to William Dean who was superintendent at the famous Great Western Railways workshops in Swindon where he worked on steam engines. Despite this, he was keenly aware of the work carried out by two German inventors, Gottlieb Daimler and Karl Benz, who had successfully made the four-stroke internal combustion engine a reality.

Like a great many young men around Europe at the time, HFS was bitten by the motoring bug and in 1905 left the Great Western Railways to embark on a career that would involve motors and cars. That would have been a daring move given the times in England and the risks involved—history has not apparently recorded what HFS's father thought of all of this. HFS bought a property called Chestnut Villa on Worcester Road in Malvern Link which was near the famous old spa town of Great Malvern. Morgan built a garage on some land adjoining the villa and opened an agency for Wolseley, Siddeley and Darracq cars.

The first Morgan garage opened in May 1905

The business was successful and in his spare time Morgan tinkered with the idea of a three-wheeled car. He had purchased a 7hp Peugeot engine and drew a chassis but he had nowhere to make it. Through his friendship with William Stephenson-Peach at the nearby Malvern College he arranged for his chassis to be built in the school's workshops. A feature of the design was its independent front suspension, something of a rarity in cars of any description in those days and especially so in something as basic as the car Morgan had in mind. Morgan conceived a compact and light sliding pillar type of suspension with coil springs providing the suspension medium. He patented the design in 1909.

The general configuration of what he conceived was to remain in production at Morgan for decades. In his tri-car he positioned the air-cooled Vee-twin Peugeot engine transversely across the front of the chassis just behind the front wheels with the drive shaft running through a backbone tube to a bevel box. From there the drive went to the single rear wheel by a chain on each side that was engaged by a dog clutch. It gave a very simple two-speed drive system with one flaw—there was no reverse gear!

A tiller steering mechanism was positioned to the driver's right and the gearchange lever to the left and there was a throttle lever (not an accelerator as such) with the only pedal being for the rudimentary cable brakes. The fuel tank was placed above the engine with gravity feed to the carburettor.

There was virtually no bodywork as such and certainly no weather protection which might amuse people today knowing what England's weather was generally like—you always took your umbrella! In the first prototype there was room only for the driver.

In November 1910 the Cycle and Motor Cycle manufacturers Trade Union held its first show at Olympia and Morgan debuted his production tri-car at the show, this vehicle having an English 8hp air-cooled Vee-twin JAP engine as its power source. That was the biggest

CHAPTER FOURTEEN • A LITTLE COMPANY HISTORY

change from prototype to production although many details of the design were modified as need demanded. At no stage did HFS consider building his own engines; with the excellent JAP engine readily available there was no need.

By August of 1911 the vehicle was officially known as the Morgan Runabout and now had seating for the driver and a passenger. At the same time the tiller steering system was replaced by a conventional steering wheel with a motorcycle type throttle lever attached to one of the spokes. Styling changes included a rather crude semblance of a body although there were no doors or weather protection but there was a near-vertical windscreen.

First production Morgan, debut at Olympia Show, November 1910

The Runabout achieved overnight fame when the racing motorcyclist Harry Martin drove it to victory in the International Cyclecar Race at Brooklands. The resulting publicity soon had Morgan's order books full-to-overflowing.

Through the next few years the pattern of slow evolution became part of the culture at the Morgan Motor Company, HFS having registered the business name on April 1, 1912—April Fool's Day! Buyers had the choice of a narrow or wide body, and side- or overhead valve engine of JAP manufacture. In 1916 a further engine option was made available, a watercooled MAG unit made in Switzerland, to counter criticisms from some people about their Runabout overheating.

First factory at Malvern Link

Responding to requests Morgan came out with the 4-seater Family version in 1920. The added demand for the Family model in addition to the Runabout meant that the original factory space was bursting at the seams and a larger premise was necessary. HFS acquired a parcel of land on Pickersleigh Road, still in Malvern Link, where he had ample room to expand as the business grew.

178

This is the site where the Morgan Motor Car Company is located today.

The release of the Austin 7 in 1922 had a significant impact on the British motor industry, and on those manufacturers who were making vehicles for those on low incomes. Morgan was one of several manufacturers adversely affected. Despite the setback, Morgan came out with the Aero model in 1923, a model name that has gone into Morgan folklore. It featured a 976cc side-valve JAP engine, up from 964cc, had a more pointed tail and twin aero screens (hence the name).

By 1927 the range had been expanded to include the De Luxe as well as the continuing Family and Aero models. The body was now 3-inches wider and several inches longer while larger 7-inch diameter front drum brakes were now fitted. A self-starter followed in 1928.

The Great Depression fell upon the world in 1929 and this had a significant effect on Morgan production but nevertheless the company pushed on by introducing the low chassis Super Aero, and modifying the propeller shaft from a single-piece unit to a two-piece. By the end of the Depression, 1932, the company introduced a rear-mounted three-speed manual gearbox that included a reverse gear. This meant that a single chain was all that was now needed to drive the car. With this momentous change came a range of 1096cc JAP engine options: side-valve or overhead valve, air-cooling or water-cooling.

Advert for the Morgan Super Aero, 1927

The following year, 1933, saw the arrival of the F-type, the first Morgan three-wheeler powered by a four-cylinder engine. HFS had been toying with the idea since 1929 when he built a prototype powered by a 750cc Coventry Climax side-valve engine. Between the

Morgan F-Type, 1933

prototype and production many details changed. The bonnet was lengthened and louvered, the doors were cutaway and the tail was rounded while at the front was a new look—a flat sloping back radiator that was destined to be a Morgan signature until the 1950s. The most important part of this model was the engine—a 933cc side-valve Ford engine powered the production range. HFS forged a relationship with Ford at this time that has endured to this day.

As if the Austin 7 was not enough, the Government added its burden in 1935 with a reduction in the Road Fund License fee to owners of small cars from £8 a year to £6. It might not seem like much today but it was a significant blow to tiny Morgan. During the same year Morgan introduced the F2 model as a 2-seater with the option of the larger 1172cc 10hp Ford side-valve engine, the Girling brakes still being cable operated.

By 1938 Morgan was the only surviving company making three-wheeled cars, the others having succumbed to the intense competition generated by the big-selling Austin 7 and the responses to it from both Morris and Ford.

The last Morgan three-wheeler left the Malvern Link factory on July 29, 1952 after a production life of 42 years.

Always the tinkerer HFS built the first prototype four-wheeled Morgan in 1934 based on the existing Ford-engined F-type with the flat radiator, a decoupled Meadows four-speed gearbox joined to the engine by a rigid tube, a short propeller shaft to the Moss-built live rear axle suspended by quarter elliptic leaf springs. Naturally the chassis was new, consisting of almost parallel pressed steel rails reaching back from the sliding pillar front suspension with several cross braces.

A second prototype was built in 1935, longer and wider than the first with a 1-litre Coventry Climax overhead inlet-side exhaust engine and an under-slung rear axle; a third prototype was built in the same year. The main difference between the two was the much neater styling of the latter car as HFS tweaked the details to get it aesthetically right. Most of the development regarding the car's styling took place on the second prototype while development road mileage was built up on the third. The biggest problem was resolving the curvature of the front wings and running boards and the placing of the Lucas free-standing headlights. HFS also decided to provide two spare wheels and tyres, these being carried on a bracket and partially sunk into the pressing for the fuel tank.

By a simple process of trial-and-error, HFS arrived at the definitive form that would stay with Morgan for the next seventy years. It would comprise a Coventry Climax engine of 1122cc capacity producing 34bhp at 4500rpm, the de-coupled Meadows four-speed manual gearbox and the flat radiator.

The Morgan 4-4 as it was known, a name apparently given it by works manager George Goodall that meant 4-cylinders and 4 wheels, was released to an expectant public on January 3, 1936—mid-winter! All the early cars were two-seaters that sported a flying M on the top of the radiator (discontinued post-war) and a rigid torque tube connecting the engine to the gearbox. Semi-elliptic leaf springs were used at the rear, their mounting being inboard of the chassis rails, while the brakes were cable operated Girling drums of just 8-inches diameter. Intriguingly, the wooden floor slats were bolted to the underside of the chassis which meant that the gearbox and drive shafts were above it, effectively inside the car's interior! The body frame, and the dashboard, were made from locally grown ash and covered by hand-formed metal sheets; the dash instruments were positioned in a central crackle finish metal panel allowing dash pockets at either end, there being no tachometer as a standard fitting. The large central Smiths speedometer was flanked by dials having two gauges each—amps and oil pressure in one, water temperature and fuel in the other.

First Morgan 4-4, 1936

This configuration, with periodic changes of engine, would remain largely unchanged until 1972. This was an amazing achievement, unparalleled in the annals of automobile history.

Just over eighteen months later (August 1937) a four-seater was introduced following many requests from obviously satisfied clients. The extra space was achieved by re-arranging components behind the front seats, reshaping the panel work and taking away one of the spare wheels.

A year later came the 4-4 drophead coupe. While the prototype body had been built by Avon Bodies in Warwick, the production bodies were built in house. Several improvements came with the drophead, improvements that would gradually be incorporated into the other models. The most notable was the use of Silentbloc engine mounts and the interior boasted walnut trimming on the dash and door cappings. During this time the Meadows gearbox was replaced by one sourced from Moss although if a buyer specifically wanted a Meadows gearbox it would be provided. From 1949 until 1972 the Moss gearbox was standardised across the range.

Mid-1939 saw the introduction of the Standard Ten OHV four-cylinder engine as an option to the Coventry Climax unit. This came about because John Black (later Sir John) offered HFS an overhead valve conversion of his engine especially for Morgan, much as he was doing for William Lyons at SS Cars in Coventry. At 1267cc the Standard engine had more capacity, power—39bhp at 4200rpm versus 34bhp at 4500rpm—and slightly more torque.

This same year saw the release of the Le Mans Replica. Powered by a 1098cc version of the Climax engine to get under the 1100cc class limit, it had cycle wings, no running boards and a modified tail to carry only one spare. It was based on the car built for Miss Prudence Fawcett who had raced at the 1938 Le Mans and finished 13th overall.

The company stopped manufacturing of the 4-4 with the outbreak of war in September 1939 and did not re-commence its manufacture until March 1946 with essentially the same car in roadster and drophead format. What did change was the writing of the car's badge: it was now displayed as 4/4, and has stayed that way ever since. Apart from a handful of Coventry Climax powered post-war cars, HFS settled on the OHV Standard-sourced engine.

New for 1951 was the Morgan Plus 4, a sports car that took advantage of the post-war government's "export or die" mantra and events at the Standard Motor Company where the production of the previous range of four- and six-cylinder engines ceased in 1948 with the arrival of the Standard Vanguard saloon. One of the best features of this car, and one that would outlive the car by many years, was its all-new engine. A 2.1-litre OHV unit, it possessed a cast iron cylinder block with easily removable "wet" cylinder liners and a cylinder head with eight large ports for good breathing. Even though Peter Morgan, now working alongside his father, did investigate engines from Vauxhall and Austin who both declined his inquiries, it was the Vanguard unit that was ideal for their next generation of sports car released in September 1950.

The Plus 4 was in most ways a grown up 4-4. The Z-frame chassis was lengthened in the wheelbase by four-inches (from 92-ins to 96-ins), width was increased by one-inch and wheel tracks by three-inches. In this process the chassis was strengthened with box section cross members as well as reinforcing of the front sliding pillar suspension assembly and modifying the geometry of the kingpins. However, by far the most significant engineering change (other than the engine) was the adoption of full hydraulic Girling drum brakes.

Morgan range 1951 to 1952

There was a new polished wood dashboard with a rounded-end rectangular metal instrument panel finished in black crackle paint that contained two large dials with cream faces and black graphics. At the right-hand end (for a right-hand drive car) was the speedometer with integral clock and at the other end was the combination dial with four separate gauges—fuel contents, amps, oil pressure and water temperature. In between them was a bevy of pull-on/push-off switches and that icon of British cars of the 50s, the ivory/cream Bakelite rotary switch from Lucas that doubled as the lights switch and ignition.

Shown at the 1953 London Motor Show was a revised look Plus 4. There was a curved and slatted grille on a cowled radiator and a new front panel that hid the front suspension components from view allowing the headlights to be incorporated in the landing between the fender and radiator. Morgan was probably the last adherent to the '30s style of mounting its headlights on arms projecting from the radiator brackets. The flat radiator models continued until mid-'54. Morgan had to re-design the redesign within six months because of new headlight mounting height regulations (they had been unaware of them when carrying out the original redesign) and once this had settled into production the definitive style had been arrived at and is arguably still with us today.

This was a time of extreme activity at Pickersleigh Road because not only was the company finalising the design of the future Plus 4 but it was also reviving the 4/4 as an important second model line.

During 1954 the Plus 4 was fitted with the slightly smaller capacity 1991cc 90bhp Triumph TR2 version of the Vanguard engine. The engine had been developed for Triumph's TR2 sports car that went on to father a dynasty of well-loved sports cars; the capacity was reduced to allow the TR2 to compete in the under-2 litre class racing. Having displayed a four-seater prototype twice Morgan finally released it for the '54 model year; the main difference between it and the regular two-seater was the carrying of only one spare wheel. Luggage space, too, was minimal.

Morgan Plus 4 with round nose, 1954

A new dashboard came in 1955. For this iteration, a tachometer was placed to the right of the steering wheel (in a right-hand drive car) and clearly visible to the driver; to the left of the wheel was a matching diameter combination dial and on the far left, virtually in front of the passenger, was the speedometer. Between the latter two dials were the myriad switches.

For 1956 the Plus 4 adopted the more powerful TR3 100bhp engine, this change being accompanied by a new fuel tank with only one spare wheel recessed into it. The following year saw the last vestige of the original 4-4 disappear with the deletion of the fold-down windscreen, a feature that had been a Morgan staple since 1936. Two years later the fuel filler was repositioned to the left side of the car, a chromed "Morgan" badge appearing on the other side, while by mid-'59 Girling front disc brakes were at long last available as an option, this also being accompanied by a reduction in wheel size from 16" down to 15" with 5.60 tyres.

In 1958 Peter Morgan had been appointed managing director of the Morgan Motor Company although he had been intimately involved in all product development for most of the decade and had effectively been running the company following the death of George Goodall. With the company coming up to its fiftieth year in business it would have been fitting had the man who started it all been there to join in the celebrations. Sadly HFS died shortly before the event and so Peter was elevated to the position of chairman.

While the late '50s through the early '60s proved to be a tough time for Morgan, by 1966 the company was in the coveted position of having a very full order bank to the point where supply of an ordered car could be a year or more into the future. The catalyst for this happy situation was Chris Lawrence who had been very successfully campaigning a Plus 4 in races across the length and breadth of England. The peak of this activity came with his triumphant class win at Le Mans in 1962. In 1960 Morgan catalogued a lower cowled aluminium panelled light weight model, the Super Sports, that was powered by a Lawrencetune-assembled and modified Triumph TR3 engine. The engine was fully balanced with polished combustion chambers and ports and fitted with dual side draft Weber 45 DCOE carburettors. This fettling yielded a further 15-20bhp with complete reliability.

Peter Morgan sitting in a car in 1949

In early 1961 Triumph released the TR4 that was powered by an enlarged capacity engine, it now being 2138cc although actual power remained at 100bhp. The Lawrencetune version of this engine delivered 125bhp. Owners who wanted to run with the 1991cc engine for competition purposes were still able to order it. Six years later Triumph announced the TR5 that had the company's 2.5-litre OHV six-cylinder engine taken from the 2.5PI saloon. For Morgan it meant the end of what had been a sometimes tense relationship with the Standard Motor Company because the four-cylinder engine had been taken out of production after a career lasting twenty years. It was certainly one of the British motor industry's better post-war engines that proved to be amazingly versatile, rugged and reliable.

CHAPTER FOURTEEN • A LITTLE COMPANY HISTORY

The last Triumph-engined Plus 4 was built in late 1968 closing an eventful chapter in the history of the Morgan Motor Company.

Released in 1955 was the resurrected 4/4 model line. Designed to fit below the Plus 4 in marketing terms, the two were almost indistinguishable from each other. Those with a keen eye would notice that the 4/4 was ever-so-slightly lower at the cowl because of the lower height of the Ford 100E side-valve four-cylinder engine that powered it. Unfortunately the 100E engine came with a three-speed manual gearbox to which Morgan attached its own remote floor shifter. With only 36bhp available performance was not great although as the press pointed out at the time, it was the cheapest true sports car on the market. The major difference between the two models was the dashboard. On the 4/4 the speedometer was to the right of the steering wheel with a matching size combination dial to the left and a panel of switches in the centre. No tachometer was fitted.

The modern buildings of todays Morgan factory

For 1961 a revised 4/4 was announced. It was still Ford-powered, but now by the new "Kent" in-line OHV four-cylinder engine. The 4/4 now had the 105E 1-litre 39bhp engine from the Ford Anglia, and its matching four-speed manual gearbox. As with the Plus 4, the 16" road wheels gave way to 15" and the body tub was widened by around two-inches although the actual width of the 4/4 remained unchanged.

A year later the 4/4 was the recipient of the larger capacity 109E 1340cc engine from the Consul Classic; power was up to 54bhp and Girling disc brakes were now fitted to the front wheels. Another year and the 4/4 received the Cortina's 116E 1.5-litre engine with 60bhp and, at last, a four-speed all synchromesh manual gearbox. With this model a tachometer was now included in the instrumentation. Soon after the release of the 4/4, Morgan announced the Competition version that was powered by the Cortina GT 118E engine with 78bhp. Another year and another engine change as Ford constantly uprated its engine line; for 1968 Morgan released the 4/4 1600 using the new Mark II Cortina crossflow version of the venerable Kent engine. However, the Competition 4/4 outsold the standard model by a huge margin to the point where Morgan made the former Competition model its standard 4/4 offering and discontinued the lower performing version in mid-'71.

By 1970 came another dashboard, this one having a tachometer included and the pull-push switches had been replaced by the rocker type in deference to new US regulations; a collapsible steering column was now fitted for the same reason. In fact throughout the Seventies the 4/4 (and the other Morgan models) were to be constantly upgraded to allow them to conform to ever-increasing regulatory requirements from its key US market as well as the EEC. There were now also anti-burst door locks, "earless" wheel spinners and separate driver and passenger seats; by 1977 there was another dash design now with equal-sized speedometer and tachometer either side of the steering column directly in front of the driver with the auxiliary gauges lined up across the centre of the dash and the rockers switches lined up below them. A buyer could specify either vinyl or leather covering for the dash which was all vaguely Jaguar-ish in design.

Morgan Plus 4 Plus

By the middle of the decade Morgan faced another engine supply problem. Ford, in line with every other manufacturer, was in the process of switching from in-line engines driving the rear wheels to transverse engines and front-wheel drive. An additional spur (for Ford) was the fact that the Kent engine could not economically be made to comply with forthcoming EEC emission requirements.

187

After considering several engine-gearbox combinations from various English and European manufacturers, Morgan introduced their re-engined 4/4 at the 1981 Earls Court Show with a Fiat DOHC 1.6-litre four-cylinder engine together with its five-speed manual gearbox. Ford, however, was keen to continue the association with Morgan and engineered a "north-south" version of the new Escort XR3 1.6-litre single overhead camshaft CVH engine for installation in the 4/4 chassis mated to the old Cortina four-speed manual gearbox that was later replaced by the newer design (and five-speed) Sierra unit.

Both Fiat and Ford-engined 4/4s were on offer, the Fiat version being significantly more expensive and as a consequence few were built.

In 1992 the 4/4 actually went out of production temporarily while Morgan awaited supplies of the completely new Ford DOHC Zetec fuel injected engine that complied with all EEC requirements. Following its introduction, several important component changes occurred: the Girling braking system was replaced by a Lockheed system which was then standardised on all Morgans and the Salisbury rear axle was superseded by a stronger (and cheaper) Australian-made BTR unit. The 4/4 four-seater reappeared in 1999 and continues to this day as does the Ford Zetec-powered 4/4—referred to in-house as a "traditional Morgan" to differentiate it and its Plus 6 brother from the new Aero 8—and is proving to be as popular as it ever was.

In the eyes of the Morganists of this world, the company has made only one mistake in its long history—the Plus 4 Plus. Was it too civilised, too "modern," too radical for traditional Morgan buyers? Certainly it was considerably more expensive than the Plus 4 on which it was based. The mainstream press were enamoured with it and liked its smooth easy loping performance but in the event only 26 were built over an almost five year period. Morgan would have probably lost money on each one and old HFS, who counselled Peter not to do it, would have been heard saying, "I told you so." With the passage of forty years the Plus 4 Plus is perhaps not the aberration it was claimed to be but that does not alter the fact that it was by far the least successful post-war Morgan.

Announced at the 1968 London Motor Show was another Morgan that would enjoy a long and fruitful life of 36 years, the Plus 8. With the engine supply situation in a state of flux following the takeover of Triumph by Leyland in 1961 and its subsequent change of focus for the company, Morgan needed to look for another supplier of engines. Consideration was given to the Ford "Essex" V6 in 3-litre form but it was too tall and too heavy; the Ford-based Lotus DOHC engine used in the Lotus-Cortina was also investigated but was found to be not only too expensive but insufficiently robust. Then by chance Peter Morgan met Peter Wilks from Rover and the subject of their new 3.5-litre aluminium alloy V8 was raised. Morgan was interested

Morgan Plus 8 in period colour

A Buick version of the V8 was obtained from the defunct Gordon-Keeble company and, with new recruit Maurice Owen, installed in a modified Plus 4 chassis. The path to production was littered with twists and turns as Morgan had to negotiate its way through the General Motors legal department—it had to have permission to use the engine as GM held the rights to it—and Rover took quite a while to get it into production at Solihull. As that was happening Rover became part of the Leyland Group and before you could blink an eye Leyland had swallowed up the ailing British Motor Corporation (BMC) bringing all the main players under the ownership of one ill-equipped, inadequately financed and ineptly managed industrial conglomerate. Peter Morgan had been offered the Triumph Stag SOHC 3-litre V8 but he was not to be persuaded, for which every Morgan owner and enthusiast must be eternally grateful.

The Rover V8 was only an inch or so longer than the Triumph four and only a few pounds heavier but it was much wider. The Plus 8 chassis was two inches longer in the wheelbase, 8

CHAPTER FOURTEEN • A LITTLE COMPANY HISTORY

inches longer overall, one-inch wider and the wheel tracks were 1.5- and two-inches wider front and rear respectively; the suspension was strengthened as was the chassis by using welded-in sheet steel gussets for the floor in place of wood, and beautiful magnesium alloy road wheels replaced the previous wire spoke type.

Subsequently tested by every member of the media who could get his hands on it, the 160bhp Plus 8 was something of a rocket-ship up to its maximum of 120-125mph. The old Moss gearbox (still with non-synchromesh first gear!) was regarded as something of an anachronism but it did suit the olde worlde charm and character of the car.

Even though it was powered by an ex-GM V8 engine and possessed the kind of raw power and performance that Morganists love, it was not tuned or developed to cope with any of the Federal emission requirements that were slowly creeping into America. Morgan as a company was far too small to be able to fund the kind of development that would have been necessary and so it had to wait until Rover went through the certification process. This meant that its release on the American market was delayed until 1970 when Rover introduced the 3500 P6B there; by 1972 Rover was disillusioned with its sales performance and withdrew from the market taking Morgan with it.

In true Morgan tradition, small but significant details were modified and improved over the car's long model life. In 1971 new 6.5 x 15 alloy road wheels became available—they were the same design but used far better quality castings—and there were new taillight units; 1972 saw the demise of the old faithful Moss gearbox and in its place was fitted the Rover P6B four-speed all-synchromesh manual unit that was bolted directly up to the engine and not mounted remotely as was the case with the Moss, reducing somewhat the amount of foot room in an already tight cabin; this same year saw stronger front stub axles and a larger capacity radiator specified. Little changed until the 1976 model year when the ex-Rover SD1 155bhp V8 engine was installed along with the new and stronger "77" five-speed manual gearbox. The following year came a new dashboard design that was virtually the same as that fitted in the 4/4.

To meet the EEC emission requirements in 1982, the twin SU carburettors were replaced by twin Stromberg units, and in 1984 the old Cam Gears steering system was replaced by a Jack Knight Developments rack and pinion system that brought new precision to the driving of a Morgan. The new system used a central take-off point from the rack so that the steering arms were of equal length both sides. By now the Plus 8 was fitted with the 190bhp fuel injected Rover Vitesse engine which was a very tight squeeze under the bonnet.

By the end of the decade (1990) Morgan offered the 190bhp 3.9 litre EFI V8 engine from the Range Rover Vogue; this engine was available with 3-way catalytic converters and with Range Rover now established on the American market, Morgan judged it time to return with the Plus 8. Mechanical developments continued, with the old lever arm rear dampers being replaced by modern telescopic units in 1991; three years later the Plus 8 was specified with a Lockheed disc/drum braking system and the newer and stronger R380 gearbox from the Range Rover fitted, the benefit for owners being far smoother shift quality and greater reliability.

The next most significant change arrived for the 1998 model year when the whole body was made from hand-formed aluminium panels rather than the previous steel or, in some cases, steel and aluminium. At the same time the doors were lengthened slightly, the dashboard was moved forward and the seats given more runner movement as the car was prepared for the installation of optional SRS airbags; a minor redesign of the dash took place with the auxiliary gauges now positioned two-above-two in the centre (they had previously been spread out in a line) and a substantial stainless steel reinforcing bar was mounted out of sight under the dash, its role being to assist passenger safety in a side impact collision. A larger capacity 220bhp 4.9 litre version of the venerable Rover V8 was made available as an option to the 3.9 litre unit that had been Federalised.

The Plus 8 had been homologated for the American market until 2003 (the last was built in March 2004) but with the Rover V8 engine in decline as stocks were used up Morgan elected to build a special series of 200 Anniversary models to celebrate the Plus 8's 35th year in production. It was a fitting end to a great sports car.

Introduced for the 2004 model year was the Plus 8's replacement, the Roadster. Essentially the same body and chassis, the Roadster was powered by the Ford Mondeo ST220 Duratec DOHC 3-litre V6 engine that developed 217bhp and gave the car the same level of performance as the model it replaced.

Morgan's model range today consists of three "traditional" sports cars, the 4/4, Roadster and the 4-seater and the Aero 8 that initially stood alone and was regarded as something quite special within the Morgan Motor Company, its dealers and owners. It was supplemented by the limited edition AeroMax coupe for the 2009 Centenary year and has now been superseded by the daring SuperSport.

Marvellous celebrations were held for the company's Centenary, the principal one being at the Three Counties fairground near Great Malvern where over several days Morgan enthusiasts and owners came to witness the event. It augured well for the future with the showing in more recent times of the EvaGT powered by a twin-turbocharged BMW six-cylinder engine and the cute Threewheeler with its V-twin engine exposed up front just like the original. Good times continue at Malvern Link.

Chapter Fourteen • A Little Company History

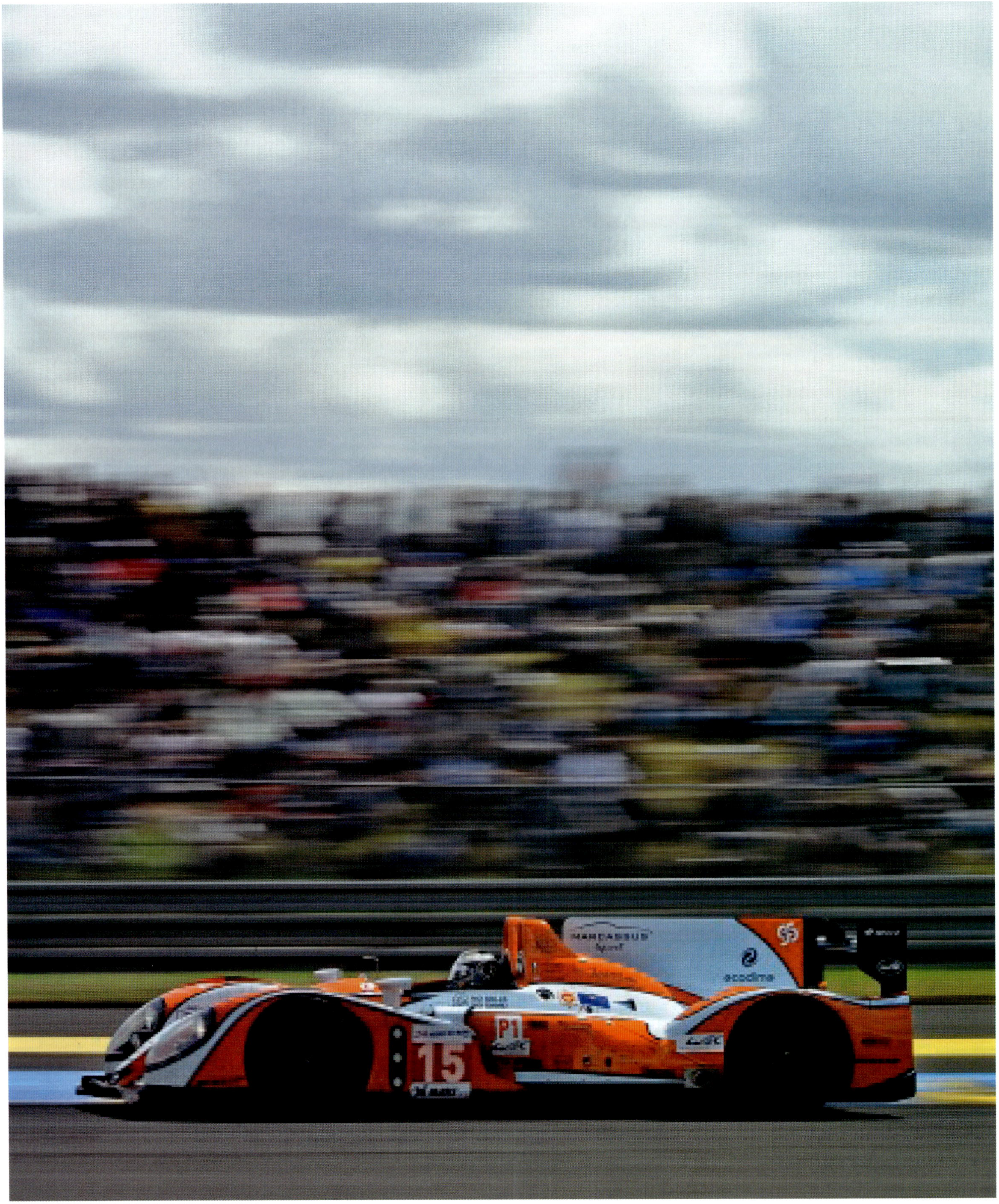
P1
15
ecodime

POSTSCRIPT

In 2012 Morgan Motor Company and OAK Racing joined forces in endurance racing and entered into a partnership that saw the new 2012 OAK LMP2 cars competing as Morgan LMP2s. The race car was manufactured by Onroak Automotive, OAK Racing's constructor department which was based at the Technoparc des 24 Heures in Le Mans. OAK Racing entered one Morgan LMP2 in that year's FIA World Endurance Championship where they sought to emulate the achievements of the Morgan Super Sport that took class victory at the 1962 Le Mans 24 Hours. 2012 marked the fiftieth anniversary of that success and the company wanted to celebrate the landmark in style.

OAK Racing 2012, Morgan LMP2

Charles Morgan, Chairman of the Morgan Motor Company said, "I am thrilled to be able to announce our partnership with Jacques Nicolet and OAK Racing. It is a source of great pride that we have the opportunity to work with a racing car designer and constructor who has achieved such success on the international stage. Whilst Morgan sports cars enjoy a great history we have also gained a reputation for pioneering new technology and I believe the LMP2 represents a superb proving ground in which to develop innovative new methods."

The partnership presented the opportunity for the next generation of Morgans to embrace new technological advances, particularly in the incorporation of materials such as carbon fibre and top level aerodynamics, elements that are key to LMP2 cars. Jacques Nicolet, President of OAK Racing commented, "I am deeply honoured and proud that OAK Racing has been able to form a partnership with Charles Morgan and the Morgan Motor Company. Like Charles, I believe our link-up places the emphasis on the future whilst also building on the strong foundations of our individual histories. In Morgan I feel the same passion that has inspired me since childhood, as well as the 'family spirit' that I hope I have been able to create at OAK Racing. Who better than Morgan to embody the gentlemen drivers' spirit needed for LMP2 competition?"

The LMP class 2 in the World Endurance Championship encouraged participation in motor sport. One of the three drivers of an LMP2 entry had to be a talented amateur. The Morgan team had some of the most talented amateurs in endurance racing. Perhaps the days of "race on Sunday, drive to work on Monday" are over but in Morgan drivers the spirit survives. Jacques Nicolet added, "What really cements this union is our common interest in both the Le Mans 24 Hours and endurance racing as a whole."

The 2012 running of the 24 Hours not only represented the fiftieth anniversary of Morgan's class win at the race but also a celebration of a new partnership.

OAK Racing 2012 Racing Program Morgan LMP2

World Endurance Championship for Sports Cars

March 18th Sebring 12 Hours, USA

May 6th Spa 6 Hours, Belgium

June 16th/17th Le Mans 24 Hours, France

August 26th Silverstone 6 Hours, England

September 16th Sao Paolo 6 Hours, Brazil

September 30th Bahrain 6 Hours, Bahrain

October 14th Fuji 6 Hours, Japan

October 28th Shanghai 6 Hours, China

European Le Mans Series

April 1st Le Castellet 6 Hours

15th July Donnington 6 Hours

9th September Brno 6 Hours

Conquest Racing 2012 Program Morgan LMP2

American Le Mans Series

March 17th Sebring 12 Hours

April 14th Long Beach 2 Hours

May 12th Laguna Seca 6 Hours

July 7th Mosport 2 Hours 45 minutes

August 4th Mid Ohio 2 Hours 45 minutes

August 18th Elkhart Lake 4 Hours

September 1st Baltimore 2 Hours

September 15th Virginia 4 Hours

October 20th Atlanta 10 Hours The 15th Petit Le Mans

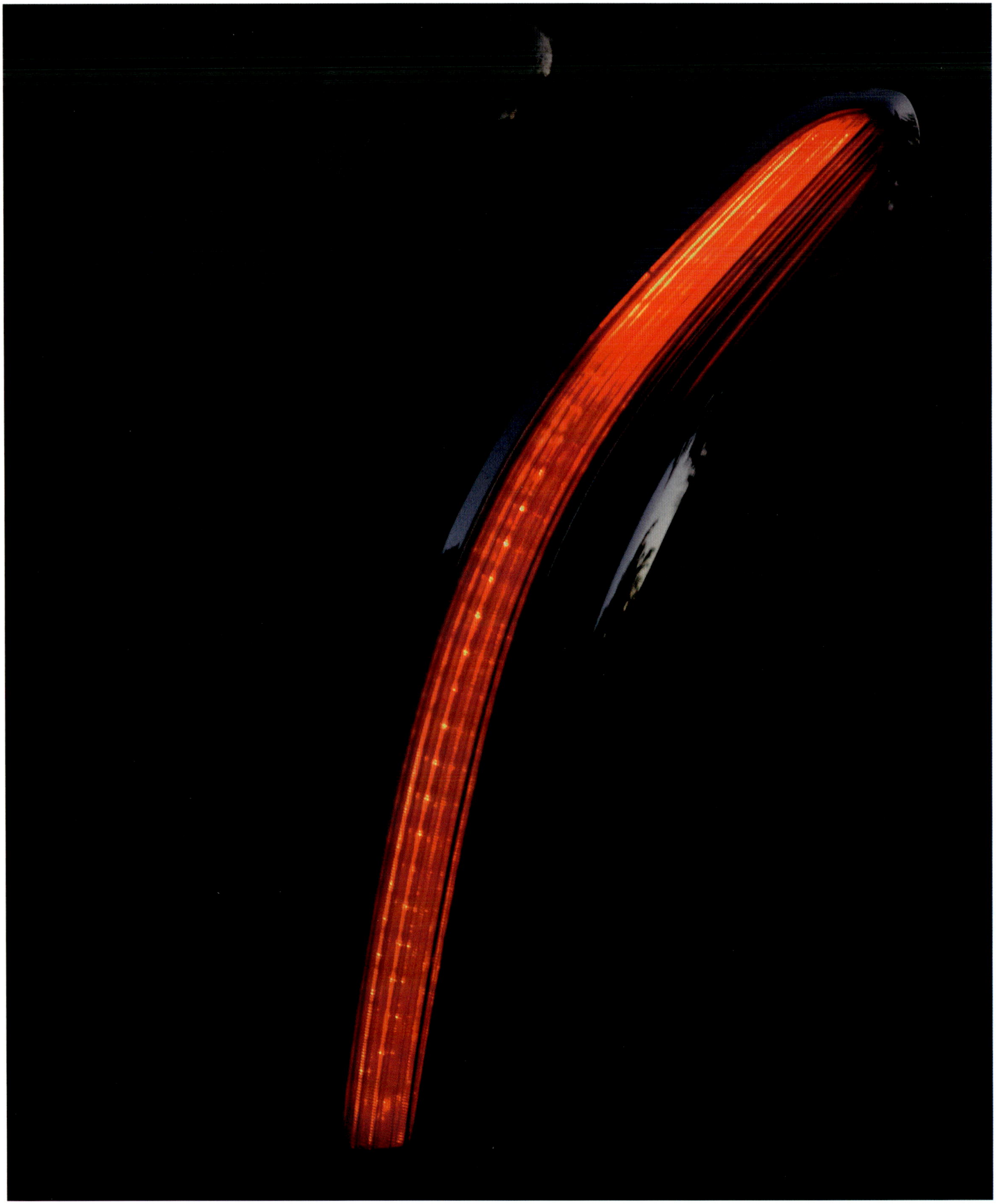

SPECIFICATIONS

AERO 8 SPECIFICATIONS

ENGINE: BMW M62B44 V8 featuring aluminium alloy cylinder block and heads; dual chain-driven overhead camshafts per cylinder bank; four valves per cylinder; Bosch DME electronic engine management, "VANOS" variable intake timing.

Bore x stroke	92 x 82.7mm
Capacity	4398cc
Compression ratio	10.0:1
Power	286 bhp (210kW) at 5500rpm
Torque	322 lbs-ft (430Nm) at 3700rpm

TRANSMISSION: Getrag S6 D429G six-speed all-synchromesh manual

Ratios:	1st 4.227; 2nd 2.506; 3rd 1.669; 4th 1.226; 5th 1.0; 6th 0.828; R 3.68
Rear axle:	BTR limited slip unit, 3.08:1

MPH/1000rpm 28.44

SUSPENSION:
Front: Independent, lower fabricated wishbone, upper cantilevered link, inboard Eibach coil springs over Koni tubular dampers

Rear: Independent, double wishbones, Eibach coil springs over Koni tubular dampers

STEERING: Jack Knight rack-and-pinion with variable power assistance, 2.4 turns lock-to-lock, centre-point geometry

BRAKES: AP Racing to Morgan specifications; vacuum servo assistance; ABS
Front 330mm cast iron rotors, ventilated, 4 pot alloy calipers
Rear 306mm cast iron rotors, ventilated, 2 pot alloy calipers

WHEELS: OZ magnesium alloy 5-spoke design, 9 x 18-inch with peg drive centre lock hubs; changed to Speedline 5-stud wheels mid-production

TYRES: Dunlop SP Sport 9000 225/40ZR 18

CHASSIS: Rigid CAD designed aluminium alloy construction bonded with Gurrit Essex adhesive and Bollhoff rivets

DIMENSIONS:

Length	162ins (4115mm)	Front track	60ins (1522mm)
Width	69ins (1753mm)	Rear track	58.5ins (1480mm)
Height	47ins (1194mm)	Weight	2200lbs (1000kgs)
Wheelbase	99ins (2515mm)	Fuel capacity	15.4 gallons (70 litres)

PERFORMANCE: Maximum speed 160mph (256km/h)   0-62mph (100km/h) in 4.8 seconds

AERO 8 Series II SPECIFICATIONS

ENGINE: BMW N62B44 V8 featuring aluminium alloy cylinder block and heads; dual chain-driven overhead camshafts per cylinder bank; four valves per cylinder; Bosch DME electronic engine management, "VANOS" variable intake timing.

Bore x stroke	92 x 82.7mm
Capacity	4398cc
Compression ratio	10.0:1
Power	333 bhp (245kW) at 6100rpm
Torque	331 lbs-ft (450Nm) at 3600rpm

TRANSMISSION: Getrag S6 D420G six-speed all-synchromesh manual

Ratios:	1st 4.05; 2nd 2.40; 3rd 1.58; 4th 1.19; 5th 1.00; 6th 0.87; R 3.68
Rear axle:	BTR limited slip unit, 3.08:1

MPH/1000rpm 27.76

SUSPENSION:
Front: Independent, lower fabricated wishbone, upper cantilevered link, inboard Eibach coil springs over Koni tubular dampers

Rear: Independent, double wishbones, Eibach coil springs over Koni tubular dampers

STEERING: Ford Granada Scorpio rack-and-pinion with electric power steering pump, 2.2 turns lock-to-lock, centre-point geometry

BRAKES: AP Racing to Morgan specifications; vacuum servo assistance; ABS
Front 348mm cast iron rotors, ventilated, 6 pot alloy calipers
Rear 332mm cast iron rotors, ventilated, 2 pot alloy calipers

WHEELS: Rimstock magnesium alloy multi-spoke design, 8.5 x 18-inch with 5-bolt hubs

TYRES: Various high performance radials, 225/40ZR 18 at the front, 245/40ZR 18 at the rear

CHASSIS: Rigid CAD designed aluminium alloy construction bonded with Gurrit Essex adhesive and Bollhoff rivets

DIMENSIONS:

Length	163ins (4115mm)	Front track	60ins (1522mm)
Width	70.25ins (1785mm)	Rear track	58.5ins (1480mm)
Height	47ins (1194mm)	Weight	2519lbs (1145kgs)
Wheelbase	99.5ins (2532mm)	Fuel capacity	15.4 gallons (70 litres)

PERFORMANCE: Maximum speed 160mph (256km/h)   0-62mph (100km/h) in 4.8 seconds

AERO 8 Series III SPECIFICATIONS

ENGINE: BMW N62B44 V8 featuring aluminium alloy cylinder block and heads; dual chain-driven overhead camshafts per cylinder bank; four valves per cylinder; Bosch DME electronic engine management, "VANOS" variable intake timing.

Bore x stroke	92 x 82.7mm
Capacity	4398cc
Compression ratio	10.0:1
Power	333 bhp (245kW) at 6100rpm
Torque	331 lbs-ft (450Nm) at 3600rpm

TRANSMISSION: Getrag S6 D420G six-speed all-synchromesh manual
Ratios: 1st 4.05; 2nd 2.40; 3rd 1.58; 4th 1.19; 5th 1.00; 6th 0.87; R 3.68
Rear axle: BTR limited slip unit, 3.08:1
MPH/1000rpm 27.76

SUSPENSION:
Front: Independent, lower fabricated wishbone, upper cantilevered link, inboard Eibach coil springs over Koni tubular dampers

Rear: Independent, double wishbones, Eibach coil springs over Koni tubular dampers

STEERING: Ford Granada Scorpio rack-and-pinion with electric power steering pump, 2.2 turns lock-to-lock, centre-point geometry

BRAKES: AP Racing to Morgan specifications; vacuum servo assistance; ABS
Front   348mm cast iron rotors, ventilated, 6 pot alloy calipers
Rear   332mm cast iron rotors, ventilated, 2 pot alloy calipers

WHEELS: Rimstock magnesium alloy multi-spoke design, 8.5 x 18-inch with 5-bolt hubs

TYRES: Various high performance radials, 225/40ZR 18 at the front, 245/40ZR 18 at the rear

CHASSIS: Rigid CAD designed aluminium alloy construction bonded with Gurrit Essex adhesive and Bollhoff rivets

DIMENSIONS:

Length	163ins (4115mm)	Front track	60ins (1522mm)
Width	70.25ins (1785mm)	Rear track	58.5ins (1480mm)
Height	47ins (1194mm)	Weight	2519lbs (1145kgs)
Wheelbase	99.5ins (2532mm)	Fuel capacity	15.4 gallons (70 litres)

PERFORMANCE: Maximum speed 160mph (256km/h)   0-62mph (100km/h) in 4.8 seconds

AERO 8 Series IV SPECIFICATIONS

ENGINE: BMW N62B48 V8 featuring aluminium alloy cylinder block and heads; dual chain-driven overhead camshafts per cylinder bank; four valves per cylinder; Bosch DME electronic engine management, Double VANOS variable valve timing and VALVETRONIC.

Bore x stroke	93 x 88.3mm
Capacity	4798cc
Compression ratio	10.0:1
Power	367 bhp (270kW) at 6300rpm
Torque	370 lbs-ft (490Nm) at 3600rpm

TRANSMISSION: Getrag S6 D420G six-speed all-synchromesh manual
Ratios: 1st 4.05; 2nd 2.40; 3rd 1.58; 4th 1.19; 5th 1.0; 6th 0.87; R 3.68
Rear axle: BTR limited slip unit, 3.08:1
MPH/1000rpm 28.44
Optional ZF 6HP26 six-speed automatic
Ratios: 1st: 4.17; 2nd: 2.34; 3rd: 1.52; 4th: 1.14; 5th: 0.87; 6th: 0.69
Rear axle: BTR limited slip unit, 3.08:1

SUSPENSION
Front   Independent, lower fabricated wishbone, upper cantilevered link, inboard Eibach coil springs over Koni tubular dampers
Rear   Independent, double wishbones, Eibach coil springs over Koni dampers

STEERING: BMW ZF rack-and-pinion with electric power assistance, 2 turns lock-to-lock, centre-point geometry

BRAKES: AP Racing to Morgan specifications; vacuum servo assistance; ABS, EBD
Front   350mm cast iron rotors, ventilated, 6 pot calipers
Rear   332mm cast iron rotors, ventilated, 2 pot calipers

WHEELS: Speedline magnesium alloy 5-spoke design, 8.5 x 18-inch with 5-bolt hubs

Rays alloys multi=spoke design, 8.5 x 19-inch with 5-bolt hubs

TYRES: Avon ZZ3 225/35 R19 front, 245/35 R19 rear

CHASSIS: Rigid CAD designed aluminium alloy construction bonded with adhesive and Bolhoff rivets

DIMENSIONS:
Length	163ins (4147mm)	Front track	60ins (1510mm)
Width	70ins (1770mm)	Rear track	58.5ins (1480mm)
Height	47ins (1200mm)	Weight	2595lbs (1280kgs) for the automatic
Wheelbase	99.5ins (2532mm)		2585lbs (1175kgs) for the manual
		Fuel capacity	15.4 gallons (70 litres)

PERFORMANCE: Maximum speed 170mph (273km/h)   0-62mph (100km/h) in 4.2 seconds for the automatic

AEROMAX SPECIFICATIONS

ENGINE: BMW N62B48 V8 featuring aluminium alloy cylinder block and heads; dual chain-driven overhead camshafts per cylinder bank; four valves per cylinder; Bosch DME electronic engine management, bi-VANOS variable intake timing and VALVETRONIC.

Bore x stroke	93 x 88.3mm
Capacity	4798cc
Compression ratio	10.0:1
Power	368bhp (270Kw) at 6300rpm
Torque	370lbs-ft (490Nm) at 3600rpm

TRANSMISSION: Getrag S6 D420G six-speed all-synchromesh manual
Ratios: 1st 4.05; 2nd 2.40; 3rd 1.58; 4th 1.19; 5th 1.0; 6th 0.87; R 3.68
Optional ZF 6HP26 six-speed automatic
Ratios: 1st: 4.17; 2nd: 2.34; 3rd: 1.52; 4th: 1.14; 5th: 0.87; 6th: 0.69
Rear axle: BTR limited slip unit, 3.08:1
MPH/1000rpm 28.44

SUSPENSION:
Front: Independent, lower fabricated wishbone, upper cantilevered link, inboard Eibach coil springs over Koni tubular dampers
Rear: Independent, double wishbones, Eibach coil springs over Koni tubular dampers

STEERING: BMW ZF rack-and-pinion with variable power assistance, 2.4 turns lock-to-lock, centre-point geometry

BRAKES: AP Racing to Morgan specifications; vacuum servo assistance; ABS
Front 330mm cast iron rotors, ventilated, 4 pot calipers
Rear 306mm cast iron rotors, ventilated, 2 pot calipers

WHEELS: Rays magnesium alloy multi-spoke design, 8.5 x 19-inch with 5-stud hubs

TYRES: Dunlop SP Sport 9000 225/35ZR 19 front, 245/35ZR 19 rear

CHASSIS: Rigid CAD designed aluminium alloy construction bonded with Gurrit Essex adhesive and Bolhoff rivets

DIMENSIONS:

Length	163ins (4147mm)	Front track	60ins (1510mm)
Width	69ins (1751mm)	Rear track	58.5ins (1480mm)
Height	49ins (1246mm)	Weight	2800lbs (1280kgs)
Wheelbase	99.5ins (2532mm)	Fuel capacity	15.4 gallons (70 litres)

PERFORMANCE: Maximum speed 160mph (256km/h)   0-62mph (100km/h) in 4.8 seconds

AEROSUPERSPORT SPECIFICATIONS

ENGINE: BMW N62B48 V8 featuring aluminium alloy cylinder block and heads; dual chain-driven overhead camshafts per cylinder bank; four valves per cylinder; Bosch DME electronic engine management, bi-VANOS variable intake timing and VALVETRONIC.

Bore x stroke	93 x 88.3mm
Capacity	4798cc
Compression ratio	10.0:1
Power	368 bhp (270kW) at 6300rpm
Torque	370 lbs-ft (490Nm) at 3600rpm

TRANSMISSION: Getrag S6 D420G six-speed all-synchromesh manual
Ratios: 1st 4.227; 2nd 2.505; 3rd 1.669; 4th 1.226; 5th 1.0; 6th 0.828; R 3.68
Rear axle: BTR limited slip unit, 3.08:1
MPH/1000rpm 28.44
Optional ZF 6HP26 six-speed automatic
Ratios: 1st: 4.05; 2nd: 2.4; 3rd: 1.58; 4th: 1.19; 5th: 1.00; 6th: 0.87
Rear axle: BTR limited slip unit, 3.08:1
MPH/1000rpm 28.44

SUSPENSION:
Front: Independent, lower fabricated wishbone, upper cantilevered link, inboard Eibach coil springs over Koni tubular dampers
Rear: Independent, double wishbones, Eibach coil springs over Koni tubular dampers

STEERING: BMW ZF rack-and-pinion with electric power assistance, 2 turns lock-to-lock, centre-point geometry

BRAKES: AP Racing to Morgan specifications; vacuum servo assistance; ABS, EBD
Front 350mm cast iron rotors, ventilated, 6 pot calipers
Rear 332mm cast iron rotors, ventilated, 2 pot calipers

WHEELS: Rays magnesium alloy multi-spoke design, 8.5 x 19-inch with 5-bolt hubs

TYRES: Avon ZZ3 225/35 R19 front, 245/35 R19 rear

CHASSIS: Rigid CAD designed aluminium alloy construction bonded with adhesive and Bolhoff rivets

DIMENSIONS:
Length	163ins (4147mm)	Front track	60ins (1510mm)
Width	69ins (1751mm)	Rear track	58.5ins (1480mm)
Height	49ins (1246mm)	Weight	2800lbs (1280kgs) for the automatic
Wheelbase	99.5ins (2532mm)		2640lbs (1200kgs) for the manual
		Fuel capacity	15.4 gallons (55 litres)

PERFORMANCE: Maximum speed 170mph (273km/h)   0-62mph (100km/h) in 4.2 seconds for the automatic

AERO COUPE SPECIFICATIONS

ENGINE: BMW N62B48 V8 featuring aluminium alloy cylinder block and heads; dual chain-driven overhead camshafts per cylinder bank; four valves per cylinder; Bosch DME electronic engine management, bi-VANOS variable intake timing and VALVETRONIC.

Bore x stroke	93 x 88.3mm
Capacity	4798cc
Compression ratio	10.0:1
Power	368 bhp (270kW) at 6300rpm
Torque	370 lbs-ft (490Nm) at 3600rpm

TRANSMISSION: Getrag S6 D420G six-speed all-synchromesh manual
Ratios: 1st 4.227; 2nd 2.505; 3rd 1.669; 4th 1.226; 5th 1.0; 6th 0.828; R 3.68
Rear axle: BTR limited slip unit, 3.08:1
MPH/1000rpm 28.44
Optional ZF 6HP26 six-speed automatic
Ratios: 1st: 4.05; 2nd: 2.4; 3rd: 1.58; 4th: 1.19; 5th: 1.00; 6th: 0.87
Rear axle: BTR limited slip unit, 3.08:1
MPH/1000rpm 28.44

SUSPENSION:
Front: Independent, lower fabricated wishbone, upper cantilevered link, inboard Eibach coil springs over Koni tubular dampers
Rear: Independent, double wishbones, Eibach coil springs over Koni tubular dampers

STEERING: BMW ZF rack-and-pinion with electric power assistance, 2 turns lock-to-lock, centre-point geometry

BRAKES: AP Racing to Morgan specifications; vacuum servo assistance; ABS, EBD
Front 350mm cast iron rotors, ventilated, 6 pot calipers
Rear 332mm cast iron rotors, ventilated, 2 pot calipers

WHEELS: Rays magnesium alloy multi-spoke design, 8.5 x 19-inch with 5-bolt hubs

TYRES: Avon ZZ3 225/35 R19 front, 245/35 R19 rear

CHASSIS: Rigid CAD designed aluminium alloy construction bonded with adhesive and Bolhoff rivets

DIMENSIONS:

Length	163ins (4147mm)	Front track	60ins (1510mm)
Width	69ins (1751mm)	Rear track	58.5ins (1480mm)
Height	49ins (1246mm)	Weight	2800lbs (1280kgs) for the automatic
Wheelbase	99.5ins (2532mm)		2640lbs (1200kgs) for the manual
		Fuel capacity	15.4 gallons (55 litres)

PERFORMANCE: Maximum speed 170mph (273km/h)   0-62mph (100km/h) in 4.2 seconds for the automatic

AERO NEW PLUS 8 SPECIFICATIONS

ENGINE:	BMW N62B48 V8 featuring aluminium alloy cylinder block and heads; dual chain-driven overhead camshafts per cylinder bank; four valves per cylinder; Bosch DME electronic engine management, Double VANOS variable valve timing and VALVETRONIC.

        Bore x stroke   93 x 88.3mm
        Capacity   4798cc
        Compression ratio   10.0:1
        Power   368 bhp (270kW) at 6300rpm
        Torque   370 lbs-ft (490Nm) at 3600rpm

TRANSMISSION: Getrag S6 D420G six-speed all-synchromesh manual
Ratios: 1st 4.227; 2nd 2.505; 3rd 1.669; 4th 1.226; 5th 1.0; 6th 0.828; R 3.68
Rear axle BTR limited slip unit, 3.08:1
MPH/1000rpm 28.44
Optional ZF 6HP26 six-speed automatic
Ratios: 1st: 4.05; 2nd: 2.4; 3rd: 1.58; 4th: 1.19; 5th: 1.00; 6th: 0.87
Rear axle: BTR limited slip unit, 3.08:1

SUSPENSION:
Front: Independent, lower fabricated wishbone, upper cantilevered link, inboard Eibach coil springs over Koni tubular dampers
Rear: Independent, double wishbones, Eibach coil springs over Koni tubular dampers

STEERING: BMW ZF rack-and-pinion with electric power assistance, 2 turns lock-to-lock, centre-point geometry

BRAKES: AP Racing to Morgan specifications; vacuum servo assistance; ABS, EBD
Front 350mm cast iron rotors, ventilated, 6 pot calipers
Rear 332mm cast iron rotors, ventilated, 2 pot calipers

WHEELS: Speedline magnesium alloy 5 spoke design, 8.5 x 18 inch with 5 bolt hubs

TYRES: Avon ZZ3 225/35 R18 front, 245/35 R18 rear

CHASSIS: Rigid CAD designed aluminium alloy construction bonded with adhesive and Bolhoff rivets

DIMENSIONS:
Length 154ins (3910mm)   Front track 60ins (1522mm)
Width 68.7ins (1746mm)   Rear track 58.5ins (1480mm)
Height 45ins (1142mm)   Weight 2595lbs (1180kgs) for the automatic
Wheelbase 99.5ins (2532mm)   2420lbs (1100kgs) for the manual
                                                Fuel capacity 15.4 gallons (55 litres)

PERFORMANCE: Maximum speed 170mph (273km/h)   0-62mph (100km/h) in 4.2 seconds for the automatic

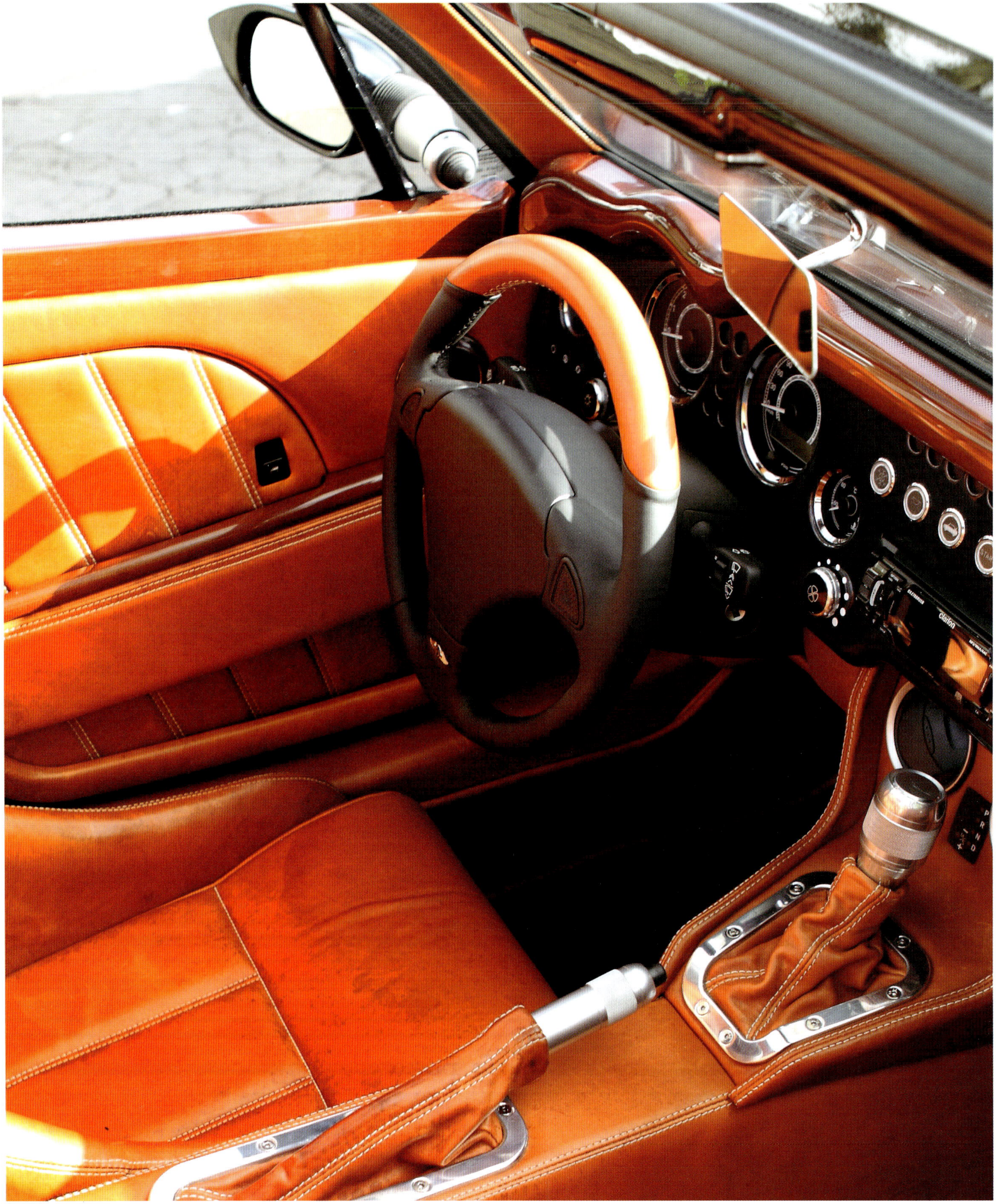
clarion

APPENDIX

Appendix 1

MORGAN AERO 8 PRODUCTION

Model	Production Start	Production Completed	Number Built
Aero 8 Series I	July 2001	October 2003	214
Aero 8 Series II	May 2003	August 2004	60
Aero 8 Series III	September 2004	December 2007	208
Aero 8 Series IV	July 2007	March 2010	178
AeroMax	August 2008	December 2009	117
Aero SuperSports	March 2010	Current	132*
Aero Coupe	March 2012	Current	10*
New Plus 8	February 2012	Current	98*
Aero 8 GTN	2004		11*

* These numbers are as at January 14, 2013

Appendix 2

MAIN COMPANY SUPPLIERS

Supplier	Product	Supplier	Product
BMW AG	V8 engine complete with Bosch ECU, steering column	Getrag	S6 D420G 6-speed manual gearbox
Alcan Aluminium	Aluminium sheets	ZF	ZF 6HP 26 6-speed automatic, steering rack from 2005
British Aluminium	Front longitudinal extrusion Suspension components extrusions	Kromberg and Schubert	Wiring loom and connectors
Radshape	Chassis complete Grille, cowl, rear over riders	Robert Bosch	Head and side lights Headlight plugs Electric window motors
GKN	Prop shaft with universals	Automotive Lighting	Rear lights

Timken	Wheel bearings	Reed Automotive	Front indicator light Central rear brake light
Jack Knight Developments	Steering rack (Series I)	LAP Engineering	Reversing light, rear fog light, number plate light, interior light
OZ	Alloy road wheels	Blaupunkt	Audio system including CD player, speakers, clock
Dunlop, Conti, Avon	Tyres	Superform Aluminium	Body wings, boot lid, airscoop for differential and gearbox, sump plug protector, front bumper and radiator intake
Koni	Suspension dampers	Pilkington and Tyneside Glass	Heated windscreen, heated side windows, heated rear window
Eibach	Suspension springs	KL	Heater/demister; air conditioner
BTR Australia	Limited slip differential	Frazero	Veneer dash
Titan Motorsport	Suspension wishbones, rod ends	Connelly	Leather for upholstery
Boysen	Exhaust manifold and pipes with catalytic converter	GM-Chevrolet	Hood latches
AP Racing	Brake disc rotors Brake callipers Brake pads Brake and clutch master cylinders	Marstons	Carpet
AP Lockheed	Brake servo unit and connectors	Autoliv	Seat belts
Motolita	Steering wheel	MB Components	Seat frames
Mulberry	Briefcase/glovebox, luggage set		

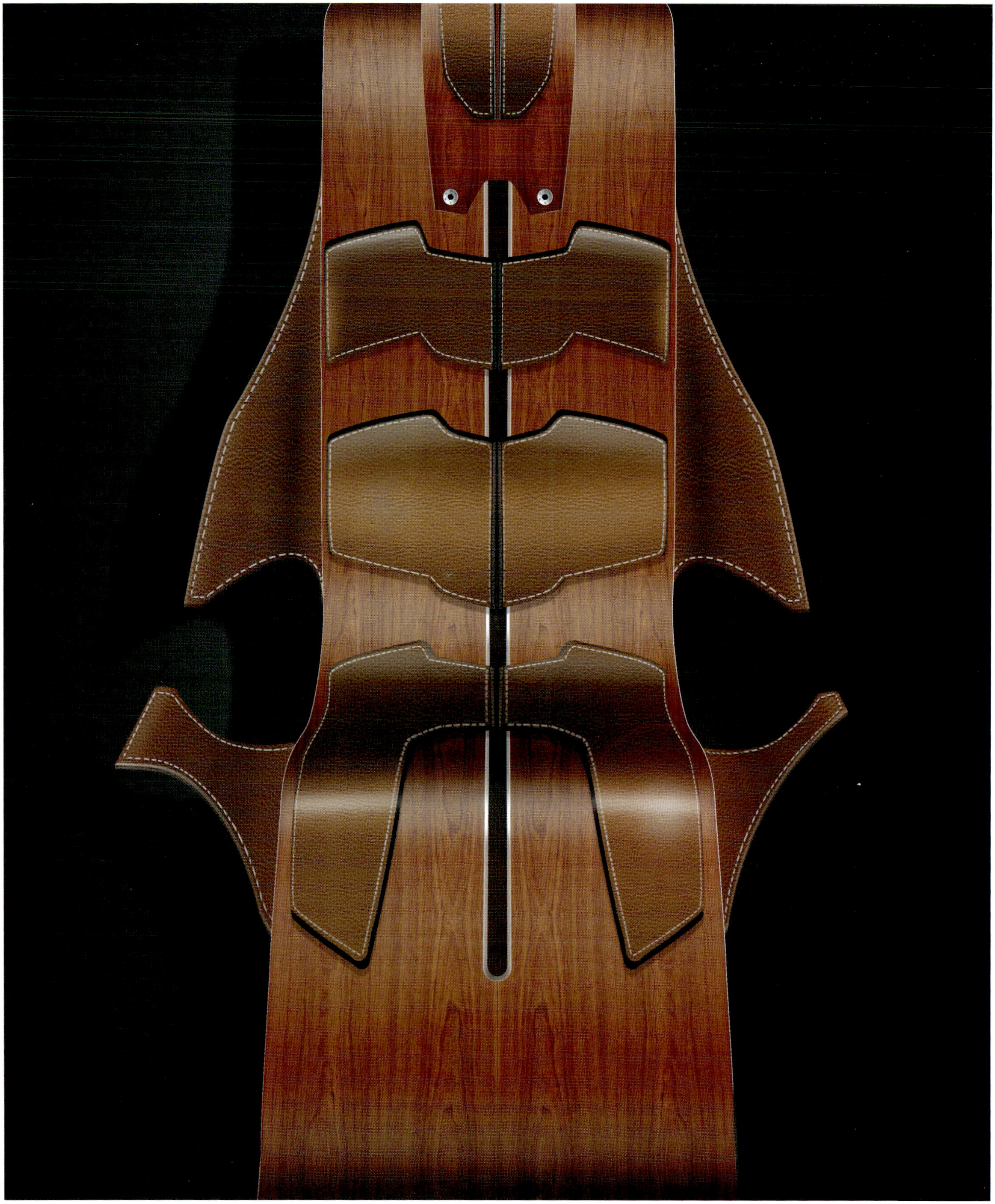

BIBLIOGRAPHY

Various motoring magazines—*CAR, Autocar, Classic and Sports Cars, Thoroughbred and Classic Cars, Road & Track, Car and Driver, Auto Express, Automobile*

Morgan 1991-2009, Brooklands Books

Morgan 1968-2001, Brooklands Books

100 Years of Morgan, Charles Morgan and Gregory Houston, Michael O'Mara Books, 2008

Morgan Maverick, Chris Lawrence, Douglas Loveridge Publishing, 2008

Morgan at Le Mans, David Dowse, Tempus Publishing Ltd, 2005

Morgan: Performance Plus Tradition, Jonathan Wood, Haynes, 2004

TOK 258 Morgan Winner at Le Mans, Ronnie Price, MX Publishing, 2005

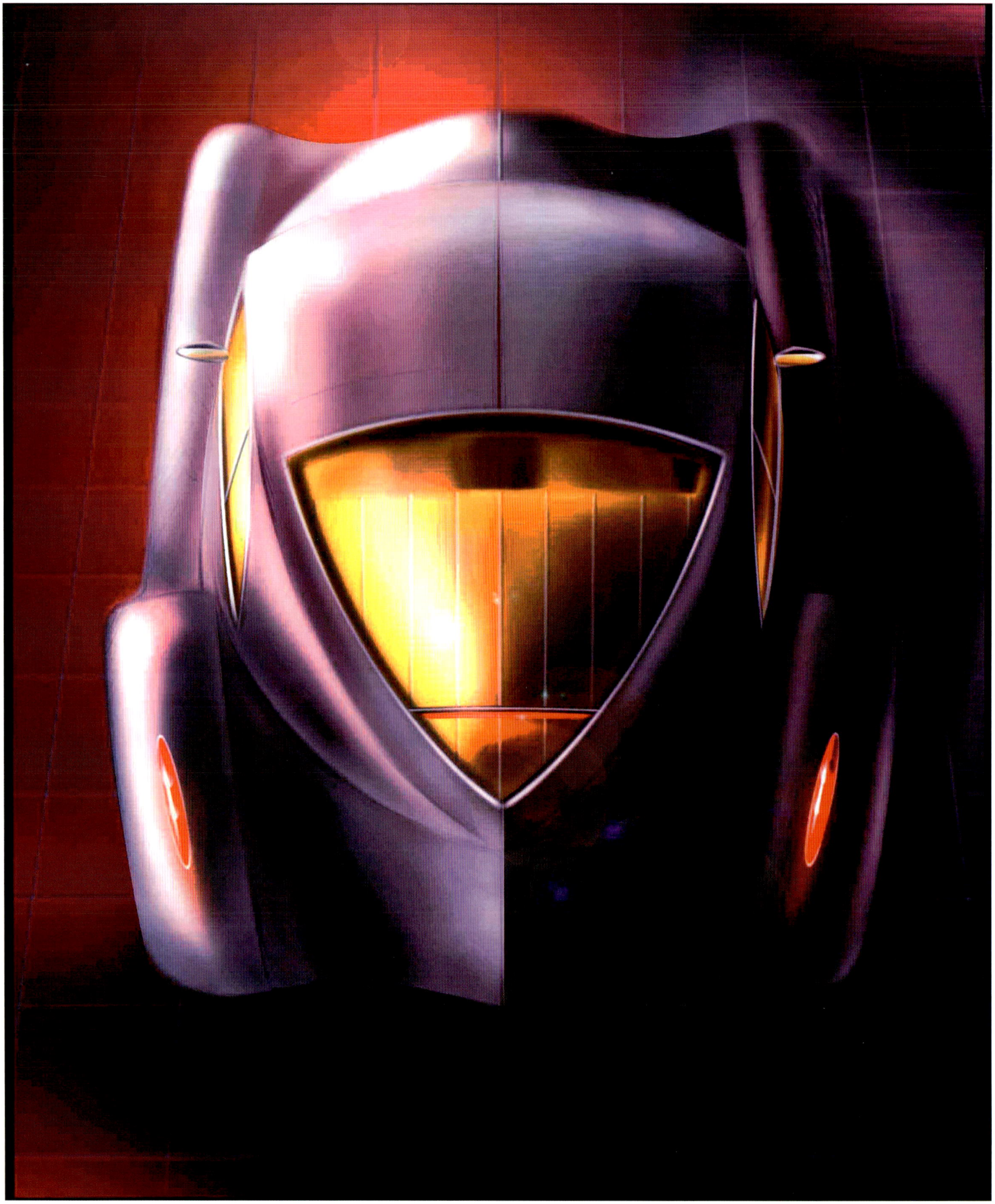

PHOTO CREDITS

Morgan Motor Company:
16, 17, 19, 20 (bottom), 22, 23, 24 (top), 28, 29, 30, 31, 35, 36, 38, 39, 40, 41, 42, 43, 44, 45, 46, 47, 51, 72, 74, 75 (bottom), 76 (both), 77, 82 (both), 83 (top), 84, 86, 87, 88 (both), 89 (both), 90, 91, 94, 95, 96, 98, 103, 108, 109, 110, 111, 113 (all), 116, 118, 119, 120 (both), 121, 123, 125, 148, 149, 152, 153 (both), 154 (all), 155, 156, 157, 159, 162, 163, 164, 170, 171, 174, 175, 176, 177, 178, 179, 181, 183, 184, 185, 189,

Richard Gilbert:
27, 50, 92, 99, 100, 102 (both), 103, 104 (both), 105, 107, 112, 113, 114 (both), 115, 117, 120 (top), 122, 124, 126, 127, 130, 131, 132, 133, 134, 135, 136, 138, 139, 140, 141, 142, 145, 146, 147, 160, 173, 187, 198

White Point: 24 (bottom)

Adrian van der Kroft: 37

Ford Motor Company: 32

Gavin Farmer: 7, 73, 75 (top), 97 (top), 166, 172, 186 (both)

Chris Lawrence: 20 (top), 168

BMW AG: 52, 56, 58, 59

Mercedes-Benz: 55 (top)

Lexus: 55 (centre)

Audi AG: 55 (bottom), 150 (top and centre)

Radshape: 78, 79, 80

Supeform Aluminium: 81

PHOTO CREDITS CONT.

Jack Knight Developments: 83 (bottom)

Frederic O'Neill: 137

MPH Communications: 128, 129, 161

General Motors-Holden: 150 (bottom)

Riversimple: 151 (both)

OAK Racing: 194, 195, 196, 197

Richard Surman: 64 (both), 65

Fred Scatley: 21 (top)

John L E Gaisford: 21 (bottom)

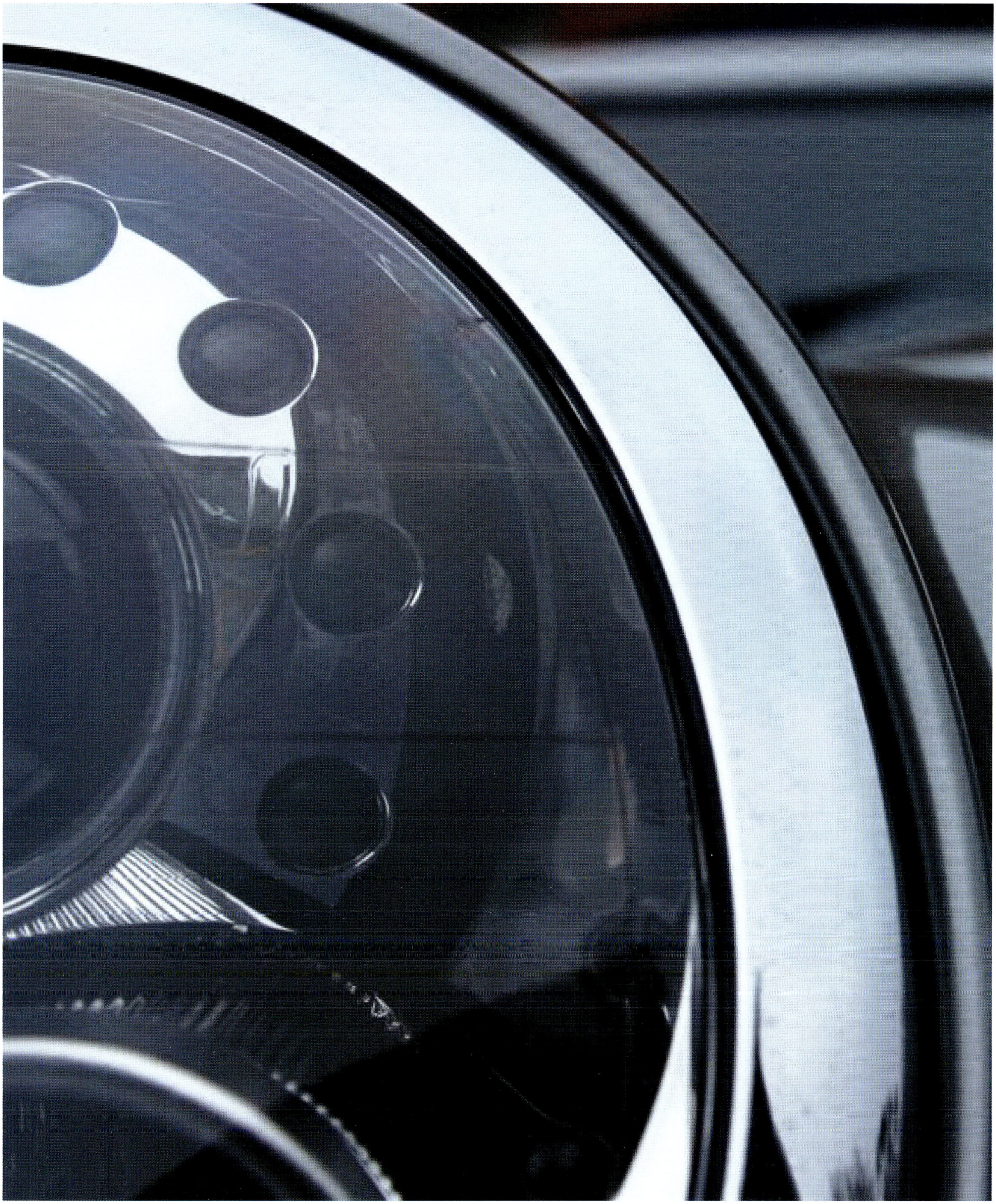

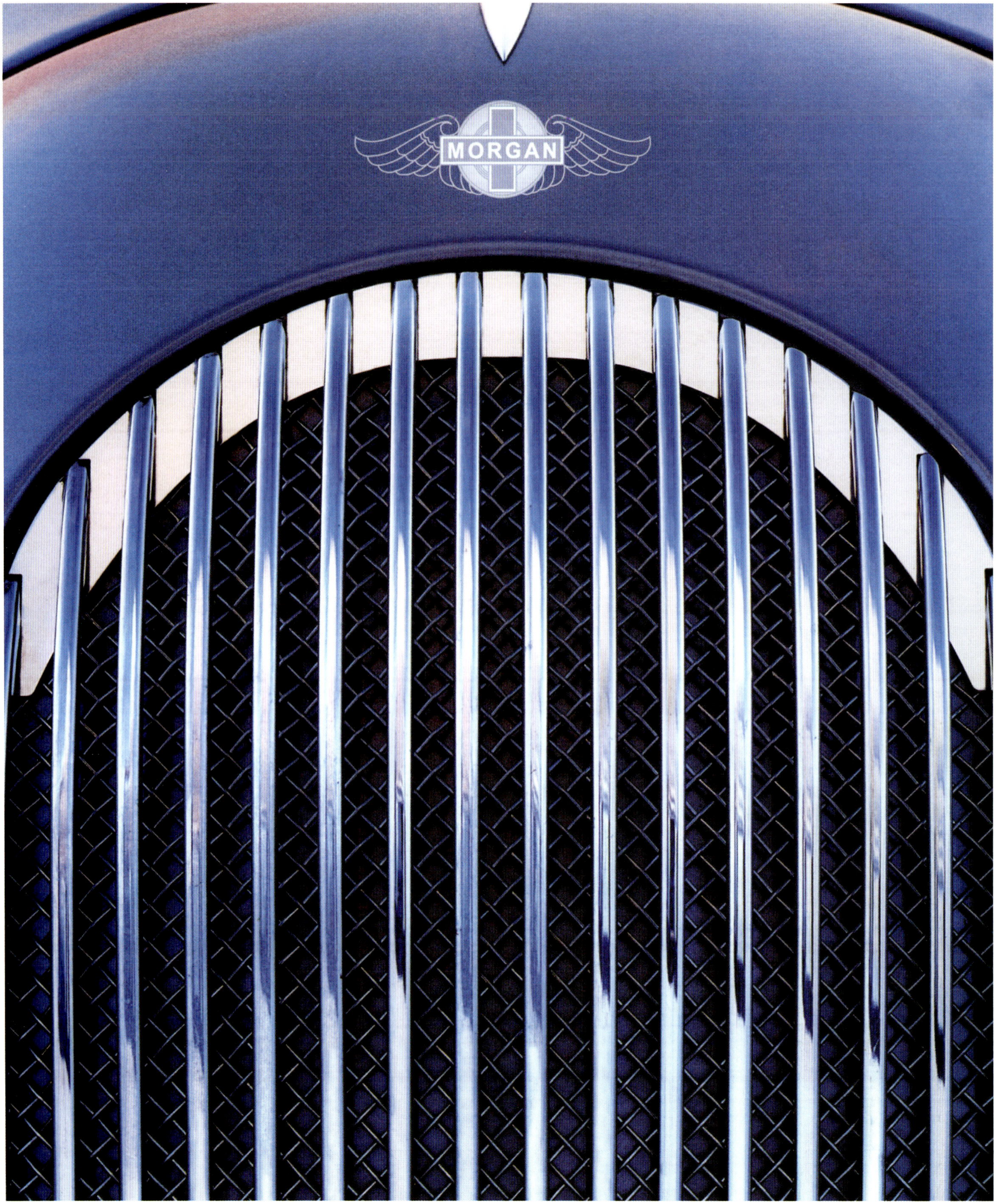
MORGAN

ALPHABETICAL INDEX

AFM 328 - 169
Ahlers, Keith - 129, 133
Alcan Aluminium - 78
Alford, Christopher - 21
AP Racing - 33, 85
Arbuckle, David - 109
Associated Motor Cycles Ltd - 168
Aston, Mark - 41
Aston Martin - 80, 83, 124, 144, 153
Audi AG - 10, 55, 134, 144
AutoGT Racing France - 136
Autocar magazine - 90, 113, 124
Auto Express magazine - 56, 103
Automobile magazine - 93
Baldwin, Mark - 23, 33, 62, 78
Baring Brothers Banque Suisse - 136
Bentley Continental GT - 124
Black, Sir John - 53, 182
BMW AG - 25, 51, 53, 55, 56, 57, 58, 59, 60, 61, 62, 63, 64, 66, 68, 69, 70, 76, 85, 88, 89, 90, 99, 100, 104, 111, 114, 115, 128, 131, 137, 144, 157, 163, 164, 169, 192
    328 - 169
    ActiveHybrid 3 - 150
    ActiveHybrid 5 - 150
BMW M GmbH - 57, 58
Boysen - 60, 76
Briche, Julien - 146
Britten, John - 21
Bugatti - 110, 124, 132, 169
Burbidge, John - 15, 49, 61, 62, 78, 98, 99, 100, 101
Cale, David - 110, 120
CAR magazine - 90
Car & Driver magazine - 96, 97
Cantab Motors - 97
Chadwick, Keith - 15, 79, 102
Chapman, Graham - 15, 77, 78, 80, 81, 88, 121
Chevrolet - 25, 26, 66, 144, 151
    Corvette - 66, 97
    Volt - 151
Christian, Manfred - 58
Cooke, Paula - 130
Coventyr Climax - 17, 179, 180, 181, 182
Cranfield University - 151, 153
Cropley, Steve - 113, 114
Cumberford, Robert - 93
Cunningham, Neil - 130, 131, 132, 133, 134, 135
Deep Sanderson - 169, 170
Dempsey, Kevin - 83
Dickinson, Christopher - 15, 78, 102
Dixon-Smith, Gregor - 42
Dollan, Craig - 121
Droitwich Aluminium - 77
Dron, Tony - 26
Edwards, David - 15, 81, 82, 113
Emptage, John - 83
Ferrari - 10, 129, 138, 171
FIAT - 55, 188
Figoni & Falaschi - 41, 44, 109
Ford Motor Company - 13, 29, 32, 49, 53, 66, 100, 140, 150, 166, 169, 180, 186, 187, 188, 189, 192
    Granada - 49
    Fusion hybrid - 150
Frazero - 85
Getrag GmbH - 76
Goodwin, David - 23, 61, 62, 88
Goschel, Dr - 76
Gray, Robin - 20, 21
Great Western Railway - 176
Gumball Rally - 36
Handlgruber, Rudolf - 56
Hardwick, George - 43, 87
Harvey-Jones, Sir John - 73, 75
Hay, Richard - 128
Hill, Nigel - 110
Honda Motor Co - 150
Houghton, David - 15, 42, 43
Humphries, Matthew - 11, 15, 102, 103,

109, 110, 113, 114, 116, 119, 120, 121, 155, 156
Hyde, Steve - 128, 134
Isis Imports - 96
Jabouille, Jean-Pierre - 10, 15, 136, 137, 139, 140, 143, 144, 146
Jack Knight Developments - 27, 30, 49, 83, 100, 191
Jaguar Cars Ltd - 33, 34, 35, 55, 103, 187
Jones, Derek - 80, 81
Kalbfell, Karl-Heinz - 25, 57, 58
Kench, Norman - 15, 42, 43
KL Automotive - 85, 211
Laffite, Jacques - 15, 130, 131, 136, 137, 138, 139, 140, 141, 143
Laffite, Margueritte - 137, 139, 141, 140, 143
Lamborghini - 10
Lancia Thesis - 111, 120, 123
Lange, Dr Karlheinz - 68
Lawrence, Carrie - 172
Lawrence, Christopher - 11, 13, 15, 18, 19, 20, 23, 24, 25, 26, 29, 33, 35, 36, 39, 41, 42, 48, 49, 53, 57, 59, 61, 62, 66, 67, 77, 83, 88, 95, 100, 127, 128, 130, 158, 167, 168, 185,
Lawrence, Stephen - 25
Lawrence, William - 168
Lawrencetune Engines Ltd - 169
Leach, Dennis - 128
Le Roch, Jean-Francois - 138, 139
Lesoudier, Gael - 127, 140, 141, 143, 144, 145, 146
Lexus (Division of Toyota) - 55, 150
    CT200h - 150
    IIS250h - 150
    GS450h - 150
    LS600h - 150
Libra Motive - 15, 45
Lotus Elite - 30
    Exige - 129
Lucas - 180, 183

Lyons, William - 182
Magliotti, Manfred - 56
Malvern College - 177
Marcos LM600 - 25, 33, 49
Marland, Simon - 78, 79, 88
Martin, Maxime - 127, 143, 144, 145, 146
McCulloch, Malcolm - 156
Mercedes-Benz - 55, 64, 97, 150
    E320 Bluetec - 150
    S400 BlueHybrid - 150
MG - 109, 169
MINI - 95, 100, 102, 103, 104, 111, 114
MIRA - 36, 45, 46, 47, 50, 89, 164
Miramas - 11, 51, 62, 63, 64, 66, 67, 81, 131, 164
Monica - 48, 171, 172
Morgan, Charles - 11, 13, 15, 21, 22, 24, 25, 26, 29, 31, 32, 33, 34, 36, 39, 40, 41, 42, 45, 47, 50, 53, 55, 56, 57, 59, 61, 62, 73, 76, 78, 81, 82, 87, 88, 95, 102, 109, 110, 111, 113, 119, 120, 127, 130, 136, 139, 143, 150, 157, 161, 167, 195, 196
Morgan, HFS - 29, 119, 175, 176, 178, 179, 180, 181, 182, 185, 188
Morgan, Peter - 17, 18, 29, 30, 31, 39, 50, 73, 119, 182, 185, 189
Morgan Motor Company - 10, 13, 19, 29, 32, 34, 49, 53, 58, 76, 78, 88, 89, 95, 109, 113, 127, 129, 157, 163, 164, 165, 175, 178, 185, 186, 192, 195, 196
Morgan cars:
    Plus 4 - 17, 18, 20, 29, 30, 53, 55, 80, 89, 96, 171, 182, 183, 184, 185, 186, 188, 189
    Plus 4 Super Sport - 18, 171
    Plus 8 - 20, 21, 22, 23, 24, 29, 31, 50, 54, 55, 56, 57, 60, 62, 63, 67, 85, 89, 95, 104, 106, 188, 189, 190, 191, 192
    GT2 - 24, 25, 26, 33, 35, 130, 131
    4-4 - 29, 181, 182, 183, 184
    4/4 - 18, 21, 55, 89, 110, 182, 184,

186, 187, 188, 191, 192
    Plus 4 Plus - 30, 188, 187
    P8000 - 26, 29, 36, 41, 42, 43, 45, 46, 47, 48, 49, 50, 66, 67, 74, 75, 77, 78, 81, 83, 104, 163
    Aero 8 - 7, 10, 13, 15, 23, 29, 30, 35, 36, 40, 43, 44, 45, 46, 47, 50, 53, 55, 59, 60, 67, 74, 75, 76, 77, 78, 79, 82, 83, 84, 85, 87, 88, 89, 90, 91, 93, 95, 96, 97, 98, 99, 100, 102, 103, 104, 106, 109, 110, 111, 114, 120, 121, 124, 127, 128, 129, 130, 131, 132, 133, 134, 135, 136, 137, 139, 140, 141, 144, 149, 153, 155, 163, 164, 170, 172, 188, 192
    AeroMax - 10, 13, 102, 103, 106, 109, 110, 111, 113, 114, 115, 116, 119, 120, 123, 144, 151, 153, 192
    SuperSport - 15, 119, 120, 123, 144, 192
    Aero 8 GTN - 127, 128, 129
    LIFECar - 119, 120, 149, 151, 152, 153, 154, 155, 156, 157, 158,
    Runabout - 178
    Family - 178, 179
    Aero 1923 - 179
    F-type -179, 180
Morris, Steve - 15, 42, 75, 76, 77, 81, 120, 121, 132
Mössner, Thomas - 61, 62
Mulberry - 47, 211
O'Neill, Frederic - 15, 136, 137 ,138, 139, 140, 141, 143, 144 ,145
Oscar - 151, 155
Owen, Maurice - 189
Oxford University - 155, 156
Parkin, Matthew - 15, 41, 88, 104, 114
Park Sheet Metal Ltd - 35, 36, 77
Pilkington Glass - 85
Porsche - 10, 18, 19, 24, 93, 97, 129, 131, 132, 134, 137, 150, 171
    GT3 - 129, 131, 132
    Panamera S hybrid - 150

QinetiQ - 151, 155, 157
Radshape - 15, 51, 66, 77, 78, 79, 80, 81, 102
Randle, James - 25, 34, 35, 39, 40, 90
Range Rover - 191
Ranzinger, Gunther - 58, 59, 60, 61, 62, 63, 64, 66, 88
Reeves, Mark - 15, 49, 50, 78, 98, 99, 100, 101, 102, 120, 123, 154, 157
Reitzle, Dr Wolfgang - 25, 57
Reuil, Dr - 76
Riversimple - 15, 151, 152, 158
Road & Track magazine - 123
Robert Bosch AG - 60, 85
Rocky Mountains Institute - 158
Rosche, Paul - 57
Rover V8 - 23, 29, 58, 163, 189, 192
Rutherford, Mike - 56
Sanderson, Joan - 168
Scheier, Johan-Boris - 137, 139, 140, 141, 143, 144, 145, 146
Sharpe, Adam - 132, 133, 134, 135
Sharpe, Robert - 133
Shepherd-Barron, Richard - 18, 19
Simanaitis, Dennis - 96, 123
Spowers, Hugo - 15, 151, 158
Sprinzel, John - 20, 171
Standard Triumph Motor Company - 53
Stanton, Richard - 127, 128, 129
Stapledon, Bruce - 21
Stevenson-Peach, William - 177
Strategem - 73, 75
Sturdza, Erich - 10, 110, 136, 144, 146
Sturdza, Georges-Alexander - 137, 138, 139, 140, 143
Survirn Engineering - 15, 42, 43, 87, 121
Summers, Steve - 42
Sunday Times, The - 91, 151
Superform Aluminium Ltd - 15, 77 81, 83, 87, 113, 114, 121
Tastevin, Jean - 171, 172
Thorby, Andrew - 155

Thorne, Richard - 15, 127, 129, 130, 132, 133
Toyota Motor Co - 13, 150
    Prius - 150
    Camry Hybrid - 150
Triumph cars:
    TR2 - 17, 184
    TR3 - 53, 184, 185
    Stag V8 - 189
TVR - 56, 134
Urbschat, Michael - 88
Van der kroft, Adrian - 25, 37, 127
Volkswagen New Beetle - 111
Wells, Robert - 15, 21, 22, 31, 32, 45, 130
Whitworth, Tim - 41
Wilks, Peter - 189
Woolmer, Tim - 156
Wykeham, Bill - 20, 21, 24, 25, 57
ZF - 66, 100, 104, 115